Africa at the Millennium

Also by Bakut tswah Bakut

SECURITY: An African Perspective

Also by Sagarika Dutt

THE POLITICIZATION OF THE UNITED NATIONS SPECIALIZED AGENCIES:
A Case Study of UNESCO

Africa at the Millennium

An Agenda for Mature Development

Edited by

Bakut tswah Bakut
Lecturer in International Relations
and Director of the African Studies Group
Nottingham Trent University

and

Sagarika Dutt
Lecturer in International Relations
Nottingham Trent University

Foreword by

Stephen Chan
Professor of International Relations and Ethics
and Dean, Faculty of Humanities
Nottingham Trent University

Selection, editorial matter and Introduction © Bakut tswah Bakut
and Sagarika Dutt 2000
Foreword © Stephen Chan 2000
Chapter 4 © Bakut tswah Bakut 2000
Chapter 13 © Sagarika Dutt 2000
Chapters 1–3, 5–12, 14 © Palgrave Publishers Ltd 2000

First published 2000 by
PALGRAVE
Houndmills, Basingstoke, Hampshire RG21 6XS and
175 Fifth Avenue, New York, N.Y. 10010
Companies and representatives throughout the world

PALGRAVE is the new global academic imprint of
St. Martin's Press LLC Scholarly and Reference Division and
Palgrave Publishers Ltd (formerly Macmillan Press Ltd).

Outside North America
ISBN 0–333–75352–6

In North America
ISBN 0–312–23519–4

This book is printed on paper suitable for recycling and
made from fully managed and sustained forest sources.

A catalogue record for this book is available
from the British Library.

Library of Congress Cataloging-in-Publication Data
Africa at the millennium : an agenda for mature development / edited by
Bakut tswah Bakut and Sagarika Dutt ; preface by Stephen Chan.
    p. cm.
  Includes bibliographical references and index.
  ISBN 0–312–23519–4
    1. Africa—Politics and government—1960- 2. Africa—Economic conditions-
-1960- 3. Africa—Social conditions—1960- 4. Twenty-first century—Forecasts.
I. Bakut tswah Bakut, 1958- II. Dutt, Sagarika, 1958-

  DT30.5 .A35325 2000
  320.96'09'049—dc21
                                                              00–033325

10   9   8   7   6   5   4   3   2   1
09   08   07   06   05   04   03   02   01   00
Printed in Great Britain by Antony Rowe Ltd, Chippenham, Wiltshire

To the children of Africa

Contents

Foreword: Maturity and Time in Africa

As we begin the twenty-first century it is ironic and, for Africa and Africans, even pleasing, to recall which country was regarded as the hopeless basket-case of the world at the beginning of the twentieth century: that was Canada. A century is both a long and short time in the histories and lessons of change.

Much has happened already in Africa in the forty years of political independence. This is a history shorter than that of post-war Europe, haunted still by Balkan conflicts, and one in which nationalisms and internationalisms have not so much developed as compressed their way forward. It is amazing that so much has worked well, rather than – as in the somewhat lazy basket-case analogy – much has not.

This volume is largely a work by Africans and those who have lived for many years in Africa, or in other parts of the Third World. It attempts something of an 'African' rather than an 'Africanist' voice. It is also a collaboration between established scholars and graduate students led, in the first instance, by Bakut tswah Bakut. It has been a pleasure to me, as Dean, to have had both the project and its energy generated in my Faculty. But, does it work? And what does it mean to be 'African', rather than 'Africanist'? What is a 'mature development'? And why is it important that the measures of time be applied here? Why is the millennium important to Africa?

It is precisely because so much commentary on Africa has been generalised and, above all, rhetorical – devised as measures by bankers and politicians, who have never seen Africa – or have seen it, and measured it, as tourists – that it is necessary to reiterate this rhetoric, before questioning and rewriting it in more complex and subtle forms that at least echo the voices of those within Africa – who themselves have not been disaster and development tourists within the West, although, given the Balkans, there is here scope for ironies at least.

That this book has several African authors lends itself to the sense of autochtonous purpose long rumbling in Africa. And, if ever there was any symbolism about a new millennium, this might as well be it: that the last sleeping continent might soon awake. It is the idea of 'mature development' that is most at stake in the new millennium. After all, Africa for Africa means Africa for all Africans – in peace and health for a start, and in freedom and plenty. But this is not an autarkic project. Africa cannot remain within Africa alone, but the Africa for and of Africans will necessarily be judged (hopefully by shared indices) in the world. A 'mature development' is, by this token, exemplary. In the twenty-first century, the hope is the world will learn from a mature Africa. The project is not therefore defensive, but positive. African studies have come a long way from disappointed returns on a kindly patronisation on the one hand, and scathing criticisms on the other. This book is a volume which expresses, not an unanchored optimism, but a 'do-ability', a non-rhetorical hope.

STEPHEN CHAN

Notes on the Contributors

Susan Adong is a doctoral candidate at the Nottingham Trent University.

Bakut tswah Bakut is the Director of the Nottingham Trent University African Studies Group.

Sagarika Dutt is Lecturer in International Relations at the Nottingham Trent University.

Christopher Farrands is Principal Lecturer in the Department of International Studies, Nottingham Trent University.

David Francis is Lecturer in International Relations at the University of Southhampton.

Oliver Furley is Honorary Research Fellow, School of International Studies and Law, University of Coventry.

Malcolm Harper is the Director of the United Nations Association, UK and Northern Ireland.

Thomas Jaye is a doctoral candidate, University of Wales, Aberystwyth.

Timothy Murithi is presently with the United Nations Institute for Training and Research (UNITAR), Geneva.

Cirino Hiteng Ofuho is Assistant Professor of Politics and International Relations, United States International University, Nairobi, Kenya, and Fellow of the Centre For Conflict Research.

Javaid Rehman is Lecturer in the Faculty of Law, University of Leeds.

Paul Rich is Professor of Politics, University of Luton.

Jack Spence is Professor of International Relations and Associate Fellow, Royal Institute of International Affairs, London.

Geepu-Nah Tiepoh is an Economic Policy Consultant with ACLAD, Canada.

Introduction

Bakut tswah Bakut and Sagarika Dutt

As we enter the twenty-first century, the impact of globalisation and its ramifications is being felt in every part of the world, including the most remote parts of Africa. These developments have led to the re-evaluation of existing structures in international relations as well as the creation of new ones which incorporate the global changes necessary, economically, socially and politically. However, the African continent seemingly still remains isolated in the global system. For the continent to benefit from the new developments, and to take part in global interactions as an equal partner and at a competitive level, there must be a new form of research and scholarship primarily focused on the nature of African societies, cultures and value systems. Up to the present time, however, this has remained a marginalised area in academic discourse and praxis.

The twenty-first century will see more complex situations in the continent, as a result of the search for effective and workable democratic principles and practices, development strategies and security in general. The pattern of things to come seems already to be emerging. On the one hand, there is the breakdown of societies as a consequence of wars, absence of civil society, and militarisation. On the other, the emerging role of African countries as initiators of peace-keeping operations in the continent and the collective search for a continental solution through regional and continental integration strategies. These issues call for a new approach in the study of the dynamics influencing the developments in the continent. The new approach should take into consideration the linkages between human rights, the environment, democracy, and development requirements and strategies. The importance of these issues in the developments of the continent was re-emphasised at the First Annual Africa Governance Forum held in Addis Ababa in July 1997,

1

a conference sponsored by the United Nations Development Programme (UNDP) and the United Nations Economic Commission for Africa.

This book is aimed at providing a framework on which research into African issues should focus in the twenty-first century. From the emergent complexities in the continent, to the role of the United Nations and nongovernmental organisations (NGOs) in the twenty-first century, and the willingness of these institutions to restructure their programmes to cater for both socio-economic needs and cultures of African societies. The search for sustainable democratic principles and practices, workable strategies for development, and the maintenance of peace and security should focus on both the individual and collective levels of analysis. Some of the chapters were first presented as conference papers at a conference organised by the African Studies Group, Nottingham Trent University and the United Nations Association (Nottingham Branch) in November 1997 on the theme: 'Africa: Agenda for Development'. Most of the chapters, however, have been written or adapted specifically for the book to cover areas that were not addressed at the conference and to ensure a co-ordinated and sequential flow of the issues involved in the quest for development in Africa.

The book is divided into three parts. Part I focuses on the Development and Economic Integration process in the continent. It is concerned with the historical marginalisation of Africa in the Global Economy and Politics. In Chapter 1, Paul Rich, while acknowledging the negative impact of the end of the Cold War era on Africa – because of the non-existence of super-powers to be played off against one another – argues that the experiences of political marginalisation are not homogeneous. African states have been affected differently. While the cases of failures are higher, there have been relative successes since the end of the Cold War era, as in other continents. Rich also argues that the overly simplistic and deterministic analysis of Africa by analysts often fail to take the nature of African states' political and economic marginalisation into consideration. To provide a contextual understanding, he traces the historical roots of the peripheralisation of African states and their attempts to break out following decolonisation. Suggesting possible areas of developing solutions, Rich considers the development of a coherent African diplomacy as a leverage to exert over the agenda of North–South relations, and concludes with a cautious optimism regarding the ability of African states to break out of the current stranglehold of peripheralisation.

Following a similar line of argument, Geepu-Nah Tiepoh takes issue in Chapter 2 with those who advocate an exclusive 'internal solution' for

African economic problems through domestic economic growth. While the argument remains valid, Tiepoh argues, the issues of external debt and economic growth are not only complex but are also symptomatic of the broader problem of lack of economic development in Africa. Thus the external debt and lack of economic growth complex must be understood in terms of causality running in both directions. Tiepoh argues that while lack of economic growth can explain Africa's external debts crisis, the overhanging huge external debt burden has over the years allowed the adoption of adjustment policies that have helped to undermine domestic economic growth efforts. As a solution to African external debt and economic growth problems, there must be a successful shift from asymmetric and rapid adjustment policies focusing on restructuring only domestic variables. Tiepoh suggests that these policies, focusing on achieving external equilibrium, should be redirected towards a balanced and long-term adjustment process aimed at improving the productive capacities and structural transformations of African economies.

Christopher Farrands argues in Chapter 3 that technologies may be combined with the important human resources of sub-Saharan Africa to promote more effective development. Because of their diversity and fragility, he does not attempt to offer a common prescription for all countries labelled 'sub-Saharan'. However, he seeks to illustrate the case that if appropriate technologies and effective management systems can be combined with human skills, expertise and experience, then real and sustainable growth is possible.

While Chapters 1–3 deal with the need for a continental approach at political, economic and technological levels, Bakut tswah Bakut focuses in Chapter 4 on the Abuja Treaty of 1991 establishing the African Economic Community (AEC). Bakut examines the Treaty and attempts to locate the theoretical framework on which the Treaty is based. He argues that while functionalism as an integration framework has its attractions and appears to be successful in the European Union (EU) experience, neo-functionalism (the European version of functionalism) is not appropriate for Africa, because of its nature and stages in development, politically, economically and technologically. As a solution, Bakut suggests that David Mitrany's classic functionalism could be a more appropriate candidate for adaptation because of its flexibility and dynamic nature. Rather than asserting a claim to be propounding a given solution, Bakut makes clear that the aim of his chapter is to generate interest and discussion among scholars, African governments and the Organisation for African Unity/African

Economic Community (OAU/AEC) Secretariat regarding the framework for pursuing the African Economic Community dream. All the chapters in Part I, entitled 'Development and Economic Integration', relate the consequences of marginalisation and the impact of technology and globalisation on the continent, and consider the African governments' strategy of action to attain an Economic Community by 2030.

Part II focuses on the conflict variables exacerbating the marginalisation and underdevelopment in the continent under the title 'Democracy, Conflict and Human Rights'. Cirino Ofuho, commences Part II by placing his argument in the context of the concepts of sovereignty and legitimacy of African states. Cirino takes issue with the critics (especially Western scholars) of the failure of the post-colonial state in Africa. While not denying the failure, and indeed absolving the African leadership, he argues that any discussion of the failure of the Westphalian state system in Africa requires not only fairness but also objectivity based on the impact of imperialism on the continent and the imposition of an inappropriate state system. To establish his point, he traces and examines the obstacles that arose during the formative years of the African states, arguing that while the European state system was relevant to the socio-political and cultural values of the Europeans, it also had ample time to develop. The African states, on the other hand, apart from their inappropriateness to the socio-political and cultural values, were imposed without any regard to the organic nature of the nations within the colonial territories. Democratisation, therefore, is not a panacea to the African states' problem. For a solution to be found, Ofuho proposes a philosophical deconstruction and reconstruction of the neo-colonial states to fit current economic and political trends in the continent and the understanding of ethno-national conflicts as a rationalisation of the colonial and post-colonial state. Post-colonial conflicts, he concludes, must be viewed as another process in purging the bad legacy of colonialism.

In Chapter 6, tracing the origins of, and elements influencing, the move towards democracy, while acknowledging the impact of international pressure on African governments to democratise, Oliver Furley argues that African people themselves play a crucial role in the shift of their governments to democracy. Taking Uganda as a case study of Africans' influencing the process of democratisation, he traces the transitional and democratic transformation in that country, outlining the prospects and problems. Furley concludes his analysis by arguing that in spite of the shortcomings (which are surmountable) of the Ugandan experience, it provides an example of the nurturing of democracy by Africans themselves.

In Chapter 7, Timothy Murithi assesses the phenomenon of the disintegration of African states. He examines the pressures often placed on war-torn societies to democratise and argues that such pressure and the quest for democratisation often fail to question whether the democratic institutions put in place are sustainable in the medium to long term. Murithi seeks to bridge the conceptual gap between the process of conflict resolution which seeks to address ethnic disputes once activated, and the process of democratisation which seeks to manage the transition towards legitimate governance in post-conflict situations. He highlights the significant parallels that exist between conflict resolution and democratisation, and raises the question of whether the process of conflict resolution itself should be considered to be a process of democratisation? For Murithi, the electoral systems constitute an integral and important political arrangement by which ethnic groups can feel secure about their socio-cultural survival and security after the conflict. He proposes an inclusive electoral system which is genuinely proportional representative.

In Chapter 8, Thomas Jaye reflects on the role of the Economic Community of West African States (ECOWAS) in the Liberian imbroglio and argues that the ECOWAS experience could be useful for future regional intervention in violent intra-state conflicts in the continent. While accepting the influence of ethnicity in the Liberian war, he feels that it is by itself neither *the* causal/explanatory factor, nor the origin of the crisis. The causality, Jaye argues, is the lack of security in the widest sense of the word. The ECOWAS intervention experience, Jaye notes, sets a precedent for consensual and collective action by African states as well as a precedent for regional organisations' interventions in regional conflicts without United Nations' (UN) sanctions. In conclusion, he holds the view that the ECOWAS intervention was justifiable within the context of the external and internal historical conditions, considering the indifference of the international community to African conflicts.

Building on the intervention of the Economic Community of West African States (ECOWAS) in West Africa, David Francis, in Chapter 9, locates his discourse in the role of ECOWAS, as a regional organisation, in maintaining international peace and security. Francis focuses on the Economic Community of West African States Monitoring Group (ECOMOG) as an example of a positive contribution of regional groupings in international relations. The ECOMOG experience, Francis argues, is an example of how African governments have shown the capacity to harness their national resources into meaningful development. The success of the ECOMOG experience, albeit qualified, has shown the definite possibility of Africans' ability to solve their problems and set an example for replication by other regions, both in the continent and outside it.

In the concluding chapter of Part II, Chapter 10, Javaid Rehman takes issue with the concept of 'peoples' rights' in international law. He argues that, while African states have been the leading proponents of the concept of 'peoples' rights', in practice they remain equivocal and uncertain. Although the African Charter of Human and Peoples' Rights (1981) remains the leading international and regional instrument dealing with the subject of 'peoples' rights', Rehman argues that it is, not possible to find a definitive meaning for the term 'peoples'. The practice of African states and the African Charter, while acknowledging the existence of 'peoples', have not provided a clearer definition as to their constitution, but strongly condemn any views of self-determination that negate the established principle of *uti posseditis juris*. The term 'peoples' in the African context, Rehman concludes, is applicable to national, ethnic, tribal and religious groups within the independent states. Thus, the 'peoples' have a right to equality and existence, but so also has the entirety of the population of the states. The term 'peoples' therefore remains problematic in definition.

As a conclusion and a proposal for an agenda for the twenty-first century, Part III takes as its theme 'Towards an International Role in the twenty-first Century'. The essays focus on the United Nations, the World Health Organisation (WHO) and the United Nations Educational, Scientific and Cultural Organisation (UNESCO), and the need to initiate and promote programmes of development, conflict resolution and human rights that are relevant for the continent. In Chapter 11, Malcolm Harper frankly assesses the UN's work in Africa and suggests ways in which it should redefine its role. Commenting on some of the major concerns in Africa, he argues that there must be a much more open assessment of the quality of governance in many parts of Africa. The process of democratisation and the strengthening of civil society are major priorities. The UN Security Council must treat the democratisation process of Africa more seriously than it has done in the past. It must be willing to understand democracy within the cultures and traditions of African people and not seek to impose a broad Western model upon them. Another issue he addresses is that of international peace and security: the UN has an obligation, under its Charter, to deal with situations that are a threat to international peace and security. However, in recent years the Security Council's attitude towards conflicts in Africa has shown a lack of interest. The UN's failure in Somalia marked a change in the attitudes of the governments of key members of the Security Council towards UN peace-keeping operations elsewhere. On the other hand, the OAU offered its fullest possible support to the efforts of the UN in the Rwandan crisis. Harper argues that the UN Security Council is not functioning very effectively and has failed to take action on a number of occasions because of delays and pusillanimity. The Council needs to be restructured and made more representative of the membership of the UN and the international community, and with Africa having a permanent seat in it. The UN must also help the OAU to build its own capacity. Harper also recommends that the UN should try to promote greater acceptance by both donors and recipients of genuine sustainable development and environmental protection programmes which prioritise poverty reduction as their overriding objective. Finally, the UN must develop a massive programme for human rights education, awareness and implementation. He concludes that the UN needs consistent political and practical support from its members in order to function effectively.

Harper's concerns about the North–South divide are echoed by Susan Adong in Chapter 12 on the topic of international health and Africa. She writes that international health has been a rather neglected area of research in international relations, and goes on to explain how the onset of Acquired Immune Deficiency Syndrome/human immuno deficiency virus (AIDS/HIV) has shown sub-Saharan Africa to be an area marginalised by the World Health Organization's rhetoric on 'universal health for all by the year 2000'. The failure of the WHO to provide for the needs of the people in the Third World, especially sub-Saharan Africa, has meant that African states must come up with their own solutions to health-related problems. Adong argues that, historically, public health has always been the responsibility of the state, and the Ugandan government, for one, has rejected a World Bank proposal for privatisation of its entire health sector. The incidence of AIDS/HIV is on the decrease in Uganda as a result of culturally sensitive state action since the mid-1980s. The message is that state action, and not WHO's prescription, is the most effective tool in the provision of health. Adong also asserts that regional alliances are more likely to be successful than the traditional regional demarcation set up by the WHO. The Great Lakes Regional AIDS Control Programme started by Uganda, Rwanda and Burundi is one example of an African initiative that was set up on the basis of cross-border co-operation. This initiative has shown that African regional co-operation based on the willingness of governments to find a common solution can, and does, work.

On the other hand, UNESCO fully recognises that Africa's development is, first and foremost, the responsibility of the governments and people of Africa themselves, but also that international partners could enhance the development prospects of Africa through an understanding and appreciation of Africa's development efforts. In Chapter 13, Sagarika Dutt traces the history of UNESCO's involvement in Africa's development in response to African member states' needs and expectations, and UN initiatives. She argues that UNESCO's approach to peace and development is particularly appropriate for Africa as it stresses the development of endogenous capacities and the cultural dimension of development rather than the neo-liberal models of development often imposed on African countries by international financial institutions. Since the late 1980s, UNESCO has considered Africa to be a priority and this trend is likely to continue well into the twenty-first century. In recent years, UNESCO has taken this one step further and its programmes for Africa in the late 1990s were based on the recommendations that were made and targets and standards that were set by the Africans themselves at a conference held in Paris in 1995.

Part III is summed up with an essay on the emerging role of the continent in the twenty-first century, suggesting areas of research necessary for Africa's inclusion in the Global Environment. In Chapter 14, the concluding chapter, Jack Spence summarises the major themes in the debate about Africa's future. He argues that capacity building at both national and local levels is crucial, as are education and training in all areas of public and private activity. In the long term an enabling environment can and should be created, in which African leaders and their peoples are able to maximise their potential.

The decision to focus on the topics covered in the book aims at setting an agenda for a mature discussion of African affairs from an innovative world view, based on a 'mix and match' strategy. Hence, contributors have been drawn from among 'older/younger' European Africanist and African scholars, particularly, 'young' and emerging scholars. The aim is also to encourage future research in these and other emerging areas. Scholarship on Africa for the twenty-first century should be orientated more towards problem-solving. It should be based on a mature approach in the search for effective and workable solutions, against the current academic-interest orientation.

Although this book seeks to present issues from an innovative and Africentric world view, the contributors are not all necessarily Africanist, but are academics and practitioners who have shown an interest in articulating issues relating to Africa from an African-centred perspective. It is our view that this book will pioneer a new form of research into African issues. It is a book that students and researchers in International Relations, Politics, Development Studies, and Security and Cultural Studies will find useful as a reference book, resource material and a research document. Charity organisations and other non-governmental organisations will also find it useful. While a number of books have been written on Africa covering some of the areas addressed here, the existing works have not been written from an African-centred world view, or drawn writers from different backgrounds and schools of thought. Existing works tend to focus on the 'known facts' on Africa without setting an agenda or suggesting strategies upon which research can be focused in search for solution(s) to the problems. This book is different, in that it argues that previously marginalised areas of research require in-depth study. It also introduces new areas of interest that have been absent from existing works. The book pays particular attention to the relative success of African countries and regions in their attempt to find solutions to Africa's 'problems', and the changing role of African states in international relations and their attempt to find a continental solution through co-operation. The book will therefore be very useful, and represent pioneering work in the development of a mature approach and new areas of studies on Africa, relevant to the twenty-first century.

Part I

Development and Economic Integration

1
The Peripheralisation of Africa in Global Politics

Paul Rich

Sub-Saharan Africa faces rather a bleak future of growing international indifference and neglect in the wake of the collapse of Cold War ideological divisions in global politics. The Cold War division of the international system into a bipolar model of conflict ensured that the newly-emerging African states in the period after 1945 could exert a considerable degree of political leverage on the rival Western and Communist blocs. Post-colonial states in Africa were provided with a high degree of external political, economic and ideological support, which tended to some degree to disguise or distort the more general process of economic and political marginalisation of the continent from the rest of the global economy.

The collapse of the Soviet bloc and the end of the Cold War has removed the rather thin veneer of legitimacy that these post-colonial regimes were able to secure during the Cold War era. They can no longer play off rival super-powers and, since at least the mid-1980s, a rather more dismal picture has begun to emerge in various parts of the continent of a crisis of political legitimacy, state disintegration and ethnic fragmentation.[1] For realists in International Relations, sub-Saharan Africa confirms that statehood which has been secured largely through juridical means and the force of international legal and moral opinion is always a rather insecure foundation for long-term political legitimation. Such states are always liable to fail the ultimate empirical test of survival against military threats, whether internally or externally.[2] In effect, African regimes find themselves forced to be marginalised from the global mainstream as their standards of statehood are found wanting.

While there may be some truth in this view, this chapter argues that it is overstated. The African continent experiences political and economic marginality in different ways and with diverse outcomes. Some states may well be able to secure quite respectable levels of economic growth over the next few years in conditions of political stability, while others may be destined to experience continued political and economic fragmentation. In other words, Africa – like other continents – has both successes and failures, suggesting that analysts need to get away from any analytical illusion that there are continentally-based characteristics that can be ascribed to all African states.

This more complex picture in contemporary African political economy should encourage analysts to avoid making overly simplistic and deterministic analyses, as those in development studies have been all too likely to do. The continent has clearly not lived up to the expectations of some modernisation theorists of the 1950s and early 1960s, who hoped that political independence and the establishment in power of new post-colonial elites would lead to a long-term process of 'nation building' and the creation of economies structured largely on North American lines. It is important here not to construct a straw man of such modernisation, since by no means all the post-war generation of Africa analysts were wholly convinced that African nationalism would copy the model of nationalism found in other continents. James Coleman, for example, warned as early as 1954 of the forces of disintegration as well as integration: 'The principle forces,' he wrote, 'currently operating to shape Africa's emergent nations are either tribalism or a nationalism following artificial imperial boundaries; and, with few exceptions, neither of these is directed towards the creation of political units which the geographer or economist would classify as ideal. In this respect, of course, Africa is not unique.'[3]

In contrast, radical analysts did not do much better than modernisationists when it came to predicting future outcomes in sub-Saharan Africa. The confident ideas of the 1970's theorists of dependency and underdevelopment, that the continent could in some manner break away from the structures of global capitalism and challenge the dominant financial institutions of the West into forging a New International Economic Order, now look distinctly dated, though few of those writing at this time have been humble enough to admit their mistakes. Indeed, to the extent that parts of sub-Saharan Africa have become peripheralised from the global economy, they have done so in a manner that some analysts have termed 'delinking by default'.[4]

Peripheralisation in Africa is an uneven process that varies according to the size and capacity of the state concerned and the degree to which it has maintained links with the former colonial power. For world-system theorists, peripheralisation is an endemic feature of the operation of the global capitalist system and its hierarchical differentiation into core, semi-peripheral and peripheral states.[5] Such an approach tends to be economically reductionist and assumes that African states will for the most part be authoritarian – what Jean François Bayart has termed the 'paradigm of the yoke'. It is incapable of explaining in any particularly penetrating way current movements for democratisation in Africa. It also assumes a far greater degree of political and economic homogeneity with the global capitalist system than in fact exists.[6] It overlooks the capacity that state elites and leaders have for diplomatic and political leverage and is generally blinkered to autonomous processes at work at the level of the polity, including the varying capacities of governing elites to manage their relations with the external global economic system. Moreover, even when taken at face value, world systems theory perpetuates many of the assumptions of dependency theory and presumes that it is unequal exchange or circulation rather than production that determines the low level of production in peripheral states. The 'productionist' critique of this, by contrast, points to production being a global rather than a national process, with all nations being subjected in varying degrees to capital movements outside their control.

African states have been peripheralised for multiple reasons and it is a fallacy to suppose, as Darryl Thomas and Ali Mazrui have argued simplistically, that the continent is a victim of a complex process of 'global apartheid' that works in a racial manner to ensure that global power and privilege remain in white hands.[7] The phase of Western imperial rule was important for establishing a framework of colonial relations that has been to a considerable degree perpetuated in the post-colonial era. It would be a myth, however, to suppose that Africa was in some way free of these dependent structures before the colonial era, because large parts of it were dependent on other metropoles in Asia and the Middle East. These external factors behind African continental peripheralisation need to be seen alongside indigenous factors relating to weak state legitimacy and the lack of cohesion among post-colonial elites in many parts of the continent.

This chapter examines these themes in four sections. The first section looks briefly at the historical roots of African peripheralisation before moving in the second section to discuss the attempt to break out of this peripheralisation following decolonization. The third section discusses the development of a coherent African diplomacy and how it might exert some leverage over the agenda of North–South relations, while the final section looks at what longer-term prospects, if any, African states have for breaking out of the current stranglehold of peripheralisation.

The historical roots of African peripheralisation

It is easy at one level to ascribe most of contemporary African peripheralisation and dependency to the era of European colonial rule. The European colonial intrusion during the nineteenth century secured metropolitan structural power over the continent, in many cases through the use of military force, though this was not always especially easy. In the case of Algeria, it took the French some four decades (1830–70) to crush indigenous resistance, at a cost of over 150 000 military casualties. In South Africa the defeat of indigenous resistance in the Eastern Cape started in the late eighteenth century and was only finally completed in the 1890s. By the twentieth century such colonial conquest had become increasingly unacceptable in terms of international law, and the Fascist government of Benito Mussolini faced international sanctions following its annexation of the Ethiopian state of the Emperor Haile Selassie in 1936 (though in the event the sanctions proved to be ineffective).

European colonial intrusion did not always depend on violent military conquest, since in a number of instances it accrued from the breakdown of more informal patterns of imperial influence and was secured relatively peacefully. European colonial rule remained in many respects a militarised operation even after the ending of African 'primary' resistance. Many colonial service personnel were recruited from military backgrounds, and military force was continually held in reserve in case the structures of colonial authority were to face a significant challenge.

The European colonial rulers were, for the most part, conservative – indeed, Burkean – in orientation as they sought to preserve 'traditional' African societies from excessive contamination by the external world. They were generally loath to tamper too much with internal African affairs, and established separate codes of African law. It was in the white settler colonies of Kenya, Algeria, the Rhodesias and South Africa that rather more wide-ranging attempts at social engineering were made by the colonial state with the forcible removal of African peasants from the best farming land and their isolation into labour reservoirs variously called 'tribal trust lands', 'reserves', 'homelands' and 'bantustans'. In the process, a local pattern of capital accumulation ensued that Donald Denoon has termed 'settler capitalism', which resembles similar processes at work in other continents such as South America and Australia. Here European settlers established a local state modelled on the European metropolitan state that was designed to facilitate an expanding capitalist sector rooted in the cheap labour of the colonised indigenous population.[8] In such instances, settler capitalists were generally happy to ally themselves with doctrines of racial segregation and exclusion that secured the forcible marginalisation of the black majority on grounds of race. As research in the case of South Africa shows, this was most likely to occur during the period of primary capital accumulation lasting roughly from the 1870s to the early 1960s. Thereafter, even indigenous capitalists had a growing interest in the progressive free-ing-up of the economy and the training of a skilled and semi-skilled black work force, thus pushing them into growing opposition to the rigid implementation of apartheid.[9]

European colonialism did not peripheralise African societies uni-formly. It imposed on them different forms of structural power, begin-ning in many cases with brutal military conquest but leading to a growing emphasis on other forms of power involving knowledge, com-munications and finance. The nineteenth-century Cape colony was an interesting early model of this evolutionary development within Euro-pean colonial rule as a restructuring of social relations occurred by the middle years of the century, leading to the development of a class of Western-educated male African land-holders who had access to the franchise and civil rights.[10] The power over knowledge became an increasingly dominant feature of European colonial rule by the early years of the twentieth century and helped, in turn, to shape African pressures for education, both locally and in Europe and the USA. The educational system to which they struggled to gain access was run by missionaries who did not necessarily share the goals of the colonial authorities. Missionary institutions by the inter-war years came to form what one scholar has termed an 'international benevolent empire' linked to the imperial metropoles. This 'benevolent empire' was broadly liberal in orientation and increasingly critical of the segregationist polices pur-sued in the white settler colonies, though it was still resistant to the idea of African nationalists displacing European colonial rulers completely.[11]

The structures of European imperialism provided some limited outlets whereby small, mission-educated African elites gained access to wider political and economic resources. The colonial era thus hardly marked a complete peripheralisation of African societies. In some respects it led to far more interest in and discussion about them occurring than had previously, even if this was in the elite circles of 'Africa experts'. The imperial connections enabled African students to take degrees in Euro-pean metropoles or in the USA, and the resulting student societies (such as the West African Students' Union in Britain) provided a focus for an exiled nationalist diaspora that had a long-term impact on indigenous

African societies.[12] Imperialism thus facilitated an expansion of scale in African societies and a resultant heightening of political consciousness that led, by the end of the Second World War, to the beginnings of nationalist movements.

Decolonisation and failure to break out of peripheralisation

For some sympathetic African analysts, the period of decolonization in the 1950s and early 1960s seemed to usher in the possibility of a major break-out from peripheralisation and to mark a major entry of Africa on to the stage of world politics. Considerable hopes were invested in the figure of Kwame Nkrumah of Ghana, who spoke a language of Pan Africanism and urged the continent to unite. However, the period of political independence signalled that the reverse process was happening, as the continent underwent a phase of intensifying 'balkanisation'. In 1950 there were only four independent states: Egypt, Liberia, Ethiopia and South Africa. By 1963–4 there were more than twenty, and by 1990, over fifty. Despite warnings by prominent figures such as Kwame Nkrumah, African leaders found it hard to agree on whether this balkanisation was a positive or a negative development. While some were worried that it might lead to a chain reaction throughout the continent, others accepted that the rest of the world was divided up into separate sovereign states.[13] The formation of the Organisation of African Unity in 1963 tended to reflect this lack of agreement. It failed to pursue a Pan African ideal for the organisation doggedly and rigidly stuck under Article III of its Charter to the principle of *uti possidetis* and the non-violation of the former colonial boundaries.

Western analysts in the 1950s and early 1960s manifested considerable optimism towards newly-independent African states. During a period when much academic analysis was dominated by discussion about theories of 'modernisation', it was assumed that post-colonial African ruling elites would have the capacity to build up developing nation states on lines not too dissimilar to those taking place elsewhere in the by then fashionably termed 'Third World'. The rhetoric of Third Worldism, the 'Afro-Asian bloc' in the UN and Non Alignment failed, however, to disguise the fact that the concept of a distinct 'Third World' was really very shallow, encompassing as it did such a wide variety of states and political systems. It was indeed largely a fabrication of wider superpower rivalry in the Cold War, and could not in the long run hide the centrality of nationalism in the struggle for liberation from European colonial rule.[14]

The African independence struggle tended as a result to be misunderstood, since African nationalism at the time of independence was still in the process of political development and had nowhere secured a permanent mass political base – indeed, it is arguable that something resembling this was only secured in the context of the mass township struggles in South Africa in the 1980s allied to the trade union movement. For European colonial governments such as the UK and France (though not a weak semi-peripheral regime such as Portugal), national independence in Africa in the late 1950s was not simply a case of trying to live up to the now nearly universal norm of decolonization. Nor, for that matter, was it a cynical attempt to promote a newer form of imperialism by other means. It stemmed largely from new sets of pressures on political decision-makers in London and Paris accruing from a changing balance of political and economic power in the post-1945 world.[15]

One of the most important of these external political constraints was the reluctance of the USA, in the wake of the Suez Crisis of 1956–7, to support unconditionally European colonial empires at a time when they appeared to be increasingly anachronistic in the ideological battleground of the Cold War.[16] The upkeep of colonies moreover appeared uneconomic. By the late 1950s, governing elites had been persuaded of the political wisdom of installing relatively weak post-colonial states under compliant governing elites which, it was hoped, would be at least capable of neutralising radical demands for more far-reaching economic and political change.

The independence era accordingly hardly marked a major African attempt to break out of the continent's peripheralisation. With the notable exception of the violent Algerian war of independence during 1954–62, European structural power was not challenged in any serious military sense and even the heyday of the Algerian model was extremely brief, lasting from around 1962 up to the military coup of 1965.[17] The decolonizing process led in most instances to a remarkable continuation of the previous pattern of colonial rule as independence led to the colonial state being relegitimated on a new footing through the single party regime and the autocratic control of civil society.[18] By the late 1960s and early 1970s, as white rule apparently became entrenched in the south, the main axis of post-independence political debate shifted towards some sort of attempt at African self-reliance. This was the era that Ali Mazrui has termed 'tanzaphilia', as interest shifted to Nyerere's Ujamaa programme of self-sufficient African peasant communities in Tanzania. It invoked a rather romantic conception of African rural life and hardly amounted to a serious strategy to challenge African marginalisation at a global level. It was based more on a resigned accept-ance of the fact that large-scale Western aid to assist in the reconstruc-tion of African economies was not going to be forthcoming, and that African communities had to make the best of the situation that inde-pendence had left them with.[19]

A more coherent attempt to challenge peripheralisation thus emerged rather later than the first phase of independence, in the context of more revolutionary shifts in power in Southern Africa following the collapse of Portuguese power and the 'forced decolonization' of Angola and Mozambique in 1975–6.[20] The seizure of power by the revolutionary National Front for the Liberation of Mozambique (FRELIMO) and Peo-ple's Liberation Movement of Angola (MPLA) regimes in Mozambique and Angola, together with the revolutionary overthrow of Haile Selassie in Ethiopia in 1977, was facilitated by what Walter Goldfrank has termed a 'permissive world context' during the latter half of the 1970s following the US withdrawal from Vietnam in 1973.[21] The quadrupling of oil prices by the Organisation of Petroleum Exporting Countries (OPEC) in 1973, following the Middle East war of that year, helped to initiate at the same time a debate on a New International Economic Order (NIEO) as it appeared that the 'Third World', now renamed the 'South', had greater political leverage than formerly to renegotiate the terms of international trade. For some analysts, it even seemed feasible that Africa by the late 1970s and early 1980s might be able to engineer some form of break-out from its peripheralisation by a strategy of regio-nal self-reliance and delinking from the structures of global capitalism.[22]

The debate centred on two major documents, the World Bank's Accel-erated Development (AD) in sub-Saharan Africa and the rival Lagos Plan of Action (LPA) drawn up by the Economic Commission for Africa under the guidance of the economist Adebayo Adedeji. The former sought greater economic liberalisation of African economies and a shift to agricultural production for export, while the latter championed more conventional state-managed corporatist models geared towards estab-lishing in the longer term a greater degree of African regional self-reliance. In some senses, both documents had utopian features as AD tried to impose a neo-classical free market model drawn from European and North American experiences (and radically at variance with those of the Asian Tigers), while the LPA was notable for its failure to spell out in any detail the policy measures needed to achieve its goal of regional self-reliance and how this was to be financed.[23] This proved to be a considerable drawback in the attempt by African intellectuals and economists to resist the onslaught of structural adjustment programmes during the 1980s as the international tide turned against the earlier NIEO with the advent of the Reagan Administration in the USA and the Thatcher Government in Britain. The 'South' proved to have little political leverage when it came to the question of international agenda setting in the 1980s. The US consistently pressured for the Uruguay Round and the enhancement of General Agreement on Tariffs and Trade (GATT) as a forum for debating LDC trade issues whilst also mounting a more overt ideological offensive against Southern forums by withdrawing from United Nations Educational, Scientific and Cultural Organisation (UNESCO) in 1984.[24]

At the local level in Southern Africa, a concerted effort began in the early 1980s to destabilise the revolutionary regimes of Angola and Mozambique. This occurred largely as a result of a 'hands off' approach from the highly ideological Reagan Administration in Washington that was concerned to secure limited political reform in South Africa through its policy of 'constructive engagement'. The policy in practice, however, provided the white South African regime with a green light to engage in widespread destruction and support for the rival political movements of the National Union for the total independence of Angola (UNITA) in Angola under Jonas Savimbi and the Mozambique National Resistance (RENAMO) in Mozambique.[25]

The resulting economic destabilisation did much to hasten the ideological shifts in the governing regimes in the early 1980s, away from a rigid attachment to Marxism-Leninism. By 1984, FRELIMO in Mozambique applied to join the World Bank and in a few more years (by 1990) it had even removed Marxism-Leninism from the country's constitution. An ideological counter-revolution of sorts occurred throughout the continent. The 'permissive international environment' of 1973–80 that had enabled many African radical regimes to come to power was ended during the brief renewal of the Cold War in the early 1980s. The USA for a period took on the role of Western hegemon towards Africa as it sought not simply to contain radical and Afro-Marxist influences but also to roll them back in a rather more active manner than anything it ever attempted in Europe. From a longer-term perspective, this American involvement in the continent's affairs was brief and was rapidly replaced following the revolutions in Eastern Europe and the ending of the Cold War with a new security policy by the early 1990s, in which its prime concern was to secure global order and access to resources.[26] It lasted long enough though for a mark to be made on the continent's diplomacy. In the case of Angola and Namibia, in particular, it was the US through its Under Secretary of State for African Affairs, Chester

Crocker, rather than the OAU, that orchestrated the protracted rounds of political mediation in 1988 which finally secured the phased withdrawal of Cuban troops from Angola in return for the independence of Namibia.[27] In the process it exposed major weaknesses in African diplomacy that subsequent years have done little to rectify.

The weaknesses of African diplomacy

African diplomacy from the time of independence has tended to be based on exclamatory declarations and statements of intent rather than on a more far-reaching set of political, military and economic strategies. The weak nature of African post-colonial regimes has meant that individual leaders such as Julius Nyerere, Kenneth Kaunda and Kwame Nkrumah have ended up personally dominating foreign policy and resisting any tendencies towards bureaucratisation and professionalisation.[28] This continued even after the independence of Zimbabwe in 1980, with Robert Mugabe maintaining tight control over the regime's foreign relations.[29] The problem with this personalised type of diplomacy is that it has tended to age along with its practitioners.[30] The small coterie of African diplomatic professionals has lost much of its anger and verve with advancing age and now that even the South West African People's Organisation (SWAPO) and the African National Congress of South Africa (ANC) have passed into government there are few new sources to renew the impetus behind bodies like the OAU and to resist the pressures of the 'development diplomats' of the World Bank and the International Monetary Fund (IMF).[31]

The weakness in African diplomatic leverage has been compounded by a more basic structural phenomenon that has become increasingly visible since the 1980s. To a considerable extent it is now possible to see what Christopher Clapham has termed the 'de-stating' of African external relations as conventional state-to-state relations become displaced by wider processes of globalisation and in effect privatised, as formerly diplomatic functions are performed by non-state actors such as multi-national corporations (MNCs) and NGOs.[32] In sub-Saharan Africa, as elsewhere in the global economy, a growing bifurcation has been taking place within the Southern rim of states between a 'Third' and a 'Fourth' world. The economic and political position of the governing elites of 'Third-World' states was rapidly being undermined by the spectre of 'Fourth-Worldism' involving the progressive collapse of urban-based economic systems, repeasantisation and, in the worst cases such as Somalia, Liberia and Sierra Leone, the destruction of the state itself.

This prospect did much to end earlier ideological divisions in the continent as the governing elites of post-colonial states, whatever their political complexion, clamoured for access to Western aid and investment. Programmes of structural adjustment have, as a consequence, had far-reaching implications for the political complexions of governing elites.

In one of the best-studied cases – Mozambique, the programme of structural adjustment has ensured that Western financial institutions (aided by other agencies) have effectively taken over the running of the country's economic policy while at the same time forcing the ruling FRELIMO regime to break its alliance with its former base of support among the peasantry and working class. This realignment of political forces has transformed the state's external relationship from one of clientelism to one of near political vassalage as the state's freedom of manoeuvre to bargain with rival power blocs has effectively been terminated.[33]

It would be an exaggeration though to see the weakness of the Mozambican state as being solely a result of external factors. It was also undermined by domestic political opposition that was generated by its ill-considered land reform programme in the late 1970s. Some of this opposition gravitated towards RENAMO during the 1980s. RENAMO was not simply a group of South-African-backed 'bandits', as official propaganda maintained, but located among disaffected sections of the peasantry as well as traditional healers – *curandeiros* – and chiefs who had largely been ignored by the FRELIMO regime.[34] The resulting ideological shifts by the ruling FRELIMO did not occur solely in response to external pressures but also as a result of the country's internal political dynamics. FRELIMO had come under the control of strongly vanguardist elements in the late 1970s, who tried to transform it into a Soviet-style party with close autocratic control over civil society. These elements became progressively marginalised during the late 1980s, and in 1990 a new constitution was introduced that provided for a multiparty political system. The overthrow of many Eastern European Communist regimes the previous year undoubtedly did much to tilt the scales in favour of political reform, though by this time a large section of the FRELIMO ruling elite had effectively abandoned Marxist ideology in favour of a free market economic model. To the despair of radical intellectual *co-operantes*, who in some cases had given some of the best of their careers to promoting revolution in the country, the FRELIMO elite placed its faith in the creation of a 'national bourgeoisie' as a major force in economic reconstruction.[35]

The rapid establishment of a free market orthodoxy in African political debate has been a matter for some regret among radical analysts, who have tried to retrieve what they can of some of the older Marxian paradigm. Timothy Shaw, for example, has accepted that most of the 1970s radical agenda in favour of some form of African regionalism that could break with the global capitalist system is now politically unfeasible. He has argued that much contemporary African political conflict has a class rather than a simple ethnic complexion, and that the prospect of escalating class struggle will be enough to restrain ruling elites, particularly in many 'Third-World' African states, from opting for a full-scale free market solution in favour of some variant of political corporatism.[36] This prospect appears to receive added reinforcement from the transitional settlement in South Africa in which the new government of National Unity has come under strong political pressure to forge a settlement with the well-organised black trade union movement on quasi-corporatist lines. However, it is unlikely that, even in the South African case, corporatism can be any more than a temporary mechanism in which some of the harsh social effects of structural adjustment may be forestalled.[37]

In the African 'Fourth World' on the other hand, an even bleaker picture emerges, with state breakdown and the revolt of an ideologically unfocused youth, in a complex pattern of generational and educational cleavages interacting with those of class and ethnicity. Rene Lamarchand has pointed to 'infra political' phenomena in which the cumulative pressure of oppression, economic scarcity, ethnic and factional violence produce new cultural idioms capable of shaping patterns of resistance as well as possibly long-term regeneration of civil society.[38]

This has become evident in a number of African societies since the early 1980s as the structure of mainstream civil society has begun to break up and more 'traditional' cultural phenomena re-emerge. In Mozambique, RENAMO has made considerable use of young men (*mujibas*), witchdoctors and chiefs (*regulos*) after they were ostracised by FRELIMO after independence in 1975. While this has not led to a movement that is completely anti-Western technology, the support of such elements may partially explain the ferocity with which the social infrastructure such as schools, hospitals and clinics have been wantonly destroyed as symbols of an alien urban-based regime that is in many cases as foreign to an oppressed rural peasantry as the former colonial Portuguese.[39]

Similar processes can be seen in other African societies. In Liberia and Sierra Leone the breakdown of the state structure was not so much a case of a youthful revolt replacing former ethnic and class divisions, but rather one giving them a new and added intensity. The leaders of the factions in the Liberian violence had all originally been in the Doe Government, where they had learned the art of factional and clientelist politics. They were too weak to maintain control over their own followers, or even in some cases to prevent them fighting each other.[40] The former ideological alignments of the Cold War had now broken down and the violence began to acquire a logic of its own, divorced from whatever political basis it may initially have had. In many cases, the political bases of conflict were replaced by spiritual and cultic ones that were on occasion strong enough to persuade soldiers in established armies to desert. This suggests that as the legitimacy of the post-colonial state begins to collapse it may be necessary to rethink, in parts particularly of 'Fourth-World' Africa, the basis of political legitimacy in spiritual terms whereby 'representations of power expressed in a spiritual register may be seen not as a-political, but as the necessary accompaniment of a political project'.[41]

There is a growing emphasis in the debate on African political and economic regeneration on the nature and basis of state legitimacy. Rethinking the nature of African statehood soon comes up against wider issues of democratisation that have permeated African political debate since the late 1980s. As the next section seeks to argue, legitimising African statehood involves a degree of democratisation alongside wider processes of economic liberalisation.

An African break-out from peripheralisation?

It will be a hard and protracted task for African states to break out of political and economic marginalisation. This is not made any easier by the realignments that have been occurring in the dominant political blocs which dominate many sub-Saharan African states as the state-led neo-corporatist model of development is replaced by newer sets of alliances between national interest groups and international actors operating at the global level.[42] International Financial Institutions (IFIs) such as the IMF and World Bank have welcomed such developments warmly, seeing them as a means of securing higher rates of economic growth than previously. In 1991, for example, only twenty states recorded positive per capita growth, while by 1995–6 this had almost doubled.[43]

The principles underlying structural adjustment, such as market liberalisation, openness in trade and financial orthodoxy, amount to a new and revised set of 'civilised standards' which developing states need to be seen to be fulfilling before they are accepted fully into the international society of states.[44] Black African governing elites have come to accept that various forms of macroeconomic restructuring are more or less inevitable if they are to maintain credible forms of external linkages with both IFIs and private investors. However, the dilemma they face as ruling elites is the capacity to maintain domestic security as well as the minimum level of political liberalisation that meets basic standards of human rights.

There is no inevitable link between economic and political liberalisation.[45] African politics contains both an authoritarian and a democratic strain, which might well be encouraged by the rapid processes of economic development.[46] The generally weak nature of African statehood suggests that ruling regimes may be forced to resort to growing authoritarianism in the early stages of economic development programmes in order to maintain social stability on lines similar to many states in the Asia Pacific region, such as Taiwan and South Korea. The fact too that civil society remains poorly developed in many parts of sub-Saharan Africa indicates that programmes of democratisation may fail to become institutionalised. Even when they do, a flourishing civil society may not necessarily secure a successful pattern of democratisation, since there may be politically exclusive and illiberal factions organised within it on ethnic and tribal grounds, which can threaten the stability of democratic structures.

African ruling regimes face a considerable political challenge in terms of trying to widen the narrow economic agenda of structural adjustment propagated by the IMF and World Bank in order to take on board issues of societal security and political stability. In 1992, the OAU Summit at Dakar, Senegal acknowledged that there was a 'link between security stability, development and co-operation in Africa'.[47] It has proved difficult, however, to move this issue on to the central agenda of debate, especially in the absence of direct African representation in the deliberations of the IFIs. In Washington, the Congressional Black Caucus deliberations have called on the G7 group of countries to promote a more active process of consultation with African leaders, though so far this has had little political effect.[48]

In terms of the wider issue of promoting societal security in Africa, there is a special onus on the United Nations to lay out a robust and credible international agenda of peace enforcement and collective economic security. Such an agenda would seek to tackle the UN's generally low standing on the African continent following its failure to resolve the

Angolan or Mozambican civil wars.[49] In the course of the 1990s there
has emerged a growing accord between the UN and the OAU behind an
agenda of growing regional association and dialogue. Indeed, the UN
has come increasingly to look upon regionalism as an essential compon-
ent of international peace-keeping if it is to avoid becoming overburdened itself by an excessive number of peace-keeping operations;
between 1989 and 1998, for example, the UN launched thirty-two
peace-keeping operations, of which thirteen were in Africa. The Somalia
operation, however, was the first UN operation in its history to be
withdrawn before completing its mission. In April 1998, the UN Secretary-General, Kofi Annan, in a report to the UN Security Council argued
that closer economic links between African states on a regional basis will
in turn promote greater attention to regional conflict resolution.[50]

The devolution of responsibility from the UN to regional peace-keeping associations makes a lot of sense in terms of avoiding excessive
centralisation in the complex UN planning machinery in New York. At
the same time, it leaves key decisions to more locally-based figures who
may be more familiar with events on the ground. However, the UN
approach to regionalism in Africa fails to recognise that there is nothing
innate about it as a process in international relations.[51] In order for
regionalism to have any political credibility on the African continent
it is likely to need a strong hegemonic power or group of powers to
promote it. Since the continent lacks for the most part states that have
robust and durable political structures and strong claims to empirical
legitimacy it is difficult to see how strong regional arrangements can
emerge easily. This became evident in the case of the ECOMOG intervention into the Liberian civil war, which ended up being dominated by
Nigeria and, as David Francis indicates elsewhere in this volume, was
largely an *ad hoc* enterprise. Indeed, the venture, if anything, has ended
up fomenting regional rivalries – especially between Nigeria and Ghana
– in contrast to the original aim of demonstrating a credible and effective process of regional peace-keeping.[52]

In the longer term, the strongest states in sub-Saharan Africa, led by
South Africa, will need to be organised into a regional consortium in
order to promote African collective security. The idea of promoting
continental collective security has been debated for a number of years.
It was the theme of the Kampala Document, which was collectively
issued by the secretariat of the OAU, the UN Economic Commission
for Africa and the Africa Leadership Forum following the 1991 Kampala
Conference on Security, Stability, Development and Co-operation in
Africa. However, the document failed to promote any tangible proposals

and ended with the usual declaratory diplomatic jargon such as its call: 'African governments must individually and collectively be guided by the principle of good neighbourliness and a peaceful resolution of conflicts'.[53] The issue may probably more profitably debated in a wider series of forums involving both the UN and OAU as well as the major Western industrialised countries, as suggested by Kofi Annan's 1998 Security Council report.[54] So far, the OAU has failed to mobilise any major political impetus behind a regional agenda and it is more than likely that whatever regionalism will occur will be more or less by stealth and on a small scale in response to individual crises. To this extent it is hard to envisage regionalism becoming at an early date part of a more pro-active strategy of conflict prevention in sub-Saharan Africa.

Conclusion

This chapter has argued that African continental peripheralisation has multiple causes, both external and internal. It is a fallacy for analysts to see the continent simply as a victim of external factors. Internal political processes have been of considerable significance in perpetuating the weak sovereignty of many states, and a reluctance to engage in wider political bargains that might secure a greater leverage with the external political and diplomatic environment. In some respects the continent is now at a crossroad as the fragile legitimacy has been exposed in the harsh new climate of the post-Cold War era.

However, while a debate has ensued on the need to establish societal as opposed to state security, it is hard to see how this can be accomplished easily in the form of regionalism, as organisations such as the UN and OAU imagine. An early African breakout from its current peripheralisation is unlikely to occur, though some states may be able to sustain higher rates of economic growth than those of the 1970s and 1980s. Structural adjustment too will continue, though as a programme it offers continental Africa no long-term vision of its future. The regional associations that are likely to occur will be those under the control of a powerful sub-regional hegemon such as the Southern African Development Community (SADC) under the aegis of South Africa in Southern Africa. A successful demonstration of regional peace-keeping at this level may well be extended later to other parts of the continent.

Notes and References

1 Kaplan, Robert (1994) 'The Coming Anarchy', *The Atlantic Monthly*, no. 273, pp. 43–76.

2 Jackson, Robert H. and Rosberg, Carl G. (1986) 'The Marginality of African States', in Gwendolen M. Carter and Patrick O'Meara (eds), *African Independence: The First Twenty Five Years* (Bloomington, Indiana: Indiana University Press), pp. 45–68.

3 Coleman, James (1954) 'Nationalism in Tropical Africa', *The American Political Science Review*, vol. 46, no. 2, June, pp. 423–4.

4 Wright, Stephen (1992) 'Africa in the Post Cold War World', *Transafrica Forum*, Summer, p. 28.

5 See, for example, Wallerstein, Immanuel (1979) *The Capitalist World Economy*, (Cambridge University Press).

6 Bayart, Jean-François (1993) *The State in Africa* (London and New York: Longman), pp. 2–10. See also the balanced assessment of Thomas Richard Shannon (1989) *An Introduction to the World System Perspective* (Boulder, Col.: Westview Press), esp. pp. 165–6.

7 Thomas, Darryl and Mazrui, Ali (1992) 'Africa's Post Cold War Demilitarisation', *Journal of International Affairs*, vol. 46, no. 1, Summer, pp. 173–4.

8 Denoon, Donald (1983) *Settler Capitalism: The Dynamics of Dependent Development in the Southern Hemisphere* (Oxford: Clarendon Press).

9 See, in particular, Greenberg, Stanley (1980) *Race and State in Capitalist Development* (New Haven, Conn. and London: Yale University Press).

10 Crais, Clifton (1992) *White Supremacy and Black Resistance in Pre-Industrial South Africa: The Making of a Colonial Order in the Eastern Cape* (Cambridge University Press).

11 Elphick, Richard (1987) 'Mission Christianity and Interwar Liberalism' in Jeffrey Butler, Richard Elphick and David Welsh (eds), *Democratic Liberalism in South Africa* (Middletown, Conn.: Wesleyan University Press).

12 Rich, Paul (1987) 'The Black Diaspora in Britain: Afro-Caribbean Students and the Quest for Political Identity, 1900–1950', *Immigrants and Minorities*, vol. 6, no. 2, July, pp. 151–73.

13 Neuberger, Benyamin (1976) 'The African Concept of Balkanisation', *Journal of Modern African Studies*, vol. 14, no. 3, pp. 523–9.

14 Berger, Mark T. (1994) 'The End of the Third World', *Third World Quarterly*, vol. 15, no. 2, p. 261.

15 Hargreaves, Mark T. (1988) *Decolonization in Africa* (London and New York: Longman), p. 229.

16 Boertz, Gary (1994) *Contexts of International Politics* (Cambridge University Press), esp. pp. 250–67.

17 Ottaway, David and Ottaway, Marina (1970) *Algeria: The Politics of a Socialist Revolution* (Berkeley, California: University of California Press).

18 Young, Crawford (1988) 'The African Colonial State and its Political Legacy', in Donald Rothchild and Naomi Chazan (eds), *The Precarious Balance: State and Society in Africa* (Boulder, Col. and London: Westview Press), pp. 57–60.

19 Nyerere, Julius (1973) *Freedom and Development* (London: Oxford University Press).

20 Hargreaves, *Decolonization in Africa*, pp. 212–18.
21 Goldfrank, Walter (1979) 'Theories of Revolution and Revolution without Theory', *Theory and Society*, vol. 7, esp. pp. 148–51.
22 See, for example, Shaw, Timothy (1983) 'South Africa, Southern Africa and the World System', in Thomas M. Callaghy (ed.), *South Africa in Southern Africa*, (New York: Praeger).
23 For a critical reassessment of the LPA, see John Ravenhill (1986) 'Is the Lagos Plan a Viable Alternative?', in John Ravenhill (ed.), *Africa in Economic Crisis* (London: Macmillan).
24 Livingston, Steven (1992) 'The Politics of International Agenda-Setting: Reagan and North–South Relations', *International Studies Quarterly*, vol. 36, pp. 313–30.
25 Moorcroft, Paul (1990) *African Nemesis: War and Revolution in Southern Africa, 1945–2010* (London: Brasseys).
26 Tholman, Daniel (1993) 'Africa and the New World Order', *Journal of Modern African Studies*, vol. 31, no. 1, pp. 1–30.
27 Berridge, G. R. (1989) 'Diplomacy and the Angola/Namibia Accords', *International Affairs*, vol. 65, no. 3, Summer, pp. 463–79; Rich, Paul (1993) 'The United States, Its History of Mediation and the Chester Crocker Round of Negotiations over Namibia in 1988', in S. Chan and V. Chabri (eds), *Mediation in Southern Africa* (London: Macmillan), pp. 75–96.
28 Wright, 'Africa in the Post Cold War World'.
29 Chan, Stephen (1994) 'The Diplomatic Styles of Zambia and Zimbabwe', in Paul Rich (ed.), *The Dynamics of Change in Southern Africa* (London: Macmillan), pp. 218–31.
30 Shaw, Timothy (1988) 'State of Crisis: International Constraints, Contradictions and Capitalisms?' in Rothchild and Chazan, *The Precarious Balance*, p. 315.
31 Adams, Patricia (1992) 'The World Bank and the IMF in Sub-Saharan Africa: Undermining Development and Environment Sustainability', *Journal of International Affairs*, vol. 46, no. 1, Summer, pp. 97–117.
32 Clapham, Christopher (1996) *Africa and the International System* (Cambridge University Press), pp. 256–66.
33 Bowen, Merle (1992) 'Beyond Reform: Adjustment and Political Power in Contemporary Mozambique', *Journal of Modern African Studies*, vol. 30, no. 2, pp. 255–79, reproduced in Paul Rich (ed.), *The Dynamics of Change in Southern Africa*, pp. 120–44; Plank, David (1993) 'Aid, Debt and the End of Sovereignty: Mozambique and Its Donors', *Journal of Modern African Studies*, vol. 31, no. 3, pp. 407–30.
34 Young, Tom (1994) 'From the MNR to RENAMO: Making Sense of an Africa Counter Insurgency', in Paul Rich (ed.), *The Dynamics of Change in Southern Africa*.
35 Simpson, Mark (1993) 'Foreign and Domestic Factors in the Transformation of FRELIMO', *Journal of Modern African Studies*, vol. 31, no. 2, pp. 309–37; Finnegan, William (1992) *The Harrowing of Mozambique* (Berkeley, California: University of California Press), pp. 130–2.
36 Shaw, Timothy (1992) 'Reformism, Revisionism and Radicalism in African Political Economy in the 1990s', *Journal of Modern African Studies*, vol. 29, no. 2, June, pp. 191–212.

37   Bond, Patrick (1998) *The Elite Transformation: Globalisation and the Rise of Economic Fundamentalism in South Africa* (London: Pluto).

38   Lemarchand, René (1992) 'Uncivil States and Civil Societies: How Illusion Became Reality', *Journal of Modern African Studies*, vol. 30, no. 2, pp. 177–91.

39   Finnegan, pp. 76–81.

40   Ellis, Stephen (1994) 'Liberia, 1989–1994: A Study of Ethnic and Spiritual Violence', *African Affairs*, vol. 94, no. 165, pp. 165–97.

41   Ibid.

42   Ould-Mey, Mohameden (1994) 'Global Adjustment: Implications for Peripheral States', *Third World Quarterly*, vol. 15, no. 2, pp. 319–34.

43   Camdessus, Michael (1996) 'Integrating Africa More Fully into the Global Economy', Bordeaux, May 13, Internet: http/www.imf.org/external/np/sec/mds/1996/MDS9610.HTM.

44   Gong, Gerrit W. (1998) 'Standards of Civilisation Today,' Paper presented to the Panel on Interacting Civilization at the 3rd Pan European International Relations Conference, Vienna, 16–19 September.

45   Beetham, David (1997) 'Market Economy and Democratic Polity', *Democratization*, vol. 4, no. 1, Spring, pp. 76–91.

46   Tordoff, William (1994) 'Political Liberalization and Economic Reform in Africa', *Democratization*, vol. 1, no. 1, Spring, p. 113.

47   Gambari, Ibrahim (1996) 'The Role of Regional and Global Organizations', in Edmond J. Keller and Donald Rothchild (eds), *Africa in the New International Order* (Boulder, Col.: Lynne Rienner), p. 33.

48   Washington Office on Africa (1997) 'Africans must Have Voice in Economic Policy Making', 11 June, Internet: http:/www.africanews.org/specials/19970611-feat1.html.

49   Alden, Chris (1995) 'The UN and the Resolution of Conflict in Mozambique', *Journal of Modern African Studies*, vol. 33, no. 1, pp. 103–28.

50   United Nations, Report of the Secretary-General (1998) 'The Causes of Conflict and Promotion of Durable Peace and Sustainable Development in Africa' (New York: United Nations), 16 April, p. 26, para. 100. Available on Internet: http://www.un.org/ecosocdev/geninfo/afrec/sgreport/report.htm//intro.

51   Hettne, Bjorn (1994) 'The Regional Factor in the Formation of the New World Order', in Yoshikazu Sakamoto (ed.), *Global Transformation: Challenges to the State System* (Tokyo: United Nations University Press), pp. 134–64.

52   Mortimer, Robert (1996) 'ECOMOG, Liberia and Regional Security in West Africa', in Keller and Rothchild, *Africa in the New International Order*, pp. 149–62.

53   Gambari, 'The Role of Regional and Global Organisations', p. 34.

54   United Nations, Report of the Secretary-General, 'The Causes of Conflict . . . ', p. 27, para 101.

Bibliography

Adams, Patricia (1992) 'The World Bank and the IMF in Sub-Saharan Africa: Undermining Development and Environment Stability', *Journal of International Affairs*, vol. 46, no. 1, Summer.

Alden, Chris (1995) 'The UN and the Resolution of Conflict in Mozambique', *Journal of Modern African Studies*, vol. 33, no. 1.

Bayart, Jean-François, (1993) *The State in Africa* (London: Longman).

Beetham, David (1997) 'Market Economy and Democratic Polity', *Democratization*, vol. 4, no. 1, Spring.

Berger, Mark. T (1994) 'The End of the Third World', *Third World Quarterly*, vol. 15, no. 2.

Berridge, G. R. (1989) 'Diplomacy and the Angola/Namibia Accords', *International Affairs*, vol. 65, no. 3.

Boertz, Garry (1994) *Contexts of International Politics* (Cambridge University Press).

Bond, Patrick (1998) *The Elite Transformation: Globalisation and the Rise of Economic Fundamentalism in South Africa* (London: Pluto Press).

Bowen, Merle (1996) 'Beyond Reform: Adjustment and Political Power in Contemporary Mozambique', in Paul Rich (ed.), *The Dynamics of Change in Southern Africa* (London: Macmillan).

Camdessus, Michael (1996) 'Integrating Africa More Fully into the Global Economy', Internet: http/www.imf.org/external/np/sec/1996/MDS9610.HTM.

Carter, G. M. and O'Meara, P. (eds) (1986), *African Independence: The First Twenty Five Years* (Bloomington, Indiana: Indiana University Press).

Chan, Stephen (1994) 'The Diplomatic Styles of Zambia and Zimbabwe', in Paul B. Rich (ed.), *The Dynamics of Change in Southern Africa* (London: Macmillan).

Clapham, Christopher (1996) *Africa and the International System* (Cambridge University Press).

Coleman, James S. (1954) 'Nationalism in Tropical Africa', *American Political Science Review*, vol. 46, no. 2, June.

Crais, Clifton (1992) *White Supremacy and Black Resistance in Pre-Industrial South Africa: The Making of a Colonial Order in the Eastern Cape* (Cambridge University Press).

Denoon, Donald (1983) *Settler Capitalism: The Dynamics of Dependent Development in the Southern Hemisphere* (Oxford: Clarendon Press).

Ellis, Stephen (1994) 'Liberia, 1989–1994: A Study of Ethnic and Spiritual Violence', *African Affairs*, vol. 94, no. 165.

Elphick, Richard (1987) 'Mission Christianity and Interwar Liberalism', in Jeffrey Butler, Richard Elphick and David Welsh (eds), *Democratic Liberalism in South Africa* (Middletown, Conn.: Wesleyan University Press).

Finnegan, William (1992) *The Harrowing of Mozambique* (Berkeley, California: University of California Press).

Gambari, Ibrahim A. (1996) 'The Role of Regional and Global Organisations', in Edmond Keller and Donald Rothchild (eds), *Africa in the New International Order*, (Boulder, Col.: Lynne Rienner).

Goldfrank, Walter (1979) 'Theories of Revolution and Revolution without Theory', *Theory and Society*, vol. 7.

Gong, Gerrit W. (1998) 'Standards of Civilisation Today', Paper presented to the Panel on Interacting Civilisations, 3rd Pan European International Relations Conference, Vienna, 16–19 September.

Greenberg, Stanley (1980) *Race and State in Capitalist Development* (New Haven, Conn. and London: Yale University Press).

Hargreaves, J. D. (1988) *Decolonization in Africa* (London: Longman).

Hettne, Bjorn (1994) 'The Regional Factor in the Formation of the New World Order', in Yoshikazu Sakamoto (ed.), *Global Transformation: Challenges to the State System* (Tokyo: United Nations University Press).

Jackson, Robert H. and Rosberg, Carl G. 'The Marginality of African States', in Gwendolen M. Carter and Patrick O'Meara (eds), *African Independence: The First Twenty Five Years*.

Kaplan, Robert (1994) 'The Coming Anarchy', *The Atlantic Monthly*, vol. 273.

Lemarchand, René (1992) 'Uncivil Societies and Civil Societies: How Illusion Became Reality', *Journal of Modern African Studies*, vol. 30, no. 2.

Livingston, Steven G. (1992) 'The Politics of International Agenda Setting – Reagan and North–South Relations', *International Studies Quarterly*, no. 36.

Moorcroft, Paul L. (1990) *African Nemesis: War and Revolution in Southern Africa, 1945–2010* (London: Brasseys).

Mortimer, Robert A. (1996) 'ECOMOG, Liberia and Regional Security in West Africa', in Edmond Keller and Donald Rothchild (eds), *Africa in the New International Order* (Boulder, Col.: Lynne Rienner).

Neuberger, Benyamin (1976) 'The African Concept of Balkanisation', *Journal of Modern African Studies*, vol. 14, no. 3.

Nyerere, Julius (1973) *Freedom and Development* (Oxford University Press).

Ottaway, David and Ottaway, Marina (1970) *Algeria – The Politics of a Socialist Revolution* (Berkeley, California: University of California Press).

Ould-Mey, Mohameden (1994) 'Global Adjustment: Implications for Peripheral States', *Third World Quarterly*, vol. 15, no. 2.

Plank, David N. (1993) 'Aid, Debt and the End of Sovereignty: Mozambique and Its Donors', *Journal of Modern African Studies*, vol. 31, no. 3.

Ravenhill, John (1986) 'Is the Lagos Plan a Viable Alternative?', in John Ravenhill (ed.), *Africa in Economic Crisis* (London: Macmillan).

Rich, Paul (1987) 'The Black Diaspora in Britain: Afro Caribbean Students and the Quest for Political Identity, 1900–1950', *Immigrants and Minorities*, vol. 6, no. 2, July.

Rich, Paul (1994), 'The United States, Its History of Mediation and the Chester Crocker Rounds of Negotiations over Namibia in 1988', in Stephen Chan and Vivienne Chabri (eds), *Mediation in Southern Africa* (London: Macmillan).

Shaw, Timothy, M. (1983) 'South Africa, Southern Africa and the World System', in Thomas M. Callaghy (ed.), *South Africa in Southern Africa* (New York: Praeger).

Shaw, Timothy, M. (1988) 'State of Crisis: International Constraints, Contradictions and Capitalisms?', in Donald Rothchild and Naomi Chazan (eds), *The Precarious Balance: State and Society in Africa* (Boulder, Col. and London: Westview, Press).

Shaw, Timothy, M. (1992) 'Reformism, Revisionism and Radicalism in African Political Economy in the 1990s', *Journal of Modern African Studies*, vol. 29, no. 2, June.

Shannon, Thomas Richard (1989) *An Introduction to the World System Perspective* (Boulder, Col.: Westview Press).

Simpson, Mark (1993) 'Foreign and Domestic Factors in the Transformation of FRELIMO', *Journal of Modern African Studies*, vol. 31, no. 2.

Tholman, Daniel, (1993) 'AFRICA and the New World Order', *Journal of Modern African Studies*, vol. 31, no. 2.

Thomas, Darryl and Mazrui, Ali (1992) 'Africa's Post Cold War Demilitarisation', *Journal of International Affairs*, vol. 46, no. 1, Summer.

Tordoff, William (1994) 'Political Liberalization and Economic Reform in Africa', *Democratization*, vol. 1, no. 1, Spring.

United Nations, Report of the Secretary-General (1998) *The Causes of Conflict and Promotion of Durable Peace and Sustainable Development in Africa* (New York: United Nations), 16 April.

Wallerstein, Immanuel (1979) *The Capitalist World Economy* (Cambridge University Press).

Washington Office on Africa (1997) 'Africans Must Have Voice in Economic Policy Making', June 11. Internet: http:/www.africanews.org/specials/19970611-feat1.html.

Wright, Stephen (1992) 'Africa in the Post Cold War World', *Transafrica Forum*, Summer.

Young, Crawford (1988), 'The African Colonial State and Its Political Legacy', in Donald Rothchild and Naomi Chazan (eds) *The Precarious Balance* (Boulder, Col. and London: Westview Press).

Young, Tom (1994) 'From the MNR to RENAMO: Making Sense of an Africa Counter Insurgency', in Paul Rich (ed.), *The Dynamics of Change in Southern Africa* (London: Macmillan).

2
External Debt and Adjustment: Prospects for African Economic Growth and Transformation

Geepu-Nah Tiepoh

Introduction

Amid the persistence of the debt crisis in African economies, and the inefficacy of existing international debt relief initiatives, there is a strong opinion demanding that African states should seek 'internal' solutions through promotion of economic growth. The argument is that, by improving domestic economic management, African countries can achieve adequate growth to ensure sustainability of external debt accumulation. The persistence of the debt crisis is blamed on weak economic growth caused by poor domestic economic management.[1] Such a position follows the perspective of economists such as Bulow and Rogoff (1990), who view the external debt problems of developing countries as being *symptoms* of poor economic growth rather than its *primary cause*. However, other economists, including Bacha (1992), Sachs (1990), Kenen (1990) and Krugman (1989) see external debt overhang as a major cause of stunted economic growth in heavily indebted countries. Through an econometric model, Salih (1994) has shown that high external debt stocks discourage African economic growth by their negative impacts on capital formation. Woodward (1992) has analysed the negative investment and growth implications of debt-induced adjustment in developing countries.

It is worth noting, however, that the relationship between external debt problems and economic growth is complex, with causality running in both directions. First, growth without development and structural transformation cannot provide a long-term, sustainable debt-servicing capacity. Paradoxically, however, the existence of an external debt crisis may itself necessitate an adjustment process that ignores such economic transformation, thereby undermining debt sustainability. Second, whereas poor economic growth may lead to the unsustainability of debt accumulation, the presence of excessive debt burdens can generate investment disincentives and cause a shortage of the domestic resources needed to expand productive capacity, thus inhibiting growth and development.[2] Therefore, in any analysis, the adoption of one side of the debt–growth nexus is not necessarily a negation of the other. It is possible for one to inquire into how a given low-growth situation may have an impact on debt sustainability, or how a given debt problem might affect the growth and development prospects of a country or region.

This chapter adopts the latter perspective. It analyses the impact of external debt crisis on domestic economic policy choice and sustainable development in sub-Saharan Africa (SSA). The central theme is the extent to which debt unsustainability and the adjustment process incurred by it have had a negative effect on African economic growth and transformation since the 1970s. It is argued that unless there is a successful shift from asymmetric and rapid adjustment policies focusing on restructuring only domestic variables and achieving external equilibria towards a balanced and long-term adjustment process aimed at improving productive capacity and structural transformation, African economic development will remain debt-prone. The remainder of the chapter is organised as follows. The first section presents a review of the African debt problem in terms of its origins and trends. The objective here is to highlight the immediate causes of the crisis as well as those long-term structural, institutional and political factors that have sustained it over the years. The second section applies standard rules from the growth-cum-debt literature to discuss external debt sustainability in SSA economies. The aim is to show the inefficacy of existing international debt relief initiatives for Africa. The third section demonstrates, in an informal theoretical and empirical analysis, how binding external financing constraints, resulting from the debt crisis, have led to the imposition and adoption of an asymmetric, demand-based adjustment process with negative investment and development consequences for Africa. The chapter ends with a concluding section.

The African debt crisis

Nearly two decades after the official pronouncement of the international debt crisis, most African economies still wobble under huge external debt burdens.[3] This section traces the origins of the African debt crisis and reveals its quantitative trends since the early 1970s. Four types of factor have been identified as contributing to the crisis: (i) long-term colonial–historical factors predetermining Africa's structural position in the world economy; (ii) post-colonial African state limitations; (iii) Cold War rivalry and geopolitics; and (iv) world economic turbulence and volatility during the 1970s and early 1980s. It should be cautioned, however, that serious methodological difficulties exist in drawing precise distinctions among such classifications.[4]

As will be discussed later in this section, changes in the world economic environment during the 1970s and early 1980s precipitated the international debt crisis. However, the colonial histories of African and other developing countries, which bequeathed to them a legacy of debt-prone, monocultural and imports-dependent production structures, and the incapacity of post-colonial African states to transform such structures, constitute long-term factors that aggravate their vulnerability to world economic crises. Several authors, including Rodney (1974) and Amin (1972), have detailed this colonial genesis of African economic peripheralisation and dependency, pointing out the various forms of European 'primitive accumulation' and colonial exploitation through which African economies were brought into world capitalism as mere suppliers of primary commodities and without any significant effort at structural diversification. Although it may be argued that the continent was not freed of dependency in general before the European intrusion, African economic structural dependency in the context of world capitalist evolution is rooted in the European expansion. It was then, for instance, that African industry and indigenous capital formation were systematically undermined, and an international division of labour was enforced, which sought to convert the economies of Africa into markets for products of European industry and into suppliers of agricultural and mineral raw materials. Even the limited attempts at diversification through import-substitution, made by the settler colonial states in countries such as Angola and Mozambique in order to contain the liberation movements, embodied an organic weakness in that such strategies relied on the importation of large technological and intermediate inputs from the colonial metropoles. That such a dependent and narrow industrial structure still marks Africa's economic processes is exemplified by the fact that twenty-eight out of forty-five SSA countries in 1998 have been identified as relying on primary commodities for their main source of export earnings, and for a sample of ten African countries in 1995, the percentage share of the single main commodity in total export earnings ranged from 40 per cent in Mauritania to 78 per cent in the Republic of Congo.[5]

The problem with such a monocultural dependence is that it renders African economies intrinsically vulnerable to world market demand and other exogenous changes. Thus, when copper prices plunged by a half in 1974–5, and the terms of trade deteriorated because of rising import prices, countries such as Zambia and Zaire, which depended heavily on copper, had no choice but to borrow.[6] Even the Côte d'Ivoire, a country widely regarded as an African success model for primary-export-led growth, has never been immune to such vulnerability.[7] Furthermore, the one-sided export orientation of African agriculture, by which this sector is largely confined to export crops production, undermines domestic food sufficiency and thus accentuates the continent's vulnerability to world economic crises. This is especially true as the processing, marketing and transportation of the export commodities of most African countries are largely controlled by foreign transnational corporations. There is also the question of the sustainability of a development strategy based solely on the exploitation of non-renewable mineral resources. Some African countries are already facing possible depletion of their mineral reserves. It is reported that, by the end of the year 2000, Zambia's copper mines would largely be exhausted.[8]

Africa's debt problem cannot be fully discussed apart from the larger question of what Samir Amin called its 'failure of development': the impossibility of achieving any significant economic development in the absence of a strong and democratic state capable of resisting the negative pressures from world capitalist expansion and of encouraging popular legitimacy and participation.[9] The incapacity of post-colonial African states in transforming the inherited economic structures, and their general tendency rather to reinforce them, constitute a major bottleneck in African economic progress. For some states, the availability of petro-dollars in the 1970s signalled an opportunity to foster the existing primary export-led and import-substituting industries without providing appropriate protection for agricultural modernisation and domestic food security. Moreover, as such import-substituting strategies are often biased against domestic agricultural and capital-goods production, African governments had to borrow to finance the importation of such goods from industrialised countries. When they did so, the industrialised countries passed their higher oil imports and production costs on to Africa and other developing areas. This partly explains why the external debts of oil-exporting countries, such as Nigeria and Algeria, exploded during the oil booms. Nigeria's total external debt jumped from just over $1 billion in 1973 to over $18 billion in 1984. Part of this increase may be accounted for by the growth of wheat and flour imports, from 400 000 to 1.3 million tons between 1971 and 1978. Rice imports also jumped, from 50 000 to over 550 000 tons during the same period. Such foreign-import-reliant development was sustained partly by maintaining overvalued exchange rates during the 1970s, even as inflation rose in countries such as Ghana, Sudan, Tanzania, Uganda, Zaire and Zambia. The result was that, by 1982, the real exchange rate index (1965 = 100) exceeded 200 in more than six African countries. Consequently, cheap agricultural and other imports poured into these countries, while exports contracted, thereby contributing to external deficits and debt. Overvaluation was so problematic in countries such as Ghana, Nigeria, Tanzania and Zaire that governments resorted to exchange controls in order to curtail the flow of imports. This, of course, led to the growth of parallel exchange markets in some countries.[10]

Another aspect of the debt crisis relates to the behaviour of some sections of Africa's ruling classes in perpetuating, in a different manner, the old patterns of colonial drainage of African economies. Such extraction has often assumed the form of an outright pillage and foreign transfer of national resources, or the use of economic strategies promoting such transfers. The total amount of financial resources believed to have been siphoned off by African leaders was once reported to be $200 billion, as part of total capital flight assets abroad.[11] For the period 1980–2, capital flight from developing countries is estimated at US$102 billion. Of this amount, Nigeria and Egypt alone contributed $9 billion. In 1987, capital flight assets for Nigeria amounted to $20 billion, which was 136 per cent of the country's long-term public and publicly-guaranteed debt.[12] At the end of 1984, deposits in Swiss banks by Liberian non-residents amounted to $1.5 billion, when Liberia's debt and external reserves stood at $1 billion and $1.71 million, respectively.[13] It should be noted, however, that expected devaluation as well as over-valued exchange rates may prompt foreign exchange hoarding and capital flight and, in such cases, the outflow of capital may involve not only Africans but also foreign speculators. The irony of capital flight involving African nationals is that such money is often transferred back to Africa in the form of new loans to be serviced by the continent.

For some African countries, the debt crisis also has roots in the enlistment of these nations in the Cold War and geopolitics. Countries such as Sudan and Liberia immediately come to mind. Traditionally, it is economic resource endowments, such as minerals, that attract foreign capital to developing countries. However, in the case of Sudan, whose main export is cotton, the overriding reason that attracted Western and Arab states' capital to this country was geopolitical: the need to secure the anti-Communist state of Numeiri (1969–85) as a buffer against Libya, Mengistu's socialist Ethiopia, and the presumed expansionism of Soviet policies in Africa. Thus, when Numeiri was overthrown in 1985, Sudan became one of the most heavily indebted countries in Africa, with over 80 per cent of its total debt of US$10 billion owed to official creditors.[14] Unlike Sudan, Liberia has attractive natural resource endowments, with iron ore and rubber as its main exports. While such resources have been the key magnets to foreign investors, geopolitical and other strategic concerns have also had a significant influence on foreign capital movement to the country. For example, the astronomical growth of US aid to the Doe regime during the 1980s cannot be fully explained in terms of pure economic interests. Founded in the mid-1800s as a home for freed black American slaves, Liberia has always been regarded as America's traditional ally, and this has often nurtured the political expectation that the country should always remain in the American sphere of influence. Hence the fear that the new government of Doe might come under the influence of Libya and the 'Communists' caused the Americans to rush to his aid.[15] Between 1980 and 1985, even as private investors, including US firms, were withdrawing their operations from Liberia because of gross economic mismanagement and political repression by the regime, US military and non-military aid expanded from $1.4 million per annum to $16.2 million per annum, and from $13.4 million per annum to $75.5 million per annum, respectively. Liberia's total external public debt jumped from $537 million t approximately $1.3 billion over the same period.[16] In its 1985 hearings on aid for Africa during Fiscal 1986, the US Congress Sub-Committee on Foreign Affairs accorded special treatment to Sudan, Liberia, Somalia, Kenya and Zaire for 'Congressional concern over the political instability of the regimes' in these friendly countries.[17] In this way, Western governments provided bilateral aid and assisted in securing multilateral loans for many African states, especially during the Cold War, not only for their economic interests but also for securing their influences in these states.

Regarding the immediate causes of the debt crisis, the most common explanation points to the collapse of the Bretton Woods system (1968–73) and the first OPEC oil price rise of 1973, which produced both volatility and opportunity in the global economy. As the world drowned in recession during 1974–5, and real interest rates and financial investment opportunities dwindled in most industrialised countries, the petro-dollar glut which accompanied the oil price hike became a major source of opportunity for both industrialised and developing countries.

For the industrialised countries, the opportunity came in the form of expanded capital and consumer goods markets abroad through the 'recycling' of OPEC surpluses to the developing world. Such market expansion was necessary to improve the profit margins of the banks of industrialised countries, and to pump up demands and stimulate economic recovery in these countries. As mentioned earlier, for many developing-country governments the availability of petro-dollars was seen as an opportunity to speed up their development processes and hence, contrary to the industrialised nations, they maintained expansionary policies predicated on foreign borrowing.[18]

This unprecedented influx of private foreign capital in developing countries was evidenced by the fact that, during the oil boom, total lending from Eurodollar markets around the world grew by average rates of about 25 per cent per annum, and by the end of 1983 the total debt of non-oil developing countries rose to $664 billion (an increase of 411 per cent from its 1973 level of $130 billion). The total debt of non-oil African countries grew by 436 per cent, from $14 billion in 1973 to $75 billion at the end of 1983. By the end of 1990, the aggregate debt stock of all Africa grew to $235 billion (an increase of 63 per cent from its 1985 level of $144 billion). And by the end of 1998 Africa's debt stock expanded to $287 billion (an increase of 22 per cent from its 1990 level (see Table 2.1).

As a reward for their expansion in developing economies, private banks and multinational corporations (MNCs) based in the industrialised countries realised huge profits. Over the period 1973–84, the share of the profits of the seven largest US banks flowing from operations in developing countries increased from 22 per cent to 60 per cent, and for the period 1979–85, MNC profits from developing-country operations amounted to $88 billion.[19] George (1992) estimated that, between 1982 and 1990, creditor countries extracted from developing nations a net capital outflow of $418 billion in debt-service payments alone. On the other hand, by the mid-1980s most developing countries had become deeply entrenched in debt crises, as their productive and earning capacities could no longer sustain the rising levels of debt accumulation.

A conjuncture of events in 1979, especially US high-interest-rate policy and the second OPEC oil price rise, caused this unfavourable state of affairs for developing countries. Besides pushing the world economy into recession in 1981–3, higher US interest rates made new borrowing expensive for developing nations and, because much of their debt had been contracted at floating rates, they were now faced with higher interest payments on previous loans. Moreover, as higher interest rates

Table 2.1 Regional comparison of debt indicators (1973–98), selected years (debt stocks in billions of current US dollars)

	1973[1]	1983	1973–83 (Average)	1973–83 (% change)	1985	1990	1985–90 (Average)	1985–90 (% change)	1998	1990–8 (Average)	1990–8 (% change)
Debt Stocks											
Africa	14.0	75.0	42.3	436	144.3	234.7	190.3	63	287.0	266.1	22
Asia	30.0	131.7	71.6	339	249.4	332.6	304.8	33	605.7	490.7	82
Middle East & Europe[2]	23.2	117.5	66.2	406	179.4	174.3	212.7	–3	229.3	203.8	32
W. hemisphere	44.4	247.4	127.3	457	367.2	440.8	404.0	20	716.5	579.3	31
Debt–Export Ratio (%)											
Africa	71.5	148.6	103.7		186.9	225.4	230.1		216.8	235.2	
Asia	92.9	85.4	80.7		104.9	164.3	103.0		101.1	135.2	
Middle East & Europe[2]	123.9	131.4	124.5		107.2	91.2	131.6		91.3	96.8	
W. hemisphere	176.2	242.8	201.1		292.5	265.6	300.4		226.1	261.7	
Debt Service–Export Ratio (%)											
Africa	–	–	–		27.5	27.3	25.9		24.7	25.4	
Asia	–	–	–		14.1	18.4	13.9		11.9	16.4	
Middle East & Europe	–	–	–		11.8	10.2	14.5		10.8	11.5	
W. hemisphere	–	–	–		41.8	32.6	38.9		32.6	39.7	
Debt–GDP Ratio (%)											
Africa	19.4	35.1	27.5		46.0	59.4	53.7		52.4	60.5	
Asia	19.7	27.1	22.8		26.9	31.2	28.0		26.4	30.3	
Middle East & Europe[3]	30.4	41.0	36.7		36.2	29.2	34.7		29.8	31.4	
W. hemisphere	23.0	38.6	29.2		45.5	39.9	44.2		35.3	37.2	

Notes:

1. Data covering 1973–83 are for non-oil-exporting countries. Excluded from this group are Algeria, Indonesia, Iran, Iraq, Kuwait, Libya, Nigeria, Oman, Quatar, Saudi Arabia, United Arab Emirates and Venezuela. Data covering 1985–98 refer to all countries in the regions indicated.
2. These are averages of values presented for the Middle East and Europe separately, for 1973–83.
3. These are averages of values presented for the Middle East and Europe separately, for all years.

Source: International Monetary Fund, *World Economic Outlook* (May 1983, table 32; April 1988, table A50; May 1998, table A38).

on the dollar caused it to appreciate, the real value of developing countries' debt service payments also increased. With the world in deep recession, and industrialised countries' demand for non-oil commodities diminished, export revenues for most developing countries plunged dramatically, both as a result of reduced output growth and low export prices. The real gross domestic product (GDP) for Africa dwindled from an average annual rate of 3.8 per cent in 1971–80 to 1 per cent in 1981–4.[20] It is under these conditions of rising debt services versus diminishing productive and earning capacities that the African debt crisis erupted.

In terms of absolute amounts, Africa's debt load appears modest compared to those of other regions. For example, Latin America, Brazil and Mexico each owed over $100 billion in 1988, when sub-Saharan Africa's total debt stock stood at only $146 billion.[21] As shown in Table 2.1, the average annual debt stock for African countries is less than that of every region in all periods except in 1990–8, where it exceeded only those of the Middle East and Europe. The severity of Africa's debt is fully revealed, however, when it is measured against the productive and payment capacity of the region. In terms of average debt–GDP ratios, for example, Africa leads every region in all periods, except in 1973–83 where it leads only Asia. Its average debt–export ratios are the second highest for 1985–90 and 1990–98. And in terms of debt service–export ratios, it has the second highest ratio for all periods.

Sustainability of debt accumulation

This section discusses external debt sustainability in heavily-indebted African economies and concludes that existing international debt relief initiatives have not produced significant debt reduction and sustainability for Africa. Far from achieving debt sustainability, the approach of economic adjustment underlying these measures has itself been unsustainable, resulting in negative consequences for capital formation, economic growth and transformation in Africa. Policy documents from the International Monetary Fund (IMF) assert that a country can be said to achieve external debt sustainability if it can fully meet its current and future debt service obligations without recourse to debt relief or accumulation of payment arrears, and without undermining growth in the process.[22] Conventional debt-cum-growth models show that, in order for a debt accumulation process to be sustainable, the growth rate of external debt must not be higher than that of domestic output, exports or tax revenues.[23] If we adopt the domestic output measure, this rule implies that the ratio of external debt stock to domestic output will either remain constant or decline over time. From the data in Table 2.1 it can be concluded that Africa's debt–GDP ratios indicate neither a constant nor a declining trend. In fact, the average ratios exhibit an increasing trend (from 27.5 per cent in 1973–83 to 53.7 per cent in 1985–90, and to 60.5 per cent in 1990–8).

In a formal analysis, Bacha (1992) has shown that, in order to achieve debt sustainability without compromising growth, the interest rate charged on accumulated debt must not be higher than the growth rate of domestic output. This derivation is analogous to the neo-classical rule of optimal foreign borrowing that requires the marginal rate of return to investment to be at least equal to the marginal cost of borrowing. If the interest rate is higher than the output growth rate, the debtor country will have either to receive new external finance or to decumulate existing international reserves in order to stabilise interest payments on past debt. In the absence of new loans and sufficient reserves, the debtor country must generate current trade surpluses to cover the excess of net factor payments abroad over net capital inflow.

With international interest rates, and in particular the London Inter-bank Offered Rates (LIBOR), remaining high and exceeding the growth rates of African economies throughout the 1980s, there was a need for increased net capital inflow to Africa. However, the eruption of the debt crisis removed this option, as international private investors gradually withdrew from these economies in order to reduce their risk exposures. Consequently, for most years during 1982–95, annual private capital flow to sub-Saharan Africa amounted to less than half its peak of $5.5 billion in 1982. In fact, during most of the 1990s, private loans and bond finance to the region were either negative or close to zero.[24] And while official finance has been high relative to other regions, it too declined during the 1990s. According to the Development Assistance Committee (DAC), gross bilateral disbursements to Africa fell from $13.9 billion in 1990 to $10.7 billion in 1996.[25]

In the face of higher interest payments and reduced net capital inflows, adjustment became inevitable for most African countries as the major international financial institutions (IFIs), particularly the IMF and World Bank, demanded this as a precondition for providing debt relief and a means of generating liquidity for debt repayment. As will be discussed in the third section, the IFIs' approach to adjustment has largely been focused on increasing current trade surpluses and liquidity through primary exports promotion and rapid demand deflation as opposed to increasing the long-term solvency of countries through productive capacity and structural improvement. Under IMF/World Bank-supported adjustment, African economies have been required to produce current account surpluses by constraining imports and domestic absorption, and by expanding exports. A key contradiction with such an export strategy is the fact that these institutions continue to urge primary exports expansion even though they are aware that developing countries' commodity prices are negatively sensitive to sharp increases in aggregate supply. A report by the Debt Crisis Network (DCN), *A Fresh Start for Africa*, indicates that in an effort to surmount debt-payment difficulties, African countries achieved a 50 per cent increase in export volumes and a drastic reduction in their purchase of imports after 1985. By 1992, the volume of imports per head had declined in real terms by 20 per cent of its level in 1980. These efforts were thwarted, however, by a deterioration in Africa's terms of trade, so that by the early 1990s many African countries had begun to accumulate large debt-payment arrears: while 38 per cent of debt services due in 1989–90 went unpaid, 54 per cent were unpaid in 1994. Countries such as Sudan, Somalia, Liberia, Zambia and Sierra Leone have had their drawing rights suspended because of large accumulated arrears to the IMF. The DCN report estimates that, had Africa's export prices kept pace with import prices from 1980, by 1992 the region's debt would have been 45 per cent lower.[26]

The preceding discussion suggests that adjustment, as supported by the IFIs in past decades, has failed to achieve even its basic objective of forcing the indebted economies to produce ample foreign exchange through export promotion and demand contraction, let alone the achievement of long-term solvency through economic growth and transformation. The persistence of large current-account deficits in African economies reflects this failure, which is due in part to the asymmetry of IFIs-supported adjustment that places undue emphasis on adjusting domestic economic conditions to the demands of global capital without seeking corresponding changes in existing world economic structures.[27] It should be emphasised, however, that indebted developing countries cannot generate sufficient trade surpluses and foreign exchange to meet debt obligations as long as they face unequal world economic conditions, such as restrictive international trade policies and unfavourable terms of trade. While there is a need for restructuring domestic macroeconomic and structural conditions such as fiscal and monetary policy conduct, public enterprise inefficiencies, tariff structures or labour market rigidities, such changes must be matched equally by reforms in international economic policy areas such as trade, investment and technology transfer. If external trade barriers and discriminations are not removed, and international investors and other agents remain reluctant in transferring their technologies, domestic restructuring alone will not be enough to transform African economies. To achieve sustainable growth, development, and debt sustainability, Africa's structural position in the world economy must improve, and this cannot occur without technological and capital accumulation.

While adjustment might have failed in generating adequate liquidity for sustainable debt servicing, it has led to large capital outflows from indebted African countries. The DCN report also estimates that between 1984 and the mid-1990s, governments of these countries transferred at least $96 billion to the rich countries of the North, more than one and a half times the amount owed to them in 1980. Between 1986 and 1990, the IMF alone extracted over $3 billion in debt-service payments from low-income sub-Saharan African states.[28] Countries such as Zambia and Uganda, which have been classified as heavily indebted countries, made huge net transfers to the IMF during the 1990s. Between 1991 and 1993, Zambia made a net transfer of $335 million to the Fund, while Uganda transferred $200 million between 1995 and 1998.[29]

As a way of smoothing the adjustment path, the IMF and World Bank have advocated a concerted debt relief strategy for debtor countries, involving bilateral, multilateral and commercial creditors. Although this strategy has progressed through various stages of agreements since the early 1980s, its underlying *modus operandi* has not changed fundamentally. The dominant approach continues to be the offering of debt relief: (i) through bilateral and commercial debt rescheduling under various net-present-value (NPV) debt-reduction agreements, such as the Toronto, London, Naples, and now the Heavily Indebted Poor Countries (HIPC) Debt Initiative terms; and (ii) through market-based schemes involving such debt-reduction strategies as debt buy-backs, securitisation, and debt–equity swaps (DES).[30] Until September 1996, when the two major IFIs launched their latest international debt relief strategy, HIPC Debt Initiative, all previous official debt relief strategies had been focused on only providing NPV reduction of rescheduled bilateral debt, with rescheduling agreements made contingent on debtors' commitment to seek comparable debt relief from commercial creditors. Debts owed to multilateral institutions, which account for the largest proportion of Africa's annual debt payment obligations, had never been considered seriously until then.

The stated aim of the HIPC Debt Initiative is to help each of the forty-one nations classified as heavily indebted poor countries, thirty-two of which are in Africa, to achieve debt sustainability within a period of six years and thus exit from the debt rescheduling process. Eligibility and access to the Initiative involves going through two 3-year periods. During the first three years, an HIPC applicant must establish a 'good track record' of adjustment performance as determined by the IMF and World Bank, while Paris Club bilateral creditors provide the country with flow rescheduling under Naples terms (with up to 67 per cent NPV reduction of rescheduled debt services). At the end of this period the country reaches the 'decision' point, where the Executive Boards of the two IFIs decide its eligibility for the Initiative. If it is found, on the basis of a debt sustainability analysis (DSA), that a Paris Club stock-of-debt operation on Naples terms is sufficient to bring the country to sustainability, it will not be eligible for the Initiative. But if the assessment indicates otherwise, the country will be deemed to be eligible for support under the Initiative, and will have to establish a second 3-year track record of adjustment. During this period, Paris Club and commercial creditors are to provide flow rescheduling with up to 80 per cent reduction in NPV terms. At the end of this period, which marks the 'completion point', Paris Club and commercial creditors will offer a stock-of-debt reduction of up to 80 per cent in NPV terms. Multilateral creditors are to provide additional debt relief up to a point necessary to bring the country's debt situation to a sustainable level.

At the time of writing, seven African countries (Benin, Burkina Faso, Côte d'Ivoire, Mali, Mozambique, Senegal and Uganda) have been certified as having reached their decision points under the Initiative, with Uganda having already arrived at its completion point. The total debt relief that Uganda expects to receive over time is US$650 million, or US$347 million in NPV terms, representing a 20 per cent reduction in the net present value of the country's debt. Benin and Senegal are not eligible for HIPC relief because their debts have been judged 'sustainable' with full use of traditional relief mechanisms. When Burkina Faso, Côte d'Ivoire, Mali and Mozambique arrive at their completion points, they too expect to receive 14 per cent, 6 per cent, 10 per cent and 57 per cent, respectively, in similar debt reduction.[31]

While any level of debt reduction for African HIPCs is appreciated, the amount of debt relief being provided under current plans is very limited, especially given the magnitudes of the debt burdens of African countries, and the political and economic implications of adopting such schemes. Moreover, even if sufficient funding is obtained for the above-mentioned countries, there is no guarantee that the remaining twenty-five African HIPCs will ever be reached by the Initiative, as continuation of the programme relies solely on the ability and willingness of all the concerned creditor groups to maintain their contributions. Moreover, if the principle of proportionate burden-sharing among creditors is strictly applied, there may be a deadlock. The idea of making multilateral debt relief dependent on bilateral and commercial debt reduction is likely to impede this Initiative, because some bilateral creditors may never consent to, or be able to provide, their full share of debt relief. It is worth noting also that the Initiative is not a permanent programme and, at its current rate of implementation, very few HIPCs in the world will have benefited from it by the end of the year 2000.

Of the various market-based debt-reduction strategies, the most publicised is debt–equity swaps, by which foreign investors buy a country's debt on a secondary debt market at a discount and present the purchased asset to the country for equity ownership in domestic firms. Some argue that African countries could reduce their external debts significantly by encouraging such debt–equity swaps, especially through the sale of state-owned enterprises (SOEs).[32] This view is consistent with the position of the Bretton Woods institutions, which advocates privatisation of the African public sector as a remedy for the continent's development woes. It should be noted, however, that what Africa requires is not the banishment of the state from economic function, but rather its transformation and democratisation so that it becomes more capable of, and relevant to, African development. It is also argued that privatisation, through DESs, can increase capital flow to Africa. But, as Krugman (1989) argued, a debt–equity swap neither removes a country's debt nor entails a capital inflow, because the foreign investor brings in no new foreign exchange but simply acquires an equity claim on the country to replace an existing claim. Disregarding such drawbacks of DESs, however, the question is whether Africa's external debts can be reduced significantly by selling off its public enterprises to foreign companies, or whether this is an optimal choice. Between 1991 and 1995, Zambia sold 100 of its 145 SOEs and obtained a total of only $100 million. Analysts estimated that even if Zambia had sold its remaining forty-five SOEs, the total proceeds received would have paid for only a tiny fraction of the country's $7 billion debt. As well as the low value placed on African SOEs, only few African countries have state-owned enterprises with good value.[33]

Debt, adjustment and African economic transformation

This section discusses the prospects for economic growth and transformation in heavily indebted African economies facing the unsustainability of current-account imbalances as reflected by excessive debt burdens, binding external financing constraints, and the consequent inevitability of IMF/World Bank-type adjustment. The standard theory of the balance of payments indicates that a continuation of current-account deficits, and the net real resource inflows that this reflects, can be maintained over a long run only if there exist sufficient net capital inflows or international reserves to finance the excess expenditures. If existing reserves are inadequate, and external finance is not forthcoming, the country will have to adjust by acting to reduce the deficits to a sustainable level.

Debt crisis and adjustment: an informal theoretical analysis

It is implied from the preceding point that, in the face of insufficient new finance and international reserves, the need for economic adjustment is inevitable. Under such conditions, the issue is not about adopting adjustment *per se*, but rather the approach of adjustment to be implemented. If the external financing constraint is strictly binding, and to the extent that external deficits are caused by the excess of aggregate domestic demand over aggregate output, the country will be under extreme pressure to adopt short-term adjustment measures that cause rapid demand reduction rather than implementing long-term adjustment policies that reduce the deficits slowly through structural improvement and gradual output expansion. In such a case, adjustment will be presented as a substitute for external financing. On the other hand, if international creditors are willing to continue to provide credit, the country can afford to adopt a long-term approach to adjustment that seeks to reduce the deficits gradually through structural transformation and output growth. Adjustment and external financing, in this case, will be complementary, since gradual adjustment presupposes the availability of foreign credit to finance the continuation of deficits.[34]

This brings us to a discussion of the impact of external debt crisis on the choice of adjustment approach as well as the investment and growth implications of the adopted approach. The existence of an external debt crisis implies that the country is not receiving sufficient net capital inflows (including international reserves accumulation) to cover the sum of debt service and the excess of imports over exports. Equivalently, it means that current net inflow of external finance is inadequate to sustain debt service payments and the excess of aggregate domestic absorption over aggregate output. From the savings–investment side, it also implies that savings from foreign sources are not enough to pay for debt service and the balance of domestic investment over domestic savings.[35] Under either of these constraints, if the debt burdens are very high and creditors are not willing to reduce or forgive them, and if sufficient new international capital cannot be raised, the country will be forced to remove the imbalances through adjustment, either by reducing aggregate domestic demand or increasing aggregate supply. Decreasing domestic demand requires reductions in current consumption, investment, and/or government spending, whereas output expansion requires increases and improvement in productive capacity. Since the former is relatively easier to achieve than the latter in the short run, demand suppression is often the preferred strategy when the need for adjustment is strictly binding.

The above provides the logic which underlines the IMF/World Bank-supported adjustment process that has occurred in Africa and other developing areas since the debt crisis. Faced with binding external financing constraints, heavily-indebted African countries have had to implement more rapid, demand-axing adjustment than gradual, structurally-orientated and supply-enhancing adjustment. This has entailed a greater use of macroeconomic adjustment policies, such as tighter monetary and fiscal controls and currency devaluation, aimed at fighting domestic inflation and improving the balance-of-payments position. In the event that structural reforms were supported, they were advocated mainly in such domestic policy areas as price and exchange controls, privatisation and trade liberalisation. But, as Bird (1997) has pointed out, even as these IFIs claimed that they were supporting 'structural' adjustment in developing countries, their level of financing for such programmes declined, thus raising questions about the degree of structural orientation of such adjustment. Reduced financing by these institutions only implied an adjustment process that in practice focused more on short-term, quick-acting demand management than on long-term structural economic transformation and development. Moreover, there is an issue of whether demand-based and structural-adjustment approaches, as defined and supported by the IFIs, are mutually consistent. At least from the logic of the current adjustment policies, this does not seem so. On the contrary, the application of demand-based macroeconomic adjustment policies may reduce the scope for the effectiveness of structural adjustment policies. For example, the demand-based policy of devaluation, which is aimed at improving the balance of payments through imports reduction, may counteract the effect of the structural adjustment policy of trade liberalisation aimed at removing import barriers.[36]

Even if rapid demand-suppressing adjustment is successful in bringing about quick external equilibria in the present, which is not the experience of most African countries, its negative impact on current investments in physical and human capital formation is likely to result in the strangulation of economic growth in both the short and long terms. Furthermore, by avoiding structural and supply-side transformation of the economy, demand-based adjustment is unlikely to prevent a recurrence of balance-of-payments difficulties in the long term.

Adjustment, African economic growth and transformation

The foregoing analysis does not claim that debt problems are the only cause of the need for adjustment, but that the presence of a debt crisis substantially determines the nature and pace of adjustment. This fact is clearly evident in the predominance of the international creditor institutions in the design of Africa's adjustment policies, and their persistent rejection of indigenous African policy initiatives. Over the years, African countries have prepared and adopted various long-term development plans, such as the Lagos Plan of Action (LPA); the African Priority Programme for Economic Recovery (APPER); and the African Alternative Framework to Structural Adjustment Programmes for Socio-economic Recovery and Transformation (AAF-SAP). The major IFIs have ignored these initiatives. In some cases, they responded by producing their own counter-programmes. For example, when the Organisation of African Unity (OAU) adopted the LPA, the World Bank rejected it and produced its own programme for Africa in 1981, entitled 'Accelerated Development in Sub-Saharan Africa, an Agenda for Action' (the Berg Report). Even when the APPER was adopted by the United Nations as its Programme of Action for Africa's Economic Recovery and Development (UN-PAAERD) in light of the crisis of the 1980s, the Bank and IMF produced their Structural Adjustment Programmes (SAPs). Following the publication of the AAF-SAP in 1989, the Bank launched its own major policy document on Africa in the same year, entitled 'Sub-Saharan Africa from Crisis to Sustainable Growth: A Long-term Perspective Study' (LTPS).[37]

The argument is not that the indigenous African policy initiatives have been faultless. On the contrary, some of these policy documents have failed to address certain crucial aspects of the African development question. For example, while calling on the African state to be the nationalist entrepreneur that would transform African economies through a strategy of regional self-reliance, the LPA neglected the critical political issue of the 'autonomy' and 'relevance' of that state, which is the question of its weakness in resisting negative external pressures and its lack of popular democracy, without which mobilisation for self-reliance is impossible. Apart from such limitations, however, it can be argued that the LPA provided at least a better policy framework for confronting African economic peripheralization than its rival, the Berg Report, which offered no new policy perspective on the African development crisis. Moreover, as the World Bank and IMF often assert, development policy for Africa must emanate from Africans themselves; international institutions can only assist in enriching and implementing African initiatives, but not to ignore them and substitute their own programmes.

The rejection of African policy documents has often been reflected in the absence of Africa's development objectives in the policy formulations of these institutions. Before the 1989 LTPS, Africa's concerns with such issues as human resources development, health, income distribution, poverty alleviation, good governance, democratic empowerment and environmental protection, which are necessary for the achievement of economic adjustment with sustainable development, had never been part of the adjustment designs of these institutions. Contrary to the AAF-SAP and other African initiatives, which have emphasised adjustment through long-term socio-economic transformation policies, the adjustment approach of the Bank and IMF had been preoccupied with correcting Africa's external deficits through demand-based macroeconomic policies such as those articulated in the first generation of SAPs (FGSAPs). But, as Hussain (1992) pointed out:

> African economies suffer from persistent deficits apart from the balance of payments: in education and training services, in health services, in food, in production-servicing facilities and in productive capacity, to name a few. An arithmetic correction of the external deficit alone can only be achieved at the expense of exacerbating these development-related deficits. (pp. 94–5)

It was after international organisations, such as the United Nations Children's Emergency Fund (UNICEF), challenged these institutions that they began to consider some of Africa's socio-economic concerns in their programmes, as evidenced by the grafting of SDA-type (Social Dimension of Adjustment) policies on to the 1989 LTPS report. Even then, such concerns have only been peripheral to these programmes, as improvements in human resources development, for instance, continue to be viewed as the result of effective SAPs implementation rather than as an integral part of the means of adjustment and development.[38] Thus the Second Generation of SAPs (SGSAPs), as articulated in the LTPS, has maintained the same logic as the FGSAPs.

Consequently, in recent decades African countries have been subjected to the implementation of an adjustment process that has been based largely on domestic demand contraction, state deregulation, and asymmetric economic and trade liberalisation. It is clear that such an adjustment approach has failed to achieve even its basic underlying objective of obtaining debt sustainability and external balance for African economies. Indeed, the evidence indicates that it has contributed to the undermining of African economic growth and transformation through its failure to protect physical and human capital investments during the 1980s and 1990s. Data from the IMF's *World Economic Outlook* (IMF, various years) indicates that Africa's domestic savings rates fell from 26 per cent in 1977–81 to 15.7 per cent in 1993, and the investment rate declined from 29.5 per cent to 18.1 per cent over the same period.[39] The fall in Africa's savings and investment levels during this period supports the claim that, faced with binding external financing constraints, investment spending was a main target of fiscal discipline, and that the tightened monetary policies pursued during this period also failed to improve investment results. Thus, to the degree that investments are crucial to sustained growth and development, it must be agreed that Africa's development objectives were not served by adjustment. Through a regression analysis involving thirty-three African countries implementing adjustment in the 1980s, Woodward (1992) found a clear negative impact of macroeconomic adjustment on economic growth, consumption, and investment in these countries:

> for each 1 per cent of GDP by which the annual rate of external adjustment is increased, the growth rate falls by around 0.7 per cent per year... For each additional 1 per cent of GDP per year of external adjustment, the proportion of GDP devoted to consumption falls by about an extra 0.8 per cent per year, and the proportion devoted to investment by about an extra 0.7 per cent per year. (p. 81)

It has been reported that sub-Saharan Africa has experienced economic improvement in recent years. This optimism about Africa is based on observation of the traditional macroeconomic indicators: real GDP growth averaging 4.3 per cent during 1995–7, up from 1.5 per cent in 1990–4; a drop in annual inflation from 44 per cent in 1994 to 13 per cent in 1997; a decline of overall fiscal deficits to 4.5 per cent of GDP in

1997; and a fall of current account deficits from 6 per cent of GDP in the mid-1990s to 4 per cent in 1997.[40] While these improvements should be celebrated, they are more short-term, cyclical effects of domestic macroeconomic and structural policy efficiency than a sign of a long-term shift to growth and development from balanced adjustment. As argued earlier, sustainability of growth and debt accumulation in Africa cannot be achieved without the expansion and improved utilisation of existing productive structures and capacity. The recent improvements in economic performance appear to have resulted more from improved capacity utilisation than from capacity change. Such policy efficiency is welcome, provided it is not attained by neglecting socio-economic and structural transformation. In order for African economic growth to be sustained in the long term, it must also be based on a diversified and expanded productive capacity through acquisition of new physical and human capital and technologies. This requires that economic adjustment promotes not only improved utilisation of existing productive forces through domestic policy change, but also the transfer of new technological capacity by reforming existing international trade and investment policy regimes.

Conclusion

This chapter has discussed the African debt crisis in terms of how it has influenced the adoption of asymmetric and demand-management adjustment over balanced structural transformation and development in Africa. As with other developing areas, the African debt problem has been caused and sustained by a conjuncture of colonial–historical, domestic–institutional, and world economic factors. Although the crisis was prompted by world economic turbulence and volatility during the 1970s and early 1980s, it has been sustained over the years by the fragility of economic structures bequeathed to Africa by its colonial legacy; domestic political and institutional failures; and the continuing hostility of global economic forces. In this context, one would assume that the solutions for Africa's debt and other economic crises would entail structural changes and improvement. However, the adjustment process that has been in force to deal with the debt crisis has not significantly considered this imperative in an integral manner.

On the contrary, there has been greater emphasis on providing external viability to African economies through domestic macroeconomic policy discipline without giving equal attention to the international structural factors that are also responsible for the external imbalances.

African economies cannot achieve growth and debt sustainability without having a diversified and improved productive capacity. This requires that economic adjustment not only promotes domestic macroeconomic stability and structural reforms to build and improve capacity, but also advocates changes in global trade and investment policies in order to encourage the technological and structural transformation of African economies and to ensure them fair and equal access to world markets. This is the challenge for African states and all international bodies seeking to resolve the African debt crisis in the new millennium.

Notes and References

1 See interview with Kofi Bucknor in *West Africa*, 1–14 September 1997; pp. 1432–4.
2 On the relationship between the sustainability of debt servicing capacity and economic growth, see D. Avramovic *et al.* (1964) *Economic Growth and External Debt* (Baltimore, Md: Johns Hopkins University Press), particularly pp. 10–12 and 47–84.
3 Although many developing countries began to experience debt servicing difficulties as early as the late 1970s, debt problems only became an international crisis after Mexico announced in 1982 its intention to suspend debt service payments, because of a lack of foreign exchange.
4 Other authors have applied similar methodologies in the analysis of the debt crisis. See P. Körner, *et al.* (1986) *The IMF and the Debt Crisis: A Guide to the Third World's Dilemma* (London: Zed Books), pp. 25–39, and K. Sonko (1994) *Debt, Development and Equity in Africa* (Lanham, Md: University Press of America), pp. 7–19.
5 See *World Economic Outlook* (1998), Table C; also A. Boote and K. Thugge (1997) *Debt Relief for Low-Income Countries: The HIPC Initiative* (Washington DC: International Monetary Fund), Pamphlet series no. 51, table 2.
6 P. Körner et al., *The IMF and the Debt Crisis*, pp. 34–5.
7 The Ivoirian economy was shaken by the decline in world prices of cocoa and coffee between 1977 and 1981, and since then the economy has never been immune to terms of trade fluctuations.
8 D. Mezger (1991), 'Mineral Substances on the World Market', in E. Altvater *et al.* (eds), *The Poverty of Nations: A Guide to the Debt Crisis from Argentina to Zaire* (London: Zed Books) p. 88.
9 See S. Amin (1987) 'Underdevelopment and Dependence in Black Africa', *Journal of Modern African Studies*, vol. 10, no. 4, p. 1.
10 P. Körner *et al. The IMF and the Debt Crisis*, p. 27; E. Garbrah-Aidoo and L. Osuji, (1997) 'Military Regimes and Africa's Economic Development' in F. M. Edoho (ed.), *Globalization and the New World Order: Promises, Problems and Prospects for Africa in the Twenty-first Century* (London: Praeger), pp. 38–40 and 88–9.
11 *West Africa*, 4 July 1994, no. 4005, p. 1178.
12 P. Körner *et al.*, *The IMF and the Debt Crisis*, p. 37; J. Bulow and K. Rogoff (1990) 'Cleaning up Third World Debt Without Getting Taken to the Cleaners', *Journal of Economic Perspectives*, vol. 4, no. 1, Winter, p. 37.

13   T. Tipoteh (1989) 'Debt and Structural Adjustment: A Brief Perspective Paper', Paper prepared for the Meeting of the UNESCO Advisory Panel on Adjustment in the World Economy and Implications for Policy Formulation, 6–9 March, p. 175.

14   R. Tetzlaff 'LDCs (Least Developed Countries): The Fourth World in the Debt Trap', in E. Altvater *et al.*, *The Poverty of Nations*, pp. 160–1. and Y. Farzin; (1988) *The Relationship of External Debt and Growth: Sudan's Experience, 1975–1984*, Washington, DC: World Bank Discussion Papers, p. 6.

15   Immediate US assistance to the Doe regime 'was recommended by US Assistant Secretary of State for African Affairs, Chester Crocker, after it was felt that the new PRC government in Liberia would come under the influence of Libya if the Americans were not there with cash first'. See P. Nyong'o (1987) 'Popular Alliances and the State in Liberia, 1980–85', in P. A. Nyong'o (ed.), *Popular Struggles for Democracy in Africa* (London: Zed Books), p. 235.

16   T. Tipoteh (1986) 'Crisis in the Liberian Economy (1980–85): The Role of Endogenous Variables', *Liberian Studies Journal*, vol. 11, no. 2, pp. 523 and 535.

17   See P. Nyong'o, 'Popular Alliances', p. 246.

18   P. Krugman and M. Obstfeld (1991) *International Economics: Theory and Policy*, 2nd edn, (New York: HarperCollins), pp. 644–7.

19   See Note 13, Tipoteh (1989), pp. 173–4.

20   Calculated from *World Economic Outlook*, April 1989, table A1.

21   K. Sonko, *Debt Development and Equity*, p. 7.

22   A. Boote and K. Thugge, *Debt Relief for Low-Income Countries*, p. 10.

23   See E. Bacha (1990) 'External Debt, Net Transfers and Growth in Developing Countries', *World Development*, vol. 20, no. 8, pp. 1183–92, and D. Avramovic *Economic Growth and External Debt*.

24   A. Bhattacharya, *et al.* (1997) 'How Can Sub-Saharan Africa Attract More Private Capital Inflows?', *Finance and Development*, vol. 34, no. 2, pp. 3–5.

25   S. Fischer, E. Hernandez-Cata and M. Khan (1998) *Africa: Is This the Turning Point?*, Paper on Policy Analysis and Assessment (Washington, DC: International Monetary Fund), p. 5.

26   The DCN report and figures mentioned here were cited in *West Africa*, 12–18 February 1996, pp. 217–19.

27   For a detailed discussion of the asymmetry in the global adjustment process, see D. Woodward (1992) *Debt, Adjustment and Poverty in Developing Countries*, vol. 1, ch. 6 (London: Pinter).

28   U. Ezenwe (1993) 'The African Debt Crisis and the Challenge of Development', *Intereconomics*, January/February, p. 37.

29   *West Africa*, 1–14 September 1997, p. 1432.

30   For a detailed discussion of market-based debt-reduction strategies, see P. Krugman (1989) 'Market-Based Debt Reduction Schemes', in J. A. Frenkel, M. P. Dooley and P. Wickham (eds), *Analytical Issues in Debt* (Washington, DC: International Monetary Fund), pp. 259–75; and W. A. Elali (1994) *Debt–Equity Swaps and the Alleviation of the LDCs' Debt Problem*, (Montreal: Concordia University Faculty of Commerce), Working Paper Series.

31   For a full description of the HIPC Debt Initiative, see A. Boote and K. Thugge, *Debt Relief for Low-Income Countries*. Also see 'HIPC Initiative: A Progress Report', Prepared by the Staffs of the IMF and the World Bank, 25 September 1998.

32 *West Africa*, 1–14 September 1997, p. 1433.
33 Ibid.
34 G. Bird (1997) 'External Financing and Balance of Payments Adjustment in Developing Countries: Getting a Better Policy Mix', *World Development*, vol. 25, no. 9, pp. 1409–20 and D. Woodward, *Debt Adjustment and Poverty* have discussed this trade-off between short-term, quick-acting macroeconomic adjustment and external financing, and the complementarity between long-term structural adjustment and external financing.
35 These statements assume that all non-debt factor services, such as those related to foreign direct investment and shipping, are represented in the excesses of imports over exports; domestic absorption over output; and domestic investment over savings; that is, they are already accounted for in the current account deficit.
36 For more description of the conflicts between short-term macroeconomic adjustment and structural adjustment, see D. Woodward, *Debt Adjustment and Poverty*, vol. 1, pp. 54–8.
37 B. Onimode (1992) 'The World Bank's LTPS and Africa's Transformation', in M. Turok (ed.), *The African Response: Adjustment or Transformation* (London: Institute for African Alternatives), p. 66.
38 E. Maganya (1992) 'The World Bank's New Agricultural Policy for Sub-Saharan Africa or Old Wine in a New Bottle: What Hope for Sustainable Growth?', in M. Turok, *The African Response*, pp. 77–8.
39 G. Bird, 'External Financing', p. 1420.
40 S. Fischer *et al.*, *Is This the Turning Point?*, pp. 1–2.

Bibliography

Altavater, E. (1990) *The Poverty of Nations: A Guide to the Debt Crisis from Argentina to Zaire* (London: Zed Books).

Amin, S. (1972) 'Underdevelopment and Dependence in Black Africa', *Journal of Modern African Studies*, vol. 10, no. 4.

Amin, S. (1987) 'Preface: The State and the Question of Development', in P. A. Nyong'o (ed.), *Popular Struggles for Democracy in Africa* (London: Zed Books).

Avramovic, D. *et al.* (1997) *Economic Growth and External Debt* (Baltimore, Md: Johns Hopkins University Press).

Bacha, E. L. (1992) 'External Debt, Net Transfers, and Growth in Developing Countries', *World Development*, vol. 20, no. 8, pp. 1183–92.

Bhattacharya, A., Montiel, P. and Sharma, S. (1997) 'How Can Sub-Saharan Africa Attract More Private Capital Inflows?', *Finance and Development*, vol. 34, no. 2, June.

Bird, G. (1997) 'External Financing and Balance of Payments Adjustment in Developing Countries: Getting a Better Policy Mix', *World Development*, vol. 25, no. 9, pp. 1409–20.

Boote, A. R. and Thugge, K. (1997) *Debt Relief for Low-Income Countries: The HIPC Initiative* (Washington, DC: International Monetary Fund), Pamphlet Series No. 51.

Bulow, J. and Rogoff, K. (1990) 'Cleaning up Third World Debt Without Getting Taken to the Cleaners', *Journal of Economic Perspectives*, vol. 4, no. 1, Winter, pp. 31–42.

Elali, W. A. (1994) *Debt–Equity Swaps and the Alleviation of the LDCs Debt Problem* (Montreal: Concordia University Faculty of Commerce), Working Paper Series.

Ezenwe, U. (1993) 'The African Debt Crisis and the Challenge of Development', *Intereconomics*, January/February, pp. 35–43.

Farzin, Y. H. (1988) *The Relationship of External Debt and Growth: Sudan's Experience, 1975–1984*, World Bank Discussion Papers, Washington, DC.

Fischer, S., Hernandez-Cata, E. and Khan, M. (1998) *Africa: Is This the Turning Point?*, Paper on Policy Analysis and Assessment (Washington, DC: International Monetary Fund).

Garbrah-Aidoo, E. A. and L. O. Osuji (1997) 'Military Regimes and Africa's Economic Development', in F. M. Edoho (ed.), *Globalization and the New World Order: Promises, Problems, and Prospects for Africa in the Twenty-First Century* (London: Praeger).

George, S. (1992) *The Debt Boomerang: How the Third World Debt Harms Us All*, (Boulder, Col.: Westview Press).

Hussain, M. N. (1992) 'Between Legitimacy and Dominance: The AAF-SAP versus the IMF System', in M. Turok, (ed.), *The African Response: Adjustment or Transformation* (London: Institute for African Alternatives).

Kenen, P. B. (1990) 'Organizing Debt Relief: The Need for a New Institution', *Journal of Economic Perspectives*, vol. 4, no. 1, Winter, pp. 7–18.

Körner, P. *et al.* (1986) *The IMF and the Debt Crisis: A Guide to the Third World's Dilemma* (London: Zed Books).

Krugman, P. R. (1989) 'Market-Based Debt-Reduction Schemes', in J. A. Frenkel, M. P. Dooley and P. Wickham (eds), *Analytical Issues in Debt* (Washington, DC: International Monetary Fund).

Krugman, P. R. and Obstfeld, M. (1991) *International Economics: Theory and Policy*, 2nd edn (New York: HarperCollins).

Maganya, E. (1992) 'The World Bank's New Agricultural Policy for Sub-Saharan Africa or Old Wine in a New Bottle: What Hope for Sustainable Growth?', in M. Turok (ed.), *The African Response: Adjustment or Transformation* (London: Institute for African Alternatives).

Mezger, D. (1991) 'Mineral Substances on the World Market', in E. Altvater *et al.* (eds), *The Poverty of Nations: A Guide to the Debt Crisis from Argentina to Zaire* (London: Zed Books).

Nyong'o, P. A. (1987) 'Popular Alliances and the State in Liberia, 1980–85', in P. A. Nyong'o (ed.), *Popular Struggles for Democracy in Africa* (London: Zed Books).

Onimode, B. (1992) 'The World Bank's LTPS and Africa's Transformation', in Turok, M. (ed.), *The African Response: Adjustment or Transformation* (London: Institute for African Alternatives).

Rodney, W. (1974) *How Europe Underdeveloped Africa* (Washington, DC: Harvard University Press).

Sachs, J. D. (1990) 'A Strategy for Efficient Debt Reduction', *Journal of Economic Perspective*, vol. 4, no. 1, Winter, pp. 19–29.

Salih, S. A. (1994) *Impacts of Africa's Growing Debt on its Growth* (Helsinki: UNU World Institute for Development Economics Research).

Sonko, K. N. (1994) *Debt, Development and Equity in Africa* (Lanham, Md: University Press of America).

Tetzalaff, R. (1990) 'LLDCs (Least Developed Countries): The Fourth World in the Debt Trap', in Altvater, E. *et al.* (eds), *The Poverty of Nations: A Guide to the Debt Crisis from Argentina to Zaire* (London: Zed Books).

Tipoteh, T. (1986) 'Crisis in the Liberian Economy (1980–85): The Role of Endogenous Variables', *Liberian Studies Journal*, vol. XI, no. 2.

Tipoteh, T. (1989) 'Debt and Structural Adjustment: A Brief Perspective Paper', Prepared for the Meeting of the UNESCO Advisory Panel on Adjustment in the World Economy and Implications for Policy Formulation, 6–9 March.

Turok, M. (1992) *The African Response: Adjustment Transformation* (London: Institute for African Alternatives).

West Africa (various issues).

Woodward, D. (1992) *Debt, Adjustment and Poverty in Developing Countries*, vol. 1 (London: Pinter).

World Economic Outlook (various issues).

3
Technology and the Technical Management of Human Resources: Prospects for Sub-Saharan African Development into the New Millennium

Christopher Farrands

If we look for grounds for optimism about the prospects of African development at the end of the twentieth century, they seem at first sight to be very hard to find. The problems of war, crime and corruption, the accumulated debt burden, ethnic divisions and social conflicts have added to a damaging legacy of colonialism. The lack of the kind of solid basis for development which seems to have worked in other, more successfully developing regions, such as South East Asia or even Latin America, seems to justify a continuing pessimism. The African state is in crisis, in terms of both its practical and its legitimating functions, both necessary for development to take place.[1] The development of the AIDS/ HIV epidemic, now said to be affecting up to 25 per cent of the population of Zimbabwe,[2] almost as devastating in other parts of central Africa, and widespread in regions where virtually no treatment is available because of civil conflict, adds to the pressures of underdevelopment. External aid and technical assistance, significant in themselves, are substantially outweighed by debt repayment demands. Outside 'help' in the form of knowledge and advice is often wasted because it cannot be followed through systematically, or because it is seen as being inappropriate to the society in which it is to be implanted.[3]

But this pessimistic picture, infused with stereotypes, or at least with unspoken assumptions, themselves redolent of basically racist images of Africa as dependent and inferior, is mistaken. It is not wholly wrong, for the evidence of the harmful effects of war and mismanagement layered on top of the colonial legacy are clear enough. But it is mistaken at least in the sense that it is one-sided. It omits both real achievements in Africa since independence and some of the aspects of the colonial legacy that provide a basis for development some forty or more years on. Even more significantly, it misses a profoundly important point, that two generations of effort at development have produced a body of experience on which improvements of a real, socially meaningful and relatively efficient nature can be based (what these criteria mean more exactly will be explained below). Furthermore, the lessons of this experience are being understood and shared increasingly, even if they are not always followed.[4]

This chapter aims to explore the grounds for optimism that can be found in these lessons. It looks in particular at how technology can be used to promote development, and finds in practical examples and experience a case for a much more optimistic image of the prospects for African development.[5] However, readers should note that the argument is 'much more' optimistic. It is not blindly optimistic: the obstacles of poor management, corruption, civil and international war, and inappropriate development policies remain potent barriers to development. Technologies also embody dangers, risks and costs, and we cannot argue a case for technology as a basis for development without keeping them in mind. All the same, the chapter aims to construct a case which, as will become clear, puts a particular emphasis on the human resources available and the ways in which technology and human capital can best be combined.[6] One way to begin to do this is to think of technologies as being diverse and useful when appropriately chosen; to think that a single, all-powerful 'technology' offers more solutions than problems is particularly dangerous, though it might perhaps be hoped that no one except some of its cruder critics today thinks of technology in such terms.

In addressing these questions, this chapter needs to clarify the distinction between genuinely desirable and less desirable forms of development, and between different meanings of 'technology'.[7] It was said earlier that development that is 'real', 'socially meaningful' and 'relatively efficient' might be possible. The debate on the meaning of development has been so powerful as to call into question the idea that any real 'progress' is possible at all in the developing world.[8] This is a frustrating idea. For while the traditional 'liberal developmentalist' idea of growth, grounded in the idea that developing countries needed to follow a more or less ubiquitous Western model which was easy to adapt and measurable in terms of GDP per head has failed (and had failed by the 1970s), there is still no doubt that improvements in living standards are worth having if they reflect in the quality of life, and if they can be accompanied by reductions in perinatal mortality. And by increases in life choices as well as life expectancy, and improvements in social indicators such as literacy rates and access to clean water and medical facilities. Post-modern development thinking is valuable when it throws a critical light on the reality of power relations underpinning discourses of development; but it can look distinctly silly when it pretends that, because the liberal discourse of development is seriously flawed, there is nothing to be done but adopt a critical pose and leave the world as it is. In this case, critical knowledge also has to be *practical* knowledge. More to the point perhaps, critical knowledge *can* be practical knowledge, and the most useful critical knowledge is grounded in practical experience. It is for this reason that the experience of non-governmental organisations (NGOs) and the networks and cooperative capacities they can create have so much value in assessing the importance of development work. It was also suggested earlier that development should be 'real', and this means measurable. We may criticise the fetishisation of certain measurements of GDP, and we should criticise accounts of development that use only this measure. But GDP growth per head is at least one tool that can be used to compare one country with another, and if there is an indication that one country is doing better than another we can ask why and explore the implications and lessons. But development also needs to be 'real' in the sense that people recognise improvements in their quality of life, and social indicators which measure both quality of life and how people experience it are important alongside basic economic measurements for development to count. Any account of development should also be socially meaningful: it should matter to society, not just to an elite group or to a statistician.[9] Development should be 'relatively efficient' in two senses. Short-term economic growth fuelled merely by commodity price changes does not count. Nor does development which involves a waste of resources or long-term environmental damage to be paid for later these are as inefficient as megalomaniac schemes imposed by a bureaucracy which produce measurable increases in GDP without making any contribution to the real economy in the medium to long term. In short, to be worthwhile, development needs to involve an increase in measurable economic performance, an improvement in perceived living standards and access to the means to satisfy basic needs; and to be efficient in terms of sustainability and the avoidance of waste. The kinds of relatively low-tech development advocated in this chapter can achieve this, and sometimes already has.

The chapter could put more emphasis on the potential value of regional co-operation than it will do. As B. Hettne has argued, regionalisation provides a basis for development without necessarily requiring a homogenisation of the varied experiences of different countries.[10] But regionalism is a theme of several other chapters, and this chapter will defer this issue to other contributions to this volume. However, it is worth pointing out that regional networks of co-operation are important means of sharing knowledge, and regional forms of economic integration provide a basis for trade and an incentive for investment, which are important. Many African producers cannot surmount the barriers to trading effectively on world markets; but they can export or base their factories in neighbouring countries. Regional co-operation is an important part of the picture this chapter aims to explore, but to avoid duplication the reader is asked to look to other chapters in this collection for a discussion of this question.[11]

Technology in development

Technology is increasingly difficult to define the more carefully we consider it.[12] The concept covers so much of modern social and economic organisation. What it emphatically does not mean here is machinery or, for example, computing equipment alone. Technology may include machinery; but it involves social organisation and the knowledge in which specific pieces of machinery are embedded. A given technology involves specific assumptions about its operation and a socially shared image of what it is for. Weaving techniques make sense in the context of the groups of people who use them; and this in turn makes sense of the particular forms of loom equipment they employ. Technology is properly defined to include knowledge, some of which is easily transferable but some is socially embedded expertise that may be very hard to transplant out of its context. Technology is properly defined to include both ideas and social practices and discourses. It is socially organised: if a new technique of horticulture, such as hydroponics, is to be deployed effectively, it has to be integrated into working practices and to be operated in a way that recognises group and individual identities (see below on hydroponics). Of course, these cultural and organisational factors will change from context to context. Thus 'technology' changes its meaning from one context to another, and what is practical in one context may not be effective in another.[13]

The kinds of technology this chapter explores are what used to be called 'appropriate technologies' and are now often subsumed under the label of 'sustainability'.[14] On the whole, this means relatively small-scale technologies. But size is not their key defining characteristic:

what is more important is that the technologies fit life styles and social organisation; very often the technologies will grow from these, because many of the most appropriate technologies take as a starting point the existing technologies and practices of a community. The idea of designing technologies to avoid disrupting existing communities, to build on existing practices and to respect local markets, and what are often fragile economic institutions, is not new. It owes something to E. F. Schumacher, who published *Small is Beautiful*[15] in the 1970s. But after decades of failed large-scale projects and the social engineering that has gone with them, what has changed is that development institutions have taken this kind of human-scale technological innovation on board.

The role of NGOs in promoting this shift has been important, and is discussed briefly below. But larger-scale agencies, perhaps especially the European Community (EC) in its implementation of later versions of the Lomé Convention, have found that smaller-scale and more focused kinds of technical innovation have been more effective and less damaging in terms of necessary social and economic costs.[16] The experience of famine in Africa has shown the dangers of large-scale food aid in disrupting local markets: the second great Ethiopian famine of the 1980s was caused in some measure by the impact of food aid given in response to the first. Small-scale technical help to promote aquaculture has offered one effective way of providing valuable additional supplies of protein to consumers without the risks and costs of cash crop production.[17] It is also possible to organise aquaculture on different scales and to provide (small-scale or non-intrusive) management systems that are appropriate to the ways in which village communities work.[18] Meeting basic needs became a key objective of both UN and regional development organisations in Africa in the early 1980s. However, the policy shift took some time to implement in practice. A strong emphasis of the basic needs approach has been to provide clean water to communities that did not have easy access to it, usually by small-scale, piecemeal innovations using technology which villagers could use and maintain for themselves. Apart from the importance of access to water as a part of the development process, the lessons in this case include the importance of not relying on 'experts' from outside where the expertise of local communities can be used. Development can be a part of an empowering process for local communities, and exploring how local markets, local knowledge or local networks can be used rather than stepping in with big boots from outside makes a great deal of difference to the kinds of development and the experience of commitment to it which local communities share.

Why look at technology at all? It may seem too basic a question, but economic development depends on three main elements. First, natural resources, including human capabilities: African economies are not short of resources, although these are not always in the most convenient places. Second, technology in the form of productive machinery, but also organisation and management capability integrated effectively with the machinery. Third, infrastructure: ports, roads, telecommunications and so on are important, but are not discussed here. They provide longer-term bases for development, although they may also be the focus of the corruption and political misdirection that large projects often attract. The basic answer to the question is that it is technology, organised on an appropriate scale and well managed which can produce increased trade and increased wealth, as well as employment and improved life choices and chances. As C. L. McCarthy emphasises, technology is the main factor in the possibility of economic development, improved competitiveness and a growth in regional and international trade.[19]

Knowledge and the transfer of technology

Knowledge figures as a central concept in the idea of the modern economy in general, and in development assessment in particular. Whereas in the traditional Western industrial economy, production was primarily of things, and work was primarily organised around forms of production associated with the production line and the manufacturing process, in the post-industrial (or post-modern) economy, production in general is much more often geared around knowledge and inventions, or the application of inventions. The majority of workers in the post-industrial economy produce symbolic knowledge or handle information in some way. Ash Amin has produced a valuable collection of essays which outlines the scope of this 'post-fordism' as a form of economic organisation.[20] Post-fordist production systems have two possible implications for African economies. On the one hand, they might imply an opening of an opportunity for 'old-fashioned' forms of material production to be exported to low-cost developing countries. This has certainly happened – for example, in the case of the textiles and clothing industries. But while much of the redistribution of world clothing production capacity has been to developing economies, it has gone more to South or South East Asia, or to countries of the Mediterranean region. Africa is a significant cotton producer, and African societies have a tradition of spinning and weaving as well as great skill in dyeing. Yet African cotton-producing countries have not gained very much from the restructuring of the world's clothing industries. Even though clothing production has continued, African countries' exports have not penetrated world markets effectively, and cotton continues to be exported raw or only spun so that the advantages of adding value go largely to non-African producers even if African-grown cotton is used.[21]

Two specific technologies help to illustrate the case here. Hydroponics and aquaculture (fishenes management) are taken as examples where technology has developed fairly rapidly since the 1980s, and they illustrate arguments about appropriate technology use which can also be applied to rural industrialisation or to agriculture. Neither is obviously high-tech, although they can nonetheless be inappropriately used if deployed carelessly. They seem to provide valuable models of good practice in technology management in a number of examples in African contexts.

Hydroponics is the use of water and water-borne chemicals to grow food, usually in some kind of greenhouse.[22] Although it is often called 'soil-less agriculture', the distinguishing feature of most hydroponic systems is that, because they are closed systems which recycle all their water, their net consumption of water is very little. Instead of getting nutrition from the soil, crops are grown on rock or sand which has no food value for plants but allows water to flow freely through them. The rock or sand, is, of course, virtually costless. The methods are intensive, and can be used to produce high-yield crops.[23] The initial investment is high by the standards of Third-World agriculture, but less than many industrial schemes. Food can be grown for consumption or export, and a typical scheme would grow a mixture of fruit and vegetable crops (with perhaps, flowers as well for export). For these reasons, hydroponic systems increase the food resource flexibility of the communities that use them, and provide opportunities for increasing value added. They need little land, and can be used alongside more conventional cropping. They have been developed as co-operatives in Senegal, Zimbabawe and Kenya, among other African countries.[24] They have been a particular interest of Dutch and German development horticulturists, and their presence often explains why schemes have appeared in some countries more than others. The disadvantages of hydroponic systems are that the closed greenhouse environments encourage disease, which can be difficult to control, although good husbandry can prevent it up to a point, and that the fertilisers used in suspension in the water cycle, although not particularly expensive, have to be available reliably as a failure in supply is disastrous. It is not difficult to learn to use hydroponic systems, and good practices in everyday farming transfer to it. The theory behind the systems may be quite complex but the practice is not difficult. Most important, for rural communities, hydroponics does not depend on large initial investment. It can be introduced gradually from small-scale work, and in the process people can learn to use it, to make it effective, and to feel the ownership of it for themselves.

Aquaculture provides a parallel example. Aquaculture in natural lakes and rivers is a part of the established traditional practice of some African communities (especially in West and Central Africa), and its development is hardly a high technology revolution.[25] However, it is possible to use more sophisticated techniques to intensify production, introduce new species, control pests and diseases, and avoid the environmental harm (through damaging water stocks) that aquaculture can sometimes cause.[26] In the process, a valuable additional source of protein becomes available. Also, as with hydroponics, the community gains more flexibility in both consuming and marketing its produce. The spread of knowledge in aquaculture is important, not least because bad management can lead to the loss of a whole crop of fish and a seriously damaged environment. As with hydroponics, while some of the theory behind particular aquaculture systems may be advanced, the level of expertise needed to manage a system, at least on a day-to-day basis, is appropriate for local communities provided there is expertise and veterinary care available. The latter requirements limit the countries, or perhaps more accurately the geographical location, of schemes. But, as research reports on its implementation argue, it does not suggest that aquaculture is not an important technology for development in Africa which is at once manageable and relatively low-cost, as well as something that builds on existing cultures, expertise and priorities.[27]

In looking at hydroponics and aquaculture we are looking at two examples where existing knowledge in particular communities can be developed and complemented by the introduction of expertise and specific techniques from outside. In neither case were the techniques wholly alien, and in neither case was the knowledge diffusion process one that in itself transformed the society receiving the new technology. In general, the transfer of new ideas depends on the ability of recipient institutions to absorb and understand what is new, as well as on the ability of the provider of the new technologies to communicate them.[28] In each of these examples, some African societies have been able to acquire new techniques and systems that enable relatively stable, community-friendly growth to take place. This has other advantages, in promoting forms of small-scale empowerment and possibly in spreading an interest in technical innovation beyond the specific technology introduced. Demonstrably, it helps to stabilise rural communities if they can improve their living standards without more violent forms of social disruption (such as moving to cities). And in each case, although there is a recognisable additional investment cost, it is not as great as most industrial investments, and is a cost that can be staged over a period of time as the new technology is introduced gradually.

Japanese initiatives

One distinctive view on the ways in which human and material resources can be combined to promote development in Africa is provided by new developments in Japanese aid policy. In some respects, this offers a contrast to European aid programmes, including the emphasis on technical knowledge and the diffusion of management competence and cultures. It should also be said that Japanese aid and development programmes have put more explicit emphasis on private company roles than have most Western development schemes, at least until recently. In the 1990s, Japan has become the primary aid donor in general in the global economy. In the past, the immediate concerns of Japanese aid policy have tended to focus on East and South Asia, and on multilateral co-operation through UN institutions. However, in the 1990s there has been something of a shift. Japanese development policy has become interested in Africa, and while there are multinational initiatives, a more national tone is observable in policy. Japanese initiatives have been focused around the Tokyo International Conference on African Development (TICAD), an international conference organised between Japan on the one hand and sub-Saharan Africa on the other.[29] The first TICAD was held in October 1993; the second in October 1998. The intention of these meetings was to create a process with a certain impetus and a clear set of priorities. The Japanese see themselves as having a distinctive development role in Africa: first, because they have no colonial tradition there, and so have no difficult legacy to shake off; second, because they have very considerable resources; and third, because they claim that they have an understanding of development priorities that they can put into practice most effectively in Africa. These priorities emphasise the role of private business and inward investment, the role of specific forms of technology and knowledge transfer, the need for small-scale project aid which is carefully monitored, and an emphasis on food production technologies that reflect some of the experiences of Japanese agriculture as well as a view of African needs.[30] Japanese aid policy reflects some of the priorities of national research and development policy,[31] but they also reflect priorities that are in fact not particularly original. However, the resources they can contribute make their opinions important.

The priorities of Japan's new African policy also reflect a concern to promote, within a partnership framework, a use of appropriate technology in rural development in agriculture and in micro-industrialisation. This has been a stimulus to research in Japan, but also in Senegal and Kenya, where TICAD has created development 'staff colleges' (this author's phrase) which explore how technical capability, microeconomic policy, skills development and shared management practices can be passed on, both to policy managers at a higher political level and to ordinary village workers or those who train or diffuse good practice. No doubt, as in all reports on development questions, there is some rhetoric or self-pride attached to reports of this work. But there also appears to be a sense of what is possible and what is effective, taking into account the diversity of African experience. The emphasis on good management, and on the benefits of learning across the vertical axis of policy management (in plain language, having senior and junior managers learning and training together) is characteristic of Japanese practice in both the public and private sectors,[32] but it is uncommon in practical development contexts. It may provide an important lesson in combining technology and human skills in a relatively new way, and that way is designed to be more sensitive to the specifics of local cultures and practices, although it is true to say that it is also too early to judge the outcomes of the TICAD initiatives.

Inequalities and paradoxes

In advocating a diversity of approaches to technological diffusion and to the role of technology in development in Africa, there is something that should be recognised: diverse strategies of development will inevitably produce mixed results. The 'normal' image of development is one of increasing convergence, not only between developed and developing worlds but also within the developing world. This predominantly liberal image is clearly problematic, as James Manor, among others, has shown.[33] But the corollary of the critique of the liberal argument is that as development takes place there will be increasing divergence between different countries' and communities' experience. And if we accept a divergent model of development on the grounds, among others, that this recognises different people's rights to explore different potentialities for growth, we also have to accept that some of them will get it wrong, and that some experiences of development will fail.

Human capital

There is a certain truism about any country that its greatest resource is its people. The idea has been put to work very effectively in managing economic development in the People's Republic of China since 1949, and more recently in countries short of other natural resources, such as Singapore and Hong Kong. The argument may well be put in terms of the concept of 'human capital'. People have knowledge as individuals and as groups. In groups, knowledge is embedded in social institutions, not least the family, the community-sharing grazing and hunting rights, and urban women's groups, as well as more 'formal' institutions. Just as money is not 'capital' until it is taken out from under the bed and applied through investment, so 'human capital' is not properly capital until it is applied in particular ways. Human capital has been seen by writers as diverse in their approach as Robert Reich and Ash Amin as the key to growth and employment within developed economies, but also as a critical element of development for poorer societies.[34] Knowledge embedded in communities can also be lost. Thus, for example, civil war and the break-up of community, or famine and the dispersion of people, can deprive them of access to skills and expertise that had once been assumed to be a collective birthright. The spread of HIV/AIDS infection has created large groups of young orphans in central and southern Africa. As well as losing their families, these children have lost their access to the regular transmission of collective knowledge and community-based skills.

In a specifically African context, skills and know-how are central to development potential; it is a critical problem if they are absent or have been lost.[35] But in most of the continent, and especially in societies which are trying to recover from war, such as Mozambique, as well as in others, *collectively held* communal forms of skill and knowledge remain essential resources, and collective knowledge transmission remains the basis of development potential. This has, perhaps very belatedly, come to be recognised in discussions about development policy.[36]

As Robin Clarke,[37] and more recently Ming Ivory,[38] have argued, one of the most important changes in approaches to development policy has been the gradual incremental collection of technological understanding, together with a sharper idea of how technical evaluation or assessment of projects can be achieved most effectively. M. McPherson and

S. Radelet illustrate the importance of sensitive and effective management by objectives in their study of rural development through innovative use of small-scale technologies in the Gambia.[39] Key technologies play a significant part in realising development strategies. The sense that certain basic technologies for water pumping, electricity generation or animal husbandry increase productivity and enhance economic security is important, and while some kinds of large-scale technology can break up communities, many of these kinds of smaller-scale projects are also effective in promoting community solidarity (and, among other things, in helping to limit the move from the country to the town). The use of basic but sophisticatedly targeted technologies has played, and must continue to play, a critical part in micro-level development projects. These (on the whole) work very effectively, and are now recognised as being effective even if unglamorous, in government and international development planning. This is in part what it means to say that positive lessons have been learned from failure since the 1960s. This might also include the idea that administrative procedures that are straightforward and transparent are more likely to avoid a high level of corruption. They are also more likely to be consistent with established or traditional ideas of justice and collective co-operation for development, and therefore more likely to command respect. Micro-level development programmes organised around specific, relatively short-term projects are important aspects of development policy. National governments within the developing world and those outside which, with inter-governmental organisations and NGOs, manage aid and development programmes, have come to rely on specific technical programmes operating at a micro level. They do so partly because such programmes are the easiest to evaluate and, after two or three decades of argument about the assessment of aid, Western aid donors have come to depend on what they could evaluate transparently for themselves. These criteria have also been adopted by national economics or development ministries across the continent for at least some of their own projects, partly because of conditionality in aid and partly because of the impact of Western economic training and, indeed, of Western economists. Paul Mosley has argued that certain kinds of conditionality can be focused on the realisation of social and economic objectives, and that development programmes do not need to be neo-liberal in a constricted way in order to be effective.[40] He also argues that in the specific conditions of countries such as Kenya and Tanzania, development planning can be targeted and effective and at the same time incorporate the views and priorities of local communities and the diversity of needs that they may articulate.

This becomes important when looking at how development programmes are organised and which agencies have responsibility for
which parts of the investment process. Learning how to use the institutional framework, and in particular the complex relations between
NGOs and governments, has also been important, and provides a basis
for potential future development. The involvement of NGOs in project
evaluation, which has become commonplace, helps to ensure that NGO
and governmental aid policies are co-ordinated. The use of NGOs is
intended to ensure a greater level of 'fairness' in aid and technical
assistance. But the implication of NGOs in government-led (both rich
and poor governments) programmes also opens the possibility that
NGOs are tied all the more firmly into state interests and the state
power that development aid represents. The increasing use of bodies
concerned with very specific development issues in strategic planning,
such as the role of the Save the Children Fund in Zambia and Uganda, is
designed to maintain co-ordination between the macro and micro levels
of development planning. It may work well, but it also carries risks. Save
the Children have organised a debt relief scheme in these two countries,
whereby foreign creditors have agreed to write off debts. As a condition
of the waiver, the repayments waived have then been committed to
development programmes focused particularly on children. This is an
intrinsically useful way of directing resources that have been freed
from debt repayments. It also gives the external creditors confidence
that when they agree to write off debts the repayments that would
have been theirs are committed to a good purpose which they can
justify to electors or shareholders. But this kind of programme also
demonstrates how NGOs have taken on a quasi-governmental authority, becoming implicated in difficult and morally challenging
decisions, taking over from the state roles and a negotiating position
which would more usually be associated with governments or state-led
institutions.[41] The role of NGOs in Somalia, where relief organisations
found themselves co-operating closely with UN Forces engaged in military operations to an extent that proved embarrassing to them,
provided a lesson which they seem still to be trying to absorb. In general, the 1990s have witnessed a partial breakdown of established
boundaries between NGOs, international government organisations
(IGOs) and governments in the creation of a 'developmental governance' which has certain short-term advantages in efficiency and in
enabling critical information to be communicated effectively. But
whether in the longer term it undermines the independence of NGOs,
and whether that perceived independence is not necessary for them to

continue to operate in the longer term, is a difficult, and still unanswered, question.

An increased role for the diverse range of NGO groups has also contributed to the redefinition of what counts as 'development' away from more traditional or economistic ideas which measure along only one quantitative scale. The collection of works edited by James Manor,[42] among others, shows a broadening definition of what might count as development to incorporate social goals, and to recognise the diversity of cultural concerns one would expect to find in an African society no less than in a richer country (after all, *pace* some liberal developmentalists, poorer societies are not at all less differentiated or less complex than richer ones in cultural or linguistic terms). This leads to an important question linking NGOs and the questions already examined about knowledge diffusion and innovation for development – the role of networking in African communities.

Mobilising the potential in societies: networks and social movements

Networks are a store of human knowledge. They may be a lot of other things, but as stores of expertise they are of great importance in setting frameworks within which development can take place. This is recognised in management literature, where a considerable effort was made during the later 1990s to find ways of identifying the value in networks, of finding ways of formalising and measuring this value, and of enhancing it to the advantage of the firm.[43] In the same way, where we can identify networks as stores of valuable expertise, and of human capital, there is a potential both for investment in what already exists and for its enhancement.[44]

In looking for development potential, two particular kinds of network are of especial interest. Women, particularly grandmothers, play a key role in many more-or-less traditional societies, as writers such as Mahbub ul Haq recognise.[45] They provide a focus for the family and they play a crucial economic role as traders, negotiators, and land owners or tenancy holders. In an extended sense, we can speak of 'community grandmothers' – older women with dignity and authority but also a social involvement and an understanding which enables them to play the social role of grandmother across their village or neighbourhood beyond their formal extended families. The role of women, and of women's social relationships, are integral to development processes and are recognised as being very significant in the debates among specialists in technology and development.[46] Particularly in large cities, community grandmothers take on the business of managing community action, organising social or welfare relief, providing effective role models, bringing up children, and ensuring a certain level of security. The importance of these community networks has been recognised in development programmes in the Caribbean, but is underestimated in the literature on Africa. Second, religious organisations play an economic role and have a part in assuring social stability. For example, the spread of Islam reflects (at least in part) a congruence between a long-established sense of what is just, and a deep and powerful religious commitment to social justice emphasised by the obligation to give charity. Religious networks of all kinds tend to attract discussion outside Africa only if they have some subversive or harmful purpose or if they can be labelled as agents of 'fundamentalism'. But they are also agencies of considerable power in promoting social cohesion and in providing motivation for investment or social development.

Networks in general are a precondition of development in several ways. They serve as stores of human capital;[47] and they may, through schemes to develop micro credit, credit unions, or community and co-operative banks, serve to accrue and invest 'actual' capital. Examples can be found in Cameroon, as well as in funding investment in prawn and cashew nut production for export in Mozambique.[48] Micro credit schemes have become important ways of creating stores of investment capital which are quite modest, but which are able to reach and be used by specific communities without needing substantial resourcing.[49] They may foster the conditions under which markets flourish. Through specific forms, of which grandmothers and religious networks are only two specific examples among many, among which women's group networks have been recognised since the start of the 1990s as an important potential for fruitful investment and for real development, networking activity appears to be a basis for growth as well as for the maintenance of a measure of social order.

Conclusion

This chapter has made an optimistic case for the ways in which technologies might be combined with the important human resources of sub-Saharan Africa to promote more effective development. It has tried to take into account the diversity and fragility of the very different countries covered by the label 'sub-Saharan Africa'. It has not tried to offer a common prescription across the board. Rather it has sought to illustrate the case that, if appropriate technologies and effective management systems can be combined with human skills, expertise and experience, then real but sustainable growth is possible. Much of this argument is reflected in recent literature on sustainability, and indeed in some of the literature on the negotiation of a replacement treaty to the Lomé Convention.[50] So the chapter as a whole does not pretend to be particularly original. But it does sustain three points that are insufficiently emphasised in much of the existing debate on development in African political economy. The first is that particular conceptions of technology need to be incorporated in ways in which we think about sustainable development. It is no good asserting the argument for sustainability without thinking through in detail the implications for how technologies are implemented. The second point is that the introduction of innovative technologies, albeit 'low tech' solutions of one kind or another, need particular forms of management. It is not enough to think in terms of a two-way matrix 'sustainability = forms of (appropriate) technology + forms of human capital/skills/expertise'. The matrix has to be at least three-way: local-based, specifically organised management has to be incorporated into the framework. And this in turn points to the third conclusion. That if we are talking about technology as organised and structured uses of innovation, 'organisation' here invokes culture. Human skills and endowment are elaborated in a context that is culturally specific. And effective management must, equally, incorporate a sense of the cultural potential and the cultural limitations of itself as well as of the world it addresses. In short, the particularities of cultural constraints on development processes can not be ignored. Even the most positivistic economist has to take some notice of the conclusions of culturally sensitive research in order to fulfil her/his own agenda. In this sense, in order to explore the need for diverse and particular ways of addressing development questions in political economy, post-modern and positivist scholars cannot afford to neglect each other.

Notes and References

1   Clapham, Christopher (1998) 'Degrees of Statehood', *Review of International Studies*, vol. 24, no. 2, April, pp. 143–58.

2   Speech by President Robert Mugabe of Zimbabwe reported in the *Independent*, 17 April 1999.

3   If this picture seems overly pessimistic, see G. Ayittey (1998), *Africa in Chaos* (New York: St Martin's Press) Michael Chege, (1997) 'Paradigms of Doom and the Development Management Crisis in Kenya', *Journal of Development Studies*, vol. 33, no. 4, April, pp. 552–67; Jeffrey James (1996) 'The Political

Economy of Inappropriate Technology: Industrialisation in Sub-Saharan Africa', *Development and Change*, vol. 27, no. 3, pp. 415–31; or R. Sandbrook (1993), *The Politics of Africa's Stagnation* (Cambridge University Press). A more balanced argument is sustained in S. Murithi (ed.) (1996) *Africa in Development Dilemma – The Big Debate* (Washington, DC: Press of America); and in material cited in footnotes 3, 4 and 6 following.

4   See, for the origin of central ideas in this chapter, F. Stewart, S. Lall and S Wangure (eds) (1992) *Alternative Development Strategies in Sub-Saharan Africa* (London: Macmillan); M. Fransmann and K. King (eds), (1994) *Technological Capability in the Third World* (London: Macmillan); and J. James and H. Romiji (1997) 'The Determinants of Technological Capability: A Cross Country Study', *Oxford Development Studies*, vol. 25, no. 2, pp. 189–208.

5   Clarke, Robin (1985) *Science and Technology in World Development* (Oxford University Press).

6   See Skolnikoff, Eugene B. (1993) *The Elusive Transformation: Science, Technology and the evolution of International Politics* (Princeton, NJ: Princeton University Press), pp. 144–6, for a fuller discussion of skills and technology as preconditions of global innovation and technology diffusion; also R. Reich (1993) *The Work of Nations*, (New York: Vintage Books).

7   This paragraph draws closely on Poku and Pettiford's attempts to make sense of the idea of development in the 1990s: N. Poku and L. Pettiford (eds) (1998) *Redefining the Third World* (London: Macmillan). See also D. J. C. Forsyth (1994) *Technology Policy for Small Developing Countries* (London: Macmillan).

8   Poku and Pettiford, *Redefining the Third World*.

9   Agrawal, Arun (1995) 'Dismantling the Divide Between Indigenous and Scientific Knowledge', *Development and Change*, vol. 26, no. 3, pp. 413–40.

10   See Hettne, B., 'Globalism Regionalism and the New Third World', in Poku and Pettiford, *Redefining the Third World*, pp. 69–87.

11   See also M. Blumstrom and M. Lundahl (eds) (1993) *Economic Crisis in Africa: Perspectives on Policy Responses* (London: Routledge).

12   Farrands, Chris (1999) *Technology, Globalisation and Power* (London: Routledge), ch. 7.

13   Skolnikoff, *The Elusive Transformation*, illustrates this argument at pp. 132–40 and 230–1; see also Makonnen Alemayehu (1999) *Industrialization in Africa* (New York: Africa World Press).

14   The concept is developed in W. Riedijk (1987) *Appropriate Technology for Developing Countries* (New York: Coronet Books); and B. Hazeltine, C. Bull and L. Wanhammer (1998) *Appropriate Technology: Tools, Choices and Implications* (New York: Academic Press); for a more specific African case study, see also M. J. C. Woillet (1980) *Appropriate Technology: Scope for Cooperation among the Countries of the West African Economic Community*, (Geneva: ILO).

15   Schumacher, E. F. (1976) *Small is Beautiful* (London: Paladin).

16   Lister, M. (1997) *The EU and the South* (London: Routledge). See also the EU Commission websites cited in footnote 32 below.

17   This case is discussed in more detail below. See also K. Remane (ed.) (1997), *African Inland Fisheries, Aquaculture and the Environment* (New York: UN Press); and E. A. Huisman (ed.) (1987) *Aquaculture Research in the Africa Region: Proceedings of the African Seminar on Aquaculture Organized by the International Foundation for Science* (Wageningen, The Netherlands: Wageningen Press).

18 Remane, *African Inland Fisheries*.
19 McCarthy, C.L. (1998) 'Problems and Prospects of African Economic Development', *South African Journal of Economics*, vol. 66, no. 4, pp. 421–51.
20 Amin, Ash (ed.) (1996) *Postfordism* (London: Routledge).
21 Primarily US companies in Sudan, Zimbabawe and South Africa: Economist Intelligence Unit (1996) *Survey of World Textiles, 1996* (London: EIU), and earlier editions.
22 Resh, Howard M. (1995) *Hydroponic Food Production* 5th edn; (Santa Barbara, California: Woodbridge Press). Meier Schwarz (1995) *Soilless Culture Management* (Advanced Series in Agricultural Sciences, vol. 24) (Frankfurt and New York: Springer Verlag).
23 Schwartz, *Soilless Culture Management*.
24 Schwartz, *Soilless Culture Management*, p. 215; V. Venkatesan and J. Kampen (1998) *Evolution of Agriculture in Sub-Saharan Africa*, World Bank Discussion Paper no. 390 (Washington, DC: World Bank).
25 Remane, *African Inland Fisheries*.
26 Bardach, J. E. (ed.) (1997) *Sustainable Aquaculture* (New York: John Wiley).
27 Huisman, E. A. (ed.) (1987) *Aquaculture Research in the African Region: Proceedings of the African Seminar on Aquaculture Organised by the International Foundation for Science* (Wageningen, The Netherlands: Wageningen Press).
28 See Chris Farrands (1997) 'Interpretation of the Diffusion and Absorption of Technology: Change in the Global Political Economy', ch. 7 in M. Talalay, C. Farrands and R. Tooze (eds), *Technology, Culture and Competitiveness* (London: Routledge), pp. 75–89.
29 This discussion draws on the substantial and valuable TICAD website at www.mofa.go.jp/region/africa/ticad2/ticad22.htm. On Japanese development policy in Africa, see also K. Ohno and I. Ohno (1998) *Japanese Views on Economic Development: Diverse Paths to the Market* (London: Routledge).
30 Kaplinsky, R. and A. Posthuma (1994) *Easternization: The Spread of Japanese Management Techniques to Developing Countries* (London: Frank Cass).
31 TICAD website cited in footnote 18.
32 Ibid.
33 Manor, James (1991) *Rethinking Third World Politics* (London: Longman), see also Poku and Pettiford, *Redefining the Third World*.
34 Reich, Robert (1993) *The Work of Nations*, New York: Vintage Books, and Amin, *Postfordism*.
35 B. J. S. K. Adsijobdosoo and S. Adsijobolosoo (1995) *The Human Factor in Developing Africa*, (New York: Praeger).
36 Stewart *et al. Alternative Development Strategies*, and Ming Ivory (1998) 'Doctrines of Science, Technology and Development Assistance', *Alternatives*, vol. 23, no. 3, July, pp. 321–74, both stress the importance of the collective nature of knowledge and of knowledge transmission.
37 Robin Clarke, *Science and Technology in World Development*.
38 Ming Ivory, 'Doctrines of Science'.
39 McPherson, M. and S. Radelet (eds) (1995) *Economic Recovery in the Gambia: Insights into Adjustment in Sub-Saharan Africa* (Cambridge, Mass.: Harvard University Press).

40   Mosley, Paul (ed.) (1994) *Development, Finance and Policy Reform: Essays in the Theory and Practice of Conditionality in Less Developed Countries* (London: Macmillan).
41   Save the Children website for background; specific discussion on debt management on BBC Radio 4, 14 November 1998 'The World Tonight'.
42   Manor, *Rethinking Third World Polities*.
43   See, for example, H. G. Gemunden (ed.) (1998) *Relationships and Networks in International Markets* (Oxford: Pergamon Press) on small business development J. Veciana (ed.) (1994) *SMEs: Internationalization, Networks and Strategy* (Aldershot: Avebury Publishing).
44   Forsyth, D. (1994) *Technology Policy for Small Developing Countries* (London: Macmillan), p. 110.
45   Haq, Mahbub ul (1996) 'Human Development in Sub-Saharan Africa', *Development*, no. 2, pp. 39–41.
46   Stewart *et al. Alternative Development Strategies* McPherson and Radelet, *Economic Recovery in the Gambia*, also recognise the key roles played by women. See, for a specific example, Stace Birks (1984); *Skills Acquisition in Micro Enterprises: Evidence from West Africa* (Geneva: ILO); and for a more critical account, Swasti Mitter (1997) 'Toys for the Boys', *Development*, no. 1, pp. 106–10.
47   Fransman and King, *Technological Capability*; Farrands, 'Interpretation of the Diffusion and Absorption . . . '.
48   *Financial Times*, 15 January 1991; *Financial Times*, 5 November 1996.
49   Forsyth, *Technology policy*.
50   See the DG VIII website at: http://europe.eu.int/com/dg08/index-en.htm on the development of negotiations, which have moved more rapidly since November 1998. The EU Commission published a Green Paper in 1996 which continues to be a valuable source on priorities and thinking; available at http://lucy.ukc.ac.uk/Sonja/RF/GP/lven1_t.htm.

4

The Afrikan[1] Economic Community (AEC): A Step towards Achieving the Pan-Afrikan Ideal

Bakut tswah Bakut

Introduction

As we enter the twenty-first century, discourses on globalisation versus nationalism permeate all areas of political studies. Relevant as the debate is to Afrika, the continent remains an insignificant player in the global economy, hence its exclusion from the debate. While globalisation has increasingly brought into question the relevance of the state system in the developed world, Afrikan governments fail to see the writing on the wall as the new phase of political administrative system compatible with the developments of the twentieth and twenty-first centuries emerges. Afrikan governments are still holding on tightly to the obsolescent state system even though it is quite clear that it has failed in Afrika (partly because of it historical origins and the nature of Afrikan societies). Thus, while the developed world is advancing with technology, building trading blocs and economic unions, Afrikan states are still struggling to create states to transcend or incorporate national (ethnic) loyalties. Since the loyalties of individuals to tribal or national groups (arguably) is the nature of interactions in Afrikan societies, Afrikan governments are burdened with internal divisions, which hinder their attempts to create inclusive states. The sentiment of 'nationalism' since decolonisation is generally expressed within the tribal or national aggregations rather than the states.[2] Such nationalism is based on the search for socioeconomic-cum-politicocultural interests of individuals, and differs from its traditional form (defined in relation to states).

In recognition of the need for a continental solution to the marginalisation of the continent, and the need to develop, the OAU proposed the creation of an African Economic Community (AEC) in the Abuja Treaty of 1991, based on the Lagos Plan of Action (LPA) of 1986. The

79

Afrikan governments seem to have become unwilling promoters of the Pan-Afrikanist ideal (considering their failure to accept Nkrumah's Continental Government Union proposal at decolonisation). The question, however, is how realistic and practicable are the objectives of the Abuja Treaty and the ambition to create an African Economic Community? Although the AEC ideal seems to be properly articulated and plausible, the theoretical framework follows the European model (neo-functionalism) which is based on state structure. Both Afrikan intellectuals and governments seem to be unquestioning followers of the principle of territorial sovereignty (although not based on the nature of Afrikan societies, but on European society).

This chapter discusses the Abuja Treaty in relation to the Functional approach to integration. As an approach to integration and global political co-operation, Functionalism provides an alternative to the state-centred view of international relations, particularly in its aim to control or eliminate the causes of conflicts, with their resultant consequence: war. Although the Afrikans' aim was to find a continental solution through integration, they failed to consider the conditions required for the successful integration of the continent based on the appropriate version of Functionalism. While classic (Mitranian) Functionalism may be inappropriate for European societies (because of their advanced development), it will be relevant to the Afrikan continent. A greater percentage of the people in the continent, still live in poverty and ignorance with disease and a host of other problems associated with severe underdevelopment. Therefore, while the developed world steps into the twenty-first century debating the nature of future societies, Afrika, because of the conditions prevailing there, cannot be considered as a real participant in these developments, and will perhaps remain underdeveloped, or even be reduced to worse conditions. The conditions of Afrika and the theoretical framework adopted in pursuing the AEC objectives are contradictory. For the European Union (EU) version of Functionalism to be successful, the participating economies require a degree of development and political will to share sovereignty. This, however, is not the case with Afrikan states. They still lay strong claims to the inherited dysfunctional Westphalian state system. Classic Functionalism, on the other hand, thrives in conditions of weakness. Weakness necessitates the need for rationalisation of economic and development strategies based on functional interactions already in existence within communities.[3] In essence, classic Functionalism as a theoretical framework for Afrikan continental integration is a more likely candidate (since the continent fulfils the conditions upon which rationalisation of action is required and necessary). This chapter focuses on the relevance and plausibility of the classical approach as a workable theoretical framework for the continent. It takes the peasants and the poor as its main focus: hence it side-steps the 'expensive' debates of ideologies. When discussing Afrikan issues, the tendency among academics (especially European ones), is to view Afrikan problems with Eurocentric perceptions. While this is considered to be academically sound and the mark of scholarship, it hinders a proper understanding and interpretation of the complexities in Afrikan societies. By side-stepping the discussions of ideologies, I hope to provoke a debate on the need for the development of a theoretical framework relevant to Afrika and the realities of the continent.

The Abuja (AEC) Treaty[4]: objectives and programme

The Abuja Treaty emerged from the various OAU resolutions and declarations adopted in Algiers (1968) and Addis Ababa (1970 and 1973), stipulating the need to create continental economic integration as a prerequisite for the achievement of the objectives of the OAU. In June 1991, the OAU created the African Economic Community (AEC) based on the recommendation of the Kinshasa declaration of 1976. The initial proposal of a continental common market was made in the Lagos Plan of Action (LPA) and Final Act of Lagos (1980), which reaffirmed the commitment to establish by the year 2000 an African Economic Community in order to foster the economic, social and cultural integration of the continent. Thus, at the twenty-fifth anniversary of the OAU (1989) it was recommended that the AEC be created, using existing regional and sub-regional sectoral economic co-operation as the basis for the creation of a larger and fuller economic integration, to enable a total continental development. The final decision to implement the various declarations of intentions is based on the reality of the global economy and marginalisation of the continent, hence the decision to create the African Economic Community as an integral part of the OAU.

Chapter 1 of the Treaty divided the continent into regions: North Africa; West Africa; Central Africa; East Africa and Southern Africa, while Chapter 2 outlined the objectives of the Treaty as to:

- Promote economic, social and cultural development and the integration of African economies in order to increase economic self-reliance and promote an endogenous and self-sustained development.

- Establish, on a continental scale, a framework for the development, mobilisation and utilisation of the human and material resources of Africa in order to achieve a self-reliant development.
- Promote co-operation in all fields of human endeavour in order to raise the standard of living of its peoples...and contribute to the progress, development and the economic integration of the African continent.
- Co-ordinate and harmonise policies among existing and further economic communities in order to foster the gradual establishment of the African Economic Community.

Article 6 (the Modalities for the establishment of the Community) states that the Community shall be gradually established over a transition period, not exceeding 34 (maximum 40) years sub-divided into six stages of variable duration. At each stage, specific activities shall be assigned and implemented concurrently as follows:

First stage   Strengthening of existing regional economic communities and the establishment of new ones where none exist, within a period not exceeding five years of the entry into force of the Treaty.

Second stage   Stabilisation of tariff and non-tariff barriers, customs duties and all other charges at each regional community level within a period not exceeding eight years of the entry into force of the Treaty.

Strengthening of sectoral integration at the regional and continental levels in all areas of activities particularly in the fields of trade, agriculture, money and finance...

Co-ordination and harmonisation of activities among existing and future economic communities.

Third stage   Establishment of free trade areas and a customs union through the adoption of a common external tariff at regional economic communities levels within a period not exceeding ten years.

Fourth stage   Co-ordination and harmonisation of tariff and non-tariff systems among the different regional economic communities with the view of establishing a customs union at the continental level through the adoption of a common external tariff within a period not exceeding two years.

Fifth stage   Establishment of the African Common Market within a period not exceeding four years, through:

Adoption of common policy in all areas of Agriculture, Transport, Industry...

Harmonisation of monetary, financial and fiscal policies.

Application of the principle of free movement of persons, rights of residence and establishment.

Creation of the Community's own resources.

Sixth stage The establishment of the Community within a period not exceeding five years, through:

Consolidation and strengthening of the African Common Market's structure: free movement of people, capital, goods and services, rights of residence and establishment.

Integration of all sectors: the establishment of a single domestic market and a Pan-African Economic and Monetary Union.

Setting up of an African Monetary Union, the establishment of an African central bank and the creation of a single African currency.

Setting up the Pan-African Parliament and election of its members by continental universal suffrage.

Harmonisation and co-ordination of the activities of regional economic communities.

Setting up of African multinational enterprises in all sectors.

Setting up the structure of the executive organs of the Community.

The Organs of the Community are introduced in Chapter 3 (Article 7) of the Treaty as:

1 The Assembly of Heads of States and Government.
2 The Council of Ministers.
3 The Pan-African Parliament.
4 The Economic and Social Commission.
5 The Court of Justice.
6 The General Secretariat.
7 The Specialised Technical Committee provided for under the Treaty or established in pursuance thereof.

In the pursuance of the Treaty's objectives, existing regional and subregional organisations have been strengthened. The defunct East African Economic Community – EAC (1967–77) was reactivated in 1994 in accordance with the provisions of the Treaty. The West African Economic Community (ECOWAS) Treaty was revised in 1993 to incorporate the objectives of the Treaty. For the same reasons, the former Southern Africa Development Co-operation Conference (SADCC) was transformed into Southern Africa Development Community (SADC) by the Treaty of Windhoek (1992). The Afrikans now seem determined to work towards the implementation of the Abuja Treaty. However, some scholars have dismissed the achievements made so far, while others have refused to acknowledge the integral relationship between the Abuja Treaty and the regional efforts in the continent.[5] The reasons for scepticism can be traced to the failures of previous attempts in the continent and the lack of political will to implement programmes.

Sovereignty and the AEC strategy

Since the emergence of the Westphalian state system Afrikan governments have drifted from one extreme to the other in the search for peace and development. The creation of the defunct EAC in 1967 (now reconstituted); ECOWAS in 1975 and SADC (1992) represent the articulated attempts of Afrikan governments to integrate. Although these attempts have had little success (a cause for pessimism), the experience gained formed the basis for an African Economic Community. The idea of a continental union can be traced back to Kwame Nkrumah's Pan-Afrikan ideology, which sought the creation of a Pan-Afrikan state. Nkrumah's ideology was based on the dialectics of the concept of 'nation' in the Afrikan sense, as referring to tribe or nation (ethnic group). Hence, a Pan-Afrikan state will incorporate the collective groups overshadowing their differences, while enhancing the development required in the continent. President Julius Nyerere of Tanzania articulated this assumption by stating that:

> it was...the tribe to which a man felt traditional loyalty, not the nation. Yet once the tribe unit has been rejected as not being sensible in Africa, then, there can be no stopping short of Africa itself as the political grouping. For what else is there? 'Nations' in any real sense of the word do not...exist in Africa.[6]

Pan-Afrikanism, therefore, is concerned with the creation of a continental state, on the assumption that the union of Afrika will provide a better prospect of achieving real economic independence. It involves a broad set of functional ideas, which allows the existence of territorial sovereignties, while de-emphasising their importance. Pan-Afrikanism will discourage tribalism, while encouraging communication and transaction among and between the people of the continent. The preamble of the Treaty states:

> We, the Heads of States and Governments of the Organisation of African Unity (OAU)...Recognising the various factors which

hinder the development of the African continent and seriously compromise the future of its people. Conscious of our duty to develop
and utilise the human and natural resources of the continent for the
general well-being of our people in all fields of human endeavour... -
decide to establish an African Economic Community.[7]

The Treaty establishing the Community is in recognition of the necessity to seek alternatives and realistic means of development for the
continent. It is therefore a starting point for the pursuit of economic
independence, peace and development in the continent. The objectives
of the Treaty are:

> [the promotion] of economic, social and cultural development and
> the integration of African economies... on a continental scale... [to
> enhance the] utilisation of the human and material resources of
> Africa in order to achieve a self-reliant development [by promoting]
> co-operation in all fields of human endeavour in order to raise
> the standard of living of its people, and maintain and enhance eco-
> nomic stability, foster close and peaceful relations among Member
> States... [through the co-ordination and harmonisation of] policies
> among existing and future economic communities in order to foster
> the gradual establishment of the African Economic Community.[8]

The ambition of the Community, it seems, is not to create a continental state, as proposed by Nkrumah, but rather a supranational organisation which will ensure the inclusion of tribal groups and nations
while diffusing the role state boundaries play in restricting interactions
between Afrikan peoples. Thus, without the advancement of technology, Afrikan peasants and the poor will be able to pursue their socioeconomic interests and participate in the development of the
continental territorial frontier (Afrikan states) they also identify with.
The compromise is perhaps related to the problems of colonial territorial
politics, which limits the prospects of achieving a continental state
ideal. The Treaty can be seen as a deliberate attempt by Afrikan governments to harmonise their vulnerable economies in order to achieve the
Pan-Afrikanist objectives of a united Afrika.

To understand the problems Afrikan governments will encounter in
the pursuit of the AEC objectives, we need to look at the concept of
sovereignty from a classic Functionalist perspective. Municipal law as
conceived by David Mitrany takes the individual as the unit of political
organisation. International law, on the other hand, takes the state as its

unit. Consequently, the doctrine of equality before the law applies to both units on the same level,[9] even though this is not the case in practice. While individuals in municipal law are recognised and given rights of participation in its making (duties of individuals), states, on the other hand, have the right to refuse participation (denial of obligation) in international law. Therefore the negative 'rights' of states render the concept of 'state equality' questionable. Although the concept of equality before the law forms the basis of the development of modern political systems, and the recognition of individuals 'as the source and end of government', the opposite is the case in the international system, with some states being 'more equal than others'. In other words, there is no equality of states. The state(s) with more capacity to contribute to the development of international law and watch over their enforcement, are 'more equal'[10] than those that lack such capacity. While state equality means equal entitlement and protection for all, in reality not all states have equal share in the formulation and application of such laws, so states are not equal. No Afrikan state has the capacity to influence international law or interactions unilaterally, because of weakness. However, a continental Afrika, asserting claims on the basis of a common cause and purpose, has the capacity to influence international law and interactions because of its potential (both human and material resources), which can be transformed into real power and leverage.

The doctrines of state sovereignty and equality are therefore generally concerned with the definition of the formal relationship of states in a negative sense, hence states' sovereignties are seen as being non-transferable, unless the political community – (elites) who hold power – abdicate. Based on the past failures of Afrikan governments to pursue the sovereign interest of their states (both economically and with regard to development) apart from for personal interest, such a proposition appears unthinkable and impracticable.[11] The possibility of this happening through the AEC is based on the fact that global changes and the integration of the most advanced and developed economies of the world reveals the decline in the importance of territorial sovereignty in the pursuit of economic and technological development. These developments have therefore left Afrikan governments with no option but to work towards regional and continental integration. Since the concept of sovereignty is essential in the creation of nationality – with customs, language, common experience and history, as well as corporate consciousness as the basis of identity articulation – a Pan-Afrikanist (continental) approach will be inclusive of tribal and national sentiments without impinging on the concept of sovereignty. The classification of the peoples of the continent as Afrikans makes more sense to the myriad tribes and nations than the territorially defined states created by the imperialists. A Pan-Afrikanist conception of sovereignty will enable these tribes and nations to pursue their socioeconomic-cum-politicocultural identities based on the existing functional institutions within a Functional federation. Generally, within Afrikan societies, individuals do not identify themselves by the sovereignties of states, but rather by their tribal or national groupings. While nationalism and nationality appear at first glance to be the same, a closer observation reveals a difference between the two. They are not identical and do not serve the same purpose in either domestic or international interactions. The differences in the concepts and purposes mean that national groups find themselves victims of the state system. They are unable to transform their national sentiment into state nationalism. Therefore, the continual maintenance of the colonial boundaries by Afrikan governments hinders the natural social development[12] of tribal groups and nations, consequently their total development. This prevents individuals from transnational intercourse, thereby disturbing the growth of human society in a functional way. We can say, therefore, that the state system reduces the opportunities available for individuals to pursue and achieve socioeconomic improvement. According to D. Mitrany, the major problem in the development of socioeconomic interactions is 'the notion that every authority must be linked to a given territory'.[13] Therefore, a system of interaction that takes these factors into consideration is needed. This represents the concern and mode of thinking of classic Functionalism and the AEC objectives: to build interactions on the basis of sociopsychological relations.

According to Dan Otchere, the failure of Afrikan states to develop is because of the exclusion of Afrikan peoples' cultures in designing models and programmes on development and economic growth. He maintains that unless Afrikan cultures are included in the search for development strategies in Afrika, the continent will remain underdeveloped.[14] This view seems to be the current thinking of development theorists from Afrika, focusing on the continent. Thus, the relevance of Afrikan peoples' culture in economic development remains an important aspect in the development strategies of the continent to ensure an unhindered development. In the twenty-first century, new nationalism (ethnic nationalism) will grow rapidly in the continent, further hindering development and exacerbating poverty as long as Afrikan governments maintain traditional state sovereignty rather than a Pan-Afrikanist concept of sovereignty. The removal of the colonial state system in Afrika will enable Afrikan people to interact on the basis of their existing functional institutions/associations. It is therefore necessary for Afrikan academics to carry out research into new frameworks for achieving the continental objective of the Abuja Treaty. Research on Afrika's development must take into consideration the complexities and nature of Afrikan societies rather than the unquestionable adoption of European frameworks. Having failed to transcend colonial boundaries and develop relations based on the common history of exploitation,[15] common cause (freedom from poverty, disease and ignorance), and articulate the already existing functional institutions, Afrikan governments and academics must now devote time to the search for appropriate frameworks in the pursuit of economic development and technological advancement through the AEC strategy. The continent has a long history of community relations, which can be traced back to 700 BCE,[16] upon which the basis of a continental solution can be found. The history of the Westphalian statehood in Afrika, on the other hand, is recent and a failure.

Functionalism and continental unification

The weaknesses and nature of Afrikan economies and societies necessitates the harmonisation of policies and the expunction of territorial boundaries hindering free continental interaction. This becomes paramount, because of the vulnerability of individual countries, which compromises their ability to compete unilaterally in the international system and effectively in the global economy. However, operating as a unit, Afrikan countries can build the strong leverage necessary for effective competition in the international system and the global economy. Although the provisions of the Abuja Treaty allow such unification at all levels, it seems that the socioeconomic interactions of people (an aspect of their economic activities) was not taken into consideration. The arbitrary way in which the continent was divided by the imperialist Europeans not only affected people's economic relations but also their social relations, which are fundamental to their interactions and transactions. While the ethnic groups divided into different states with a few exceptions do not seek to create separate states or make any irredentist claim[17] they conduct their interactions and transactions on the basis of ethnic homogeneity, which takes into consideration their historical relations in the conduct of socioeconomic affairs. Thus, Afrikan peoples' conduct of economic and social activities is based on cultural and historical relations, as well as on interest-motivated transactions.[18]

This is different from the socioeconomic interactions of the Europeans, where the pursuit of economic interest is individualistically centred, without any ties to tribes or nations (which do not exist as they do in the Afrikan continent). The continent, because of the tribal and national groups, is rendered appropriate for classic Functionalism (but not the European neo-functionalist framework). What is required is the articulation of the already existing functional institutions into associations or organisation, on the basis of functional needs and mutual interests. It appears that the Abuja Treaty unfortunately failed to make provision for such cross-border interaction at the lower levels of societies. In Article 4 of the Treaty, one of the objectives is the promotion of information flow among associations. However, the definition of associations excluded those that are not economic-interest-dominated (a European culturally defined concept of association based on pure economic interest). Consequently, peasant farmers and nomadic people involved in transnational interactions, are, by implication excluded from the tenets of Article 4. It seems that the only legitimate associations are those of 'businessmen, business and advertising'. The Treaty also failed to make provisions for the formation of such associations.

Classic Functionalism is concerned with social and economic changes in the world.[19] It is concerned with ways of creating a co-operative framework in the areas of economic and social interaction, based on the belief that politics is the cause of conflicts and wars, because of its divisive nature. Functionalism therefore provides a framework, which allows the balance of benefits and mutual interest through co-operation. This, it posits, will circumvent conflicts and wars in the world. Although the evolution of the Westphalian states seems to have united diversities and provided the basis for peaceful co-existence in the world, states, however, are catalysts to conflicts and wars, through territorial sovereignty claims. For classical Functionalism, a co-operative mechanism based on functional interactions already exists but requires proper co-ordination to create a peaceful world. The various forms of interaction between tribes and nations of the continent (in their pursuit of socio-economic interests) are manifestations of the existence of functional institutions (a necessity for the successful achievement of integration based on the classic framework). Classic Functionalism therefore, is a framework for co-ordinating the human habitual search for a unified formal order and the rationalisation of what is already in existence.[20] In essence, the AEC objectives can be achieved if Afrikan governments co-ordinate the existing functional interactions in a unified formal order (rationally) by including the peasants and poor in the integration programmes. In Functionalist thinking, national problems at international or continental levels are like municipal problems in the domestic environment[21] and must be so perceived and treated, to ensure the creation of a working peace system. Afrikan governments will therefore need to legitimise the existing transnational interaction of their citizens (often classified as illegal) to ensure the achievement of the AEC objectives.

The two forces (economic division of labour and state system) introduced in the nineteenth and twentieth centuries destroyed the abilities of individuals and local groups to develop communication naturally. This, however, is more pronounced in Europe than in the Afrikan continent. The new social life bound people together, through the forces of the state in European societies, thereby enfranchising individuals politically (individuals became citizens, while groups and national groups became enfranchised within the state structure). In Afrikan societies, however, although tribes and nations ceased to form the basis of nationality, an abstract 'state' was imposed to claim the loyalty and allegiance of the various peoples. But the state system failed, because Afrikan peoples have not undergone the same stages as Europeans in developing a sense of nationality based on the concept of the Westphalian state. While Europeans have transcended their various tribal and national aggregations over hundreds of years, the Afrikans have not. Thus, while it is possible for Europeans to pursue integration via the neo-Functionalist framework, it will be impossible for Afrikans to achieve the same success because of the differences in levels of societal development and stratification. Afrikan states must find ways, in the search for material efficiency and the quest for social betterment, of reconciling their deep-rooted loyalty to national collectives with the goals of states. Individuals in Afrikan societies find themselves constrained by states in their search for socioeconomic satisfaction. States restrain their abilities to pursue interests beyond the defined territories. To be able to achieve the AEC objectives, the theoretical framework must be one that takes into consideration the existing functional institutions in the continent. In this case, classic (Mitranian) Functionalism will be a more appropriate framework.

In classic Functionalism, activities, specifically selected, should be organised separately, under the conditions in which they operate naturally. The rationale is to allow freedom for practical variations in the organisation of the several functions, as well as in the working of a particular function, based on changing needs and conditions.[22] The organisation of issues, based on socioeconomic and cultural spheres, represents positive interaction. This pattern is different from the state system, which emphasises the negative aspects (politics, sovereignty and territorial claims). For the classic approach, the dimensions of functional activities should determine the appropriate organs (whether functional for the positive aspects, or 'structured' for the negative aspects) in which the functions operate.[23] Functions performed by such activities should determine the political instruments suitable for proper operation and effectiveness, thus making reforms possible at every stage. Such arrangements would allow the power needed by each respective authority, in its operation, to be easily determined. The logic is based on the conclusion that any division of authority and power, constitutionally or otherwise, not consistent with the general rules of nature, will hinder the working of the Functional system. Functional agencies will therefore possess the power to execute, rather than 'just' discuss or comment, as is the case with 'constitutional-type' structures. Functional agencies will be able to act as necessary, in line with the changing nature of the world, while pursuing their objectives.[24] Their success will be dependent on the way issues are organised and managed.

Functional arrangement therefore starts with the identification of needs, and issues organised along the lines of specific ends in accordance with the condition(s) of the time and place.[25] This means that every problem would be treated and tackled as a practical issue in itself, thereby allowing the appropriate authority to grow and develop through actual performance. And since the emphasis is on welfare, the early stages in the development of structures will be focused on the positive aspects of interactions. Functional agencies/institutions will not attack the state system frontally, but will act gradually, through reduction in the importance placed on territorial sovereignty as transnational interactions increase within the regions and continent. The gradualist approach will enable ideologies to take their place where applicable, diluting them if necessary, in line with the new and growing habit of co-operation, on the basis of functional needs and mutual interest. It will enable the achievement of the highest possible degree of co-operation, through active forces and opportunities, while touching as little as possible the latent active points of difference and opposition.[26] Since Functional agencies have their roots in the domestic environment, the development of such common activities and interest across frontiers would make a change of frontiers unnecessary. Functional institutions will therefore help the growth of positive interaction and constructive common work, common habits and interests, and render frontier lines meaningless.[27] If both domestic and continental environments are to experience the effective arrangement of issues along functional lines, it is necessary to allow a free movement of associations to satisfy socioeconomic and cultural needs, starting in this case from the regions as in the Abuja Treaty provision. In essence, activities should be arranged and organised to operate in the manner of a 'cartel', without a rigid structure of fixed rules. Negative functions (such as judiciary, security and so on.) because of their nature (fixed and static) need a formal approach and should be organised. Each Function should be arranged to achieve 'technical self-determination'.[28]

If the Abuja Treaty is to be achieved through a Functionalist framework, the pattern of Functional agencies within domestic environments should provide the forms for Functional institutions at the continental level. Since these forms of transnational interaction are already in existence, the pattern of co-ordination and management should also come about functionally – that is, based on the principle of 'form following function', in the following three stages:

1   At the domestic level, interactions should be based on the co-ordination of existing functional interactions into Functional agencies (FAs), to satisfy either technical or wider functional ends based on their functions.
2   This stage should be the co-ordination of the various FAs within domestic environments (both statewise and regionally) under larger and wider umbrellas – Functional Institutions (FIs) to represent the interests of domestic agencies at the continental level.
3   The last and widest stage in the structure is the co-ordination of all domestic FIs at the continental level under a broader mandate. Thus, at this level, management of the system will be by wider co-ordination and planning. This means that all members of the wider FIs at the Continental Functional Institution (CFI) level will be able to co-operate and collaborate, to satisfy the needs of the people they represent.

Each of these stages should have political authority enshrined in their operations. Thus political authority will not depend on a vertical hierarchy (as in the case of the political party system) but be obtained from delegation to represent, by democratic means (not conceived as in popular democracy),[29] which will be achieved through:

1   The measuring and examining of the achievement of the objectives of agencies/institutions. Since the structures will be designed to suit the issues organised, the agencies/institutions will include in their

objectives provisions for periodical evaluation by both the electorate and their representatives.

2 The monitoring of representatives based on their accountability to the issues they represent will ensure the avoidance of the exclusive accumulation of influence and power by a few, who could manipulate the system self-interestedly. The electorate will monitor the extent of the representatives' powers to control the agencies/institutions, as well as their individual interests. Hence, the electorate will have the power to select or deselect representatives before or after the periodic elections.

3 Any representative's claim to political or administrative control will therefore need to be justified to the electorate, who determine whom their representatives will be in relation to the pursuit of functional needs and mutual interests. The structures will ensure that corrective measures are in place and are applicable. Thus Afrikan people will have power over the selection and election of their representatives to office.

This arrangement will ensure that the usage of political or administrative power to harness the achievement of common tasks and ends is under common control, since the weak and vulnerable electorate will be able to participate, even if they are not directly involved in execution or control.[30] The electorate will experience a true sense of equality and democracy. Based on this, one can argue that the adaptation and application of classic Functionalist principles in the pursuit of the objectives of the Abuja Treaty will enable Afrikan governments to achieve these objectives on a practical basis.

The objectives of classical Functionalism are the reduction of the interference of national frontiers and the minimisation of the factors that exacerbate economic instability, while promoting the attainment of higher levels of health, literacy, culture and social justice.[31] These are similar to the AEC objectives, hence they can be achieved by applying classic Functionalism rather than a European neo-Functionalist framework. It means therefore that the Abuja Treaty must make provision for the transnational interactions and associations at the lower levels of Afrikan societies. This will encourage the development of business interactions by peasants, thus helping to protect and preserve their mutual interest. The creation of 'border markets' by the Nigerian government to enable transnational interaction with neighbouring countries is consistent with the principles of classic Functionalism. It will enable the people to interact at the market place level while the governments sign treaties in chancelleries.[32] Peasant producers will be able to diversify and/or change their commodities for higher profits or better yields as they interact at the lower level in pursuit of functional needs and mutual interest. Thus, unrecorded trading (smuggling) will be eliminated and the free flow of socioeconomic interactions in the region and the continent encouraged. People will be equipped to fight against their common enemies: poverty, pestilence and ignorance. In essence, the AEC strategy should divorce non-political issues from political constraints, by allowing people to tackle issues at the lower levels of interaction, thereby preparing them, as well as governments, for greater integration at the continental level. I.L. Claude's assertion (see Note 31) that the success of any functional arrangement relies on the co-operative pursuit of common interest in non-political fields, to generate political change conducive to peace, is very much necessary in the Afrikans' attempt. Therefore the AEC should seek to encourage such co-operative pursuits by allowing transnational interactions on non-political and socioeconomic issues at the lower levels, by creating conducive environments that will enable the people of the continent to pursue their socioeconomic-cum-politicocultural interests without the constraints of politics.

The economic conditions, development stages and proximity of member states' boundaries within the continent are, from a classic Functionalist point of view, conducive factors for the creation of a working system. Thus the necessary factors for the integration of the continent are already in place. The geographical proximity of member states; their homogeneity in values; their socioeconomic interactions, their shared functional interest in utilising available resources effectively; their desire to improve standards of living; the nature of transaction/interactions, based on historical alliances from kinship; their mutual knowledge of a common history of exploitation by imperial powers; the dependent nature of member states in the international system and global economy; governments' ineffectiveness, because of unsuitable systems/structures adopted; and the experiences gained from previous integration attempts since the early 1960s, should provide the basis for a successful AEC to pursue the creation of a Functional federation. The assumptions of classic Functionalism are based on the conditions of weakness and underdevelopment, hence the Afrikan continent is ripe for the application of the framework. One major limitation to the Treaty is that member states still have control of the decision-making and implementation mechanism. For the Treaty's objectives to be achieved, member states must have the political will

and vision to see beyond the destructive and narrow interests of territorial sovereignty. The formation of groups based on functional
needs should arise on the basis of need and mutual interests,[33] rather
than by governmental agreements or constructs. The role of government in the evolution of Functional agencies and institutions (FA/
Is) should be one of co-ordination within specific guidelines,
consistent with the objective of empowering the continent, both economically and technologically, to compete effectively in the twenty-first
century.

The organisation of the Community on a functional basis will
enhance intra-community acquisition of raw materials and resources
so that the Afrikans themselves could exploit unexplored markets in
the continent. Similar activities could also be co-ordinated to
decrease both overproduction and underproduction. However, such
functional interactions would mean the introduction of protectionist
policies for certain industries in the continent. Although this would
contravene the policies of trade liberalisation, since the Afrikan continent is relatively weak and therefore a low-level player in the global
economy, the protection of infant industries in the continent should
not pose any serious problem to the global economy. This assumption is
based on the current level of interaction between the developed world
and the Afrikan continent. The development of a continental trading
area and the protection of its infant industries will encourage intra-
community transactions, with more market opportunities for exploitation. J. S. Nye blamed Afrika's failure to industrialise on the tightness of
national boundaries and unstable demarcation, preventing the interaction of market forces.[34] The removal of intra-community frontiers
and the protection of infant industries would help to 'open up' the
tight and unstable demarcated boundaries, and to allow industrialisation and development in the continent. Although the Abuja Treaty
proposes to achieve such objectives, it has not separated non-political
interactions from political constraints. This lapse therefore constitutes
a grave set-back to the pursuance of the AEC ideal. However, if
member states are willing to ensure its success, they must also be willing
to allow the formation of functional groups/associations across state
boundaries, at the lower levels of interactions, without any constraint
or restrictions. Alternatively, the AEC strategy will have to make provisions to enable such interactions without any hindrance from member
states.

Another blockage to achieving the AEC ambition is the political will
of member states. Sir Dauda Jawara of The Gambia, commenting on the

reasons for the slow progress of ECOWAS, pointed out that 'there has to be enough political will for us to be able to implement the decisions we take. Really, you cannot separate political decisions from economic decisions'.[35] Lack of political will led to the collapse of the East African Community (EAC) in 1977. The lessons drawn from that attempt and other previous experiences lead to the conclusion that the prospect of achieving the objectives of the AEC is dependent on the political will of member states to 'sacrifice' both political and territorial sovereignties. While the Pan-African Parliament provision of the Treaty is an effort to curtail the powers of national governments, and empower the electorate, the composition, function, power and organisation of the Parliament are still on the drawing board. However, the objectives imply the provision of opportunities to the people, to present their worries directly to the Parliament. The Parliament is therefore aimed at curtailing the negative impact of national governments over peoples' socioeconomic activities within the continent. Article 91 of the Treaty specified the establishment of co-operative relations with socioeconomic organisations and associations directly within the Community.[36] These provisions assume that the lack of political will of any individual member state is open to challenge by other groups. Unfortunately, the Treaty restricts groups' transnational interaction by placing them under the direct influence of national governments, thus defeating the aim of the provision. Therefore, for the objectives of the Treaty to be achieved, national governments must be willing to relinquish their claims to territorial sovereignties and seek a continental sovereignty, by allowing individuals the right to form socioeconomic associations across national boundaries.

Sa'adia Touval explained that while Afrikans have struggled towards the creation of states, their real desire is freedom within their territories. Hence, after the achievement of territorial sovereignties, tribal and national consciousness awakened to assert that quest for freedom.[37] As long as the interests of these groups remain unsecured or unsatisfied, conflicts are bound to continue. The formation of organisations on the basis of functional needs and mutual interests will discourage such tribal and national consciousness, leading to cohesion within states, regions and the continent. Transnational interactions at the lower levels of societies will influence governments without resulting in conflicts, and provide a continental approach for groups with similar functional needs and mutual interests.

Conclusion

In spite of its limitations, the Abuja Treaty if fully implemented, will help to resolve the instability and constant changes of government in some parts of the continent. The growing irrelevance of the Westphalian state system, and the empowerment of nations under the principles of self-determination, provides an opportunity for Afrikan governments to seek out workable systems or structures for the continent. Functional agencies/institutions could become alternative collective aggregates, replacing tribal and national allegiances, which also permeate Afrikan party political systems. Functional agencies/institutions will be able to put pressure on state governments without resorting to a change of administration through violent means. This assertion is based on the assumption that Afrikan people are indifferent to the form of territorial sovereignty (although they will recognise a Pan-Afrikan sovereignty), and are more concerned with the pursuit of socioeconomic and politico-cultural interests. A de-emphasis of the importance of the inherited territorial sovereignty is therefore a necessary step towards the building of an African Economic Community. If the AEC is to succeed, the loyalty of Afrikans to tribal and national identities must be replaced with new forms of loyalty. As long as the pursuit of territorial interests and sovereignties remain the primary pursuit of Afrikan states, the AEC ambition will remain a dream. If, however, the AEC and Afrikan states can learn from Yoweri Musevini's new political order in Uganda (see Chapter 6 of this volume) tribal and national loyalties could easily be transferred to functional institution. Classic Functionalism can help Afrikan governments surmount conflicts and disunity among the myriad national groups in their states, regions and the continent, and empower Afrikans to become protagonist in the international system and the global economy. I hold the view that the creation of an African Economic Community is very possible and is a necessary step towards a developed Afrika, even though, more work is still required. There is, however, the need to debate the AEC proposal and development. The debate will encourage Afrikan governments to evaluate their positions in relation to the ambitions of the Treaty, and it will also enable the AEC Secretariat to devote time and resources to research better ways of achieving the AEC objectives within a globalising world and the decline in relevance of the state system. It is my hope that this chapter will provoke debates on the search for a workable system for the achievemnet of the AEC objectives in the twenty-first century.

Notes and References

1 The rationale in writing Afrika with a 'k', instead of 'c', besides my assertion of *kujichagulia* (self-determination), the 'k' is consistent with the phonetic pronunciation of Afrikan languages. The 'ka' has a spiritual meaning (a debate for another occasion) to the Ba'Ntu (Spirit humans) – the *kwa* linguistic group of Afrikan languages which form the major categorisation of Afrikans by scholars – and their habitat. For another conception of the usage of the 'k', see Sindiwe Magona's parable (short story), 'Mama Afrika', *New Internationalist*, no. 307, November 1998, pp. 22–3.

2 See C. A. Diop (1987) *Precolonial Black Africa* (trans. Harold Salemson) (New York: Lawrence Hill Books). Diop has outlined the state system of pre-colonial Black Africa as being highly structured, based on the division of labour/responsibilities. His work contests the 'tribal system' assumptions of Western scholars and argues that the retribalisation of Africa was because of the climate of insecurity brought about by the conquest of the Afrikan states, first by Islam and later by the Europeans. See also A. D. Smith (1991) *Ethnic Origin of Nations* (Oxford: Basil Blackwell); J. Reader (1998) *Africa: A Biography of the Continent* (Harmondsworth: Penguin) and S. P. Blier (1998); *Royal Arts of Africa: The Majesty of Form* (London: Lawrence King).

3 D. Mitrany (1966) *A Working Peace System* (Chicago: Quadrangle).

4 The Abuja Treaty (1991) establishing the African Economic Community (AEC).

5 See T. M. Shaw (1998) 'African Renaissance/African Alliance: Towards New Regionalism and New Realism in the Great Lakes at the Start of the Twenty-first Century', and B. Oden, 'The Not So New Regionalism in Africa', both in *Politeia*, vol. 17, no. 3.

6 A quotation from J. S. Nye (1966) *Pan-Africanism and the East African Integration* (Cambridge, Mass.: Harvard University Press), p. 14. See also S. Touval (1972), *The Boundary Politics of Independent Africa* (Cambridge, Mass.: Harvard University Press), pp. 21, 27. Touval argued that nationalism in Afrika was usually around the population of a given colonial territory, mainly ethnically heterogeneous in the pursuit of political independence.

7 The Abuja Treaty, 1991.

8 Ibid., Chapter iii, Article 4.

9 This inequality, by implication, means that the claim of the 'divine right' of the monarch has been transferred to the 'absolute state' working against cultures and customs, which discount such 'divine' concepts in politics. See D. Mitrany (1993) *The Progress of International Government* (New Haven, Conn.: Yale University Press), pp. 47, 71.

10 Ibid., pp. 53, 62.

11 The impracticability of 'surrendering' sovereignty (power) by the political elites stems from their individualistic interests. By the virtue of their positions in the polity, they are able to achieve personal benefits, which will be lost, if they surrender the sovereignty of the polity.

12 D. Mitrany (1975) 'The Prospect of Integration: Federal or Functional?', in A. J. R. Groom and P. Taylor (eds), *Functionalism: Theory and Practice* (London: University of London Press), pp. 64–6.

13 Ibid.

14   Dan Otchere is a development economist at Concordia University, Montreal, Canada. He seems to be attracting much attention and respect from Afrikan development theorists.

15   Touval, *The Boundary Politics of Independent Africa*, pp. 27–8, 31. The concept of 'nation' or 'state' has no meaning or relevance to Afrikan people, except the elites. The removal of the 'sphere of influence' imposed by the colonialists only awakened the deep-seated sense of particularity of the people. Although the situation led to disunity, Afrikan leaders found it more convenient and beneficial to pursue their objectives under the banner of territorial interest: states. This was one of the reasons why the Nkrumahist African Union Government failed. See also C. Hoskynes (1967). 'Pan-Africanism and Integration: The Situation in 1957', in A. Hazlewood (ed.), *African Integration and Disintegration: Case Studies in Economic and Political Union* (London: Oxford University Press), p. 354.

16   Scholars of Afrikan historical development generally agree that the continent was organised as far back as this period. The general conclusion is based on the military exploits of Piankhi, a Nuban (Nubian from present Sudan) as the Par-Ao (Pharaoh) of both Upper and Lower 'Egypt'. Piankhi defeated Osorkon, the 'Libyan' king of lower 'Egypt', who sought to impose his son on the Thebetan (Upper Egypt) Priesthood as High Priest. He also defeated Tefknakht, king of Heracleopolis, and Nimrod of Hermopolis, the two powerful kings of his time, who posed a challenge to the 'Egyptian' theolo-political civilisation. Piankhi instituted the twenty-seventh dynasty in 702 BCE. Some scholars, however, insist on an earlier date for Afrika's civilisation. They maintained that Afrikan historical development could be traced from 4500 BCE. See C. A. Diop (1974) *The African Origin of Civilisation: Myth or Reality*, trans. and ed. Mercer Cook (Chicago: Lawrence Hill Books); C. Williams (1987) *The Destruction of Black Civilisation; Great Issues of a Race from 4500 BC to 2000 AD*, (Chicago: Third World Press); W. Rodney (1982) *How Europe Underdeveloped Africa* (Washington, DC: Howard University Press); G. P. Murdock (1959) *Africa: Its Peoples and Their Cultural History* (New York: McGraw-Hill). See also M. K. Asante and K. W. Asante (eds) (1993) *African Culture: The Rhythms of Unity* (Trenta NJ: Africa World Press). Other interesting books are A. De Selincount (1954) *The Histories of Herodotus* (Harmondsworth: Penguin); C. H. Oldfather (1967) *Diodorus of Sicily* (London: Heinemann); J. H. Greenberg (1963) *The Languages of Africa* (Bloomington, Indiana: Indiana University Press). This is by no means a complete list of literature on Afrikan ancient historical development.

17   The drawing of boundaries by colonial administrators only took cognisance of the metropoles, disregarding the particular circumstances of the people, in terms of their socioeconomic or politicocultural aggregations. Thus the socioeconomic units that played a very important role in the inter-relations of the Afrikan people, were destroyed. These deliberate policies of 'divide and rule' or 'assimilation', weakened the foundation of Afrikan socioeconomic systems and hindered their growth or further development. See S. Touval, *The Boundary Politics of Independent Africa*, pp. 4, 21. Also, J. Chipman (1989) *French Power in Africa* (Oxford: Basil Blackwell), p. 227; and C. Hoskynes, 'Pan-Africanism and Disintegration', pp. 357, 358.

18   While socioeconomic activities in modern Afrikan cities are conducted on the basis of individualistic interest, the opposite is the case in rural areas. People in rural areas tend to conduct their socioeconomic activities on the basis of their relationship to other members of the community, or the neighbouring community, which may be in another state.

19   D. Mitrany (1948) 'The Functional Approach to World Organisation', *International Affairs*, vol. 24, July, p. 350.

20   Ibid., pp. 115, 118.

21   D. Mitrany (1946) *A Working Peace System*, 4th edn (London: National Peace Council), p. 50.

22   D. Mitrany (1975) *The Functional Theory of Politics* (London: Martin Roberts), p. 116.

23   Ibid., p. 118.

24   Mitrany, 'The Prospect of Integration ... ', p. 7.

25   Ibid., pp. 28–9.

26   Ibid., p. 31.

27   Ibid., pp. 33–5.

28   Ibid., pp. 41–3.

29   Popular democracy entails the conduct of elections, to choose the representatives of people through political parties/groups. The principle of democracy, however, does not restrict the choice of representations to the political parties/groups arrangement. The pattern of 'electing' representatives does not constitute the democratic process. Democracy entails the ability of individuals to choose representatives within a collective, regardless of the system in use. Thus the aim of the continental universal suffrage of democracy should be to encourage people to choose their representatives, and not the formation of political parties or groups.

30   Mitrany, 'The Prospect of Integration ... ', pp. 46–50.

31   I. L. Claude Jr. (1964) *Swords into Ploughshares*, 3rd edn (University of London Press), pp. 353–75.

32   Mitrany, *A Working Peace System*.

33   A. J. R. Groom, and A. Heraclides (1985) 'Integration and Disintegration', in M. Light and A. J. R. Groom (eds), *International Relations: A Handbook of Current Theory*, (London: Pinter), pp. 178–9. See also A. J. R. Groom (1994) 'Neofunctionalism: A Case of Mistaken Identity', in B. F. Nelson and A. Stubb, C-G, (eds), *The European Union* (Boulder, Col.; London: Lynne Rienner).

34   Nye, *Pan-Africanism*.

35   E. Anim *et al.* (1990) 'Born-again Diplomacy', *Newswatch Magazine* (Nigeria), vol. 12, no. 16, 29 October, pp. 16–20.

36   See AEC Treaty, 1991.

37   Touval, *The Boundary Politics of Independent Africa*.

Part II

Democracy, Conflict and Human Rights

5

The Legitimacy and Sovereignty Dilemma of African States and Governments: Problems of the Colonial Legacy*

Cirino Hiteng Ofuho

Introduction

Over the years since African states gained their independence, scholars interested in African affairs have produced a remarkable outpouring of scholarly research on African politics, though it is tied mainly to paradigms of development.[1] However, decades of preoccupation with development has yielded meagre returns, and African economies have been stagnating or regressing. Many factors have been offered to explain the apparent failure of development enterprise in Africa, and most of these explanations have been labelled as negative consequences of the colonial legacy. These include social pluralism and its centrifugal tendencies; the corruption of leaders; poor labour discipline; the lack of entrepreneurial skills; poor planning and incompetent management; inappropriate policies; the restriction of market mechanisms; low levels of technical assistance; the limited inflow of foreign capital; falling commodity prices, and unfavourable terms of trade; and low levels of saving and investment.[2] These negative features have become major problems for the African continent, and a number of African scholars and Africanists alike have been quick to blame them on either the colonial superstructure or the post-colonial African political order. Thus a sustained polarisation in debate has resulted. There are scholars who have argued that the readily made assumption about the failure of development in Africa is misleading. Claude Ake, for example, argues that the issue is not that development has failed, but rather that it was never on the agenda in the first place. What was in place was widespread political rivalry over the control of state power and its meagre resources.

Therefore such political conditions were exacerbated by the fragile state and bad government; and this in turn became the greatest impediment to development in the African continent.

It has been posited that colonialism was statist in nature, in the sense that it redistributed land and determined who should produce what and how. This chapter takes the argument further by maintaining that it was not only the state and governmental institutions established by colonialism that created the failures of the post-colonial state. The African elites themselves, who took charge of running those institutions, also contributed negatively. These ruling elites embraced the institutions and laws of the colonial state. It could be argued that these elites were the choice of their colonial mentors and that they were elevated to the leadership in order to protect the colonial interest after independence, rather than the interest of the African peoples. Thus, what succeeded colonialism was bad governance, mismanagement of the economy, ethnic chauvinism, and lack of a vision for development and progress even at the leadership level. These factors all led to the outright decay of African states and the erosion of the legitimacy of their governments. It should also be pointed out that the passivity of the African masses and the naïvety and bias of some African intellectuals has also contributed heavily to the failures of the post-colonial states and their governments. These groups (intellectuals and the African masses), though outside the centre of state power and government, have not been revolutionary enough to nip corruption and inefficient governance in the bud. A number of reasons can be advanced to explain why these groups were reluctant in probing the colonial state after independence. For one, Africa's independence was merely an introduction to what Kwame Nkrumah described as neo-colonialism. According to Nkrumah, independence was simply an avoidance of confrontation, and colonial masters sensed the risk of confrontation, fearing that vital comprador elements might become alienated and driven into socialism. Thus the swift move was made to bring formal colonial rule to a quick end so that new collaborative regimes friendly to multinational capitalism could safely be installed and lent the necessary external support.[3] In a way, the West mocked the founding fathers of Africa's independence. They were simply made to believe that they were in effective control of the post-colonial state even when it was clear that the so-called independent African countries were still closely tied to the metropole. Some of these leaders were selected on the assumption that they were a 'modernising elite', deeply impregnated with Western ideas and were also keenly aware of the economic and political progress of the West.

Theoretical discourses on sovereignty and legitimacy: some critical observations

I would like to draw attention to a brief critical comment on some specific analyses advanced about the 'African state'. I will do this by looking eclectically at some of the analyses of the 'African state' by two major International Relations (IR) scholars based in the West: Robert H. Jackson and Christopher Clapham. But first I would like to point out some of the common theoretical underpinnings about 'sovereignty' and 'illegitimacy'. Sovereignty refers to the right to own and control some area of the world.[4] This is a new meaning that has nothing to do with the old one, based on monarchy, on which the connotation of sovereignty was built. Our analysis here adopts the new Westphalian meaning, which both Jackson and Clapham use in their analyses. This is the idea of independent rule by a country or institution over a certain territory or set of political concerns. Thus the basic meaning of sovereignty is legitimacy of rule, as opposed to actual power. It is along this line that the language of the sovereignty of the people, as opposed to *de facto* rule by an elite, has been advanced.

However, it is the requirements of internal sovereignty, which scholars such as, among others, Robert Jackson and Christopher Clapham, suggest the African states have failed to fulfil. African states have enjoyed only external sovereignty. But the major problem for these scholars is that they are often inclined to locate such failure wholly within post-colonial Africa's political order. They therefore play down any negative contributions colonialism might have exerted on the African political order. It is these played down areas of analysis that this chapter also intends to bring to light.

On the other hand, legitimacy is both a normative and an empirical concept. In normative terms, to ask the question whether the state, or the government, is entitled to be obeyed or not, is tantamount to asking whether a political system is legitimate. For this reason, the idea of legitimacy is connected with the legal concepts of *de jure* and *de facto* power. Whatever the accepted grounds of political obligation may be, legitimacy refers to these. To sum it all, the uses of legitimacy and sovereignty are twofold: (a) popular legitimacy – where political rights are vested in the people whose consent is necessary for the state to be legitimate; and (b) 'positive sovereignty' – where freedom consists in being one's own master. The African states were constructed and their governments constituted, not on the basis of the consent of the peoples of the respective jurisdictions, but as contrary designs that were to continue indirect links with metropolitan governments.

I would like to specify some of the points emphasised by both Jackson and Clapham in their respective analyses of African states. On 'statehood' in general, Jackson and Clapham concur in their arguments about the causes of the collapse of the African states. Their writings on the 'quasi-statehood' of the African states are definitely the most eloquent.[5] Their major weakness is, however, that they do not dig out the root causes of this particular collapsed statehood. Instead, they simply assume the analysis and conclude that the African states have failed to fulfil the requirements for statehood, unlike their counterparts in Europe. They have done this by deliberately avoiding any negative impact that colonialism has had on the African states and their governments. This chapter argues that any analysis of the African states should not skip the history of European colonialism, because the African states are essentially constructs of European powers. Indeed, Clapham himself admits this when he writes that the ideal of statehood is 'western in derivation', then goes wrong in also arguing that, 'which the governing elites of "Third World" states sought to emulate, and which they might come more or less close to attaining'.[6] Clapham knows well that the very idea of 'state' is not African, but a construct of the West, of which many Western scholars have been proud, and it was imposed on the colonised peoples as an ideal construct. Long before the imposition of the state structure, the African peoples had their modes of organising society, which were phased out because the continent did not have any choice but to adopt the Westphalian structure designed by European powers in Berlin. The OAU Charter sanctioned the inviolability and sanctity of African borders for fear of post-colonial conflicts over borders. However, it should be noted that Article 3(1) of the OAU Charter was not a confirmation of correctness but rather a demonstration of awareness of the problems that any discussion of colonial borders might cause. So to simply cite African states as the exemplar of states that have failed in their role without digging deep into the root causes of the failure is itself both arbitrary and partisan.

While it cannot be denied that the African states have failed to meet what F. Halliday terms 'the stringent requirements for positive sovereignty',[7] the root causes of this very failure hark back to nearly a century of European colonial administration. Jackson and Clapham do not place emphasis on this, though they at times simply mention that the existence of the 'quasi-states' was ultimately sanctioned or permitted by the dominant states of the global order. And if this was the case, then the problems of statehood in the 'Third World' are partly located in the colonial superstructure and partly in the post-colonial African political structure. What is demanded is not only fairness but some kind of objectivity, if correct answers to the burning issues regarding the collapse of the African states and inefficiency of their governments are to be devised.

State formation in Africa: a colonial design

Long after the Westphalia system had been adopted in Europe, convenors of the Berlin–Africa Conference, 1884–5 decided that the African continent did not deserve to be demarcated in the same way Europe was. Instead, the continent was simply moulded in the European frame but lacked the ethnic or cultural congruence that most of Europe followed. This arbitrary demarcation of the continent into states has earned African states names: over the years, terms used to describe African states include 'patrimonial', 'neopatrimonial', 'underdeveloped', 'prebendal', 'patrimonial administrative', 'fictitious', 'juridical' and 'quasi'. Criticisms of African states were first pointed out in the early 1980s and exposed further in the 1990s. Some of the most outstanding books in political science have spearheaded the exposition of this anomaly.[8]

Both the 1648 Peace Treaty of Westphalia, which created the modern state in the European context, and the 1884–5 Berlin Conference, which carved Africa up into European colonial territories, were motivated by the interests of the European powers in promoting conditions of domestic law and order within territorially defined states. Thus the creation of states in the colonies was not done out of altruism but as a convenient structure for domination. There is a wide range of evidence backing the claim that the 'modern world' in all its aspects including its states system, has its roots in the culture of Western Christendom. Thus, as Frederick Schuman, noted:

> All the peoples of the globe have in varying measure been 'Europeanised' in the process. The contemporary State system, which covers the planet, is, in most of its essentials, European in origin, practices, and motivations. But its point of departure was early Western Christendom, in whose development the 'Dark' and 'Middle' Ages were but the sunrise and morning of a day, which is now past noon.[9]

Therefore, while tracing the history of state formation in Africa, a very important point to bear in mind is that the state structure is a design of the West to resolve a Western problem at a particular time. It has essentially been adopted as a model for framing the entire world system in our time. The historical precursors to the Western state system were not nation-states, but the city-states of ancient Greece and Renaissance Italy.[10] It is from these two major ancient traditions that the West derived its principles of internal government and that of diplomatic representation. From there, basic characteristics of nationhood developed, that qualified states to engage in international affairs. States' involvement in international relations has therefore depended on a host of conditions including the ability to pursue national interest, national security and economic strategy.[11] It has been widely held that most 'Third-World' countries have never fulfilled these conditions. And this has fuelled a debate that has preoccupied scholars of African politics and international relations for a long time.

Therefore, the Western state system came to rest upon three cornerstones: the concept of sovereignty; the principles of international law; and the politics of the balance of power.[12] The concept of sovereignty has been elevated to the status of a political theory and later to that of a juristic idea underlying the whole structure of modern international jurisprudence. The principles of international law have evolved into a system of public law in the community of nations. And the politics of the balance of power became an avowed principle of foreign policy, accepted and acted upon so consistently by all the great states that it may well be viewed as the central theme about which the web of diplomacy is woven.[13] Such is the way the European state system became established and was later simply adopted as a formula when carving out colonies, including those in Africa.

According to various sources, the emergence of African states took place after nearly four centuries of contact with Europe. The first and longest period in the history of African Studies began around the year 1500, with the establishment of trade relations between the African continent and the then emerging and European-based capitalist world economy of the Middle Ages.[14] The four hundred years of Afro-European relations were dominated entirely by the two events of colonialism: first the slave trade, which constituted the primary means of primitive accumulation; and second, trade in the raw materials needed for industrial production in Europe.[15] These were the primary concerns connecting Africa and Europe. However, the first detailed descriptions of African social formations and states were written by learned historians in the African countries bordering the Mediterranean. Writing in Arabic, they described the civilisations of the Sudan and the regions along the course of the Niger. Such scholars included El Bekri, El Idrisi, El Masudi, Ibn Hawkal, Ibn Khaldun, Ibn Battuta, Yakut, Makrisi, Al Hassan Ibn Mohammed (also Leo Africanus), and Es Sadi. Their writings revealed the existence of a series of societies, which were subsequently 'discovered' by European travellers and writers such as Drapper, Lopez, Cresque, Mungo Park, Barth and Frobenius. However, the scientific interest in the scramble for Africa won official recognition in Europe only in the nineteenth century, with the 1884–5 Conference in Berlin. The deliberations at the Berlin African Conference superseded any prior European involvement in the continent.

The scramble for Africa, its partition and independence

The 'scramble for Africa' and the continent's subsequent partition are two major events that have created contention among historians and scholars of post-independence African politics.[16] Worse still, historiography has added a pact of jostling theories such as the rise of, on the one hand, Eurocentric explanations that are often sympathetic towards the imperial powers and, on the other, an Africentric interpretation of colonial history, which takes into account the values and concerns of the African people. This has been a major divide, which will not be rehearsed here. Nevertheless, many scholars have sought to provide comprehensive interpretations of the 'scramble' and partition of Africa. And this is nowhere done better than in the two major series of publications of the *UNESCO General History of Africa* and the *Cambridge History of Africa*.[17] However, the explanations given by these sources have met with considerable criticism from some African scholars as being inadequate in their attempts to explain the events of this particular period.[18] Indeed, the complexities of the 'scramble' appear to continue to defy any general comprehensive interpretation, because the great diversity of Africa and its peoples, and the inextricable interests and motives of the European powers, preclude any single sweeping theory to explain the partition in every region of the continent.[19]

Moreover, a more meaningful and accurate understanding of the partition can yet be achieved by regarding the 'scramble' as a series of interconnected events which were conditioned by different patterns of human motivation and behaviour in each of the disparate regions of the continent. I am not intending to discuss these in detail here for reasons of both space and relevance.[20] However, a general survey of the literature on the 'scramble for Africa' shows that there were hesitant beginnings to the partition of Africa long before the Conference of Berlin. For example, the discovery of diamonds in South Africa in 1869 is alleged to have provided the incentive and capital for a large influx of Europeans, who ultimately spilled across the Limpopo River into Central Africa.[21] Another recounted event was the opening of the Suez Canal in the same year. The Canal not only made the East African coast more accessible, but also soon became the great pivotal point in British imperial strategy. Thus British interest shifted to Cairo, with repercussions as far south as the Great Lakes of Equatorial Africa and as far west as Wadai and Lake Chad.[22] Besides that, some historians still regard the 'scramble' to have started earlier, with Leopold's crusade in Brussels from 7 January to 15 September 1876, which culminated in the raising of three flags across Africa between September and June 1878.[23] Also during the period when the African Association (strictly, the 'Association for Promoting the Discovery of the Interior Parts of Africa') was formed in 1788, largely through the inspiration of Joseph Banks, then President of the Royal Society, who had accompanied Captain Cook's voyage to the Pacific in 1868. This is also regarded as marking the beginning of the European move towards Africa.[24]

Furthermore, some historians still regard the greatest triumph of the African Association as having begun with the dispatch of Mungo Park's first expedition of 1795–7, which finally established the general direction of the River Niger, that had long mystified Europeans.[25] A similar development took place nearly a century later in 1881, when the French extended their control over Tunis. Like the British in Egypt, Zanzibar and Turkey, the French had hoped to maintain their influence by supporting the government of the Bey, the Tunisian ruler, and to avoid annexation.[26] However, occupation by the French and the British are regarded, in the interpretations of Eurocentric historians, as non-signals or non-precipitators of the 'scramble for Africa'. For Eurocentrics, the partition of Africa required greater stimuli than the discovery of diamonds in South Africa or the political intrigue on the Mediterranean littoral.[27] This view posits that the pre-partition era was foreshadowed by a process of partition carried out by Africans themselves, but under the command of European officers.[28] The examples cited in support of the foregoing arguments include, *inter alia* the consolidation of Shaka Zulu's empire and the Mfecane migrations, the creation of the Trekker republics by the South African Boers, and the West African Jihads.[29]

Such views, however, have never been left unchallenged.[30] A number of sources have indicated that Africa, on the eve of colonial conquest and occupation, had its own system of governance, international relations and means of resolving its own conflicts. For example, many different forms of sociopolitical organisation existed in pre-colonial

Africa, ranging from centralised kingdoms such as Ashanti (Asante) and Benin in West Africa and the Buganda in East Africa; and stateless societies such as in Western Sudan, where Gao, Jenne, Kano, Timbuktu and Walata had been established many centuries before the advent of colonial rule.[31] Even as late as 1800, with very few exceptions, Africans enjoyed their sovereignty and were very much in control of their own affairs and destinies. Such rich evidence of pre-colonial Africa's way of life (or political order) is never acknowledged in either Robert Jackson's or Christopher Clapham's seminal works.

However, within an incredibly short period between 1880 and 1935, all of Africa apart from Liberia and Ethiopia was seized by the European imperial powers of Great Britain, France, Germany, Italy, Portugal and Spain.[32] As Thomas Pakenham has rightly put it, 'Africa was sliced like a cake, [and] the pieces swallowed by five rival nations'.[33] From that time, Africans were converted from sovereign and royal citizens of their own continent into colonial and dependent subjects, so much so that, by the 1900s, in place of the numerous traditional African societies and polities, a completely new and numerically smaller set of some forty artificially created colonies had emerged. These are historical facts, which both Clapham and Jackson have deliberately avoided recording. Governors and officials who were appointed by their metropolitan governments and were in no way responsible to their African subjects consequently administered these colonies. Upto the 1950s, the colonial system was firmly imposed on virtually the whole of Africa, and varied explanations of how this came about have since proliferated.

According to Professor Anthony Asiwaju, 'The establishment of formal colonial rule must be seen against a background of a major change in what came to be referred to as "balance of power" in Europe following the rise of Germany, and increasing political instability occasioned by African wars of the nineteenth century which came to threaten peace in the African interior, and consequently European trade in the coast'. Asiwaju therefore contends that the partition of Africa 'cannot become fully intelligible except in terms of the convergence between the new situation in Europe and the prevailing political conditions in particular parts of Africa'.[34]

The Berlin Conference, 1884–5, and the partition of Africa

It can be argued that one major issue that has caused Africa a number of problems today in their social organisation is that of the nation-state, Europe's most enduring legacy, not only in Africa but also in the rest of the world. This particular mode of political organisation is alien to

Africa and this partly explains why attempts to establish a coherent theory of the state in Africa have often failed.[35] The state originated in European diplomatic history and statecraft, and developed with major sociological changes within European societies. The genesis of the international state system as it exists today is often traced to the peace treaty of Westphalia of 1648, which ended the internecine Thirty Years' War in Europe. As we have been reminded repeatedly by historians and students of diplomacy, it was on the foundations of Westphalia that the entire superstructure of world diplomacy and international relations came to be constructed.[36] Over two centuries later, a similar event took place, when descendants of Westphalia convened the Berlin Conference to settle their disputes over territories in Africa. For a long time during the nineteenth century, European powers quarrelled among themselves over the parts of Africa that each wanted. But in 1884–5, in Berlin (then the capital of the German empire), they agreed to invade and take Africa without fighting each other. They marked out 'spheres of interest', each invading the continent within its own 'sphere'.[37] Like the Westphalia peace treaty that brought an end to the mutually destructive Thirty Years' War, and most recently in the way the Yalta Peace Treaty mitigated the frontiers of Eastern Europe after the Second World War, the Berlin Conference succeeded in settling the disputes arising from European activities in Africa. Thus it established the undisputed sway of colonialism in Africa for nearly a century. It is the legacy of European coercive rule that has inhibited post-colonial states and governments in Africa.

As a matter of fact, the Berlin Conference increased the intensity of the 'scramble for Africa'. During the Conference, European leaders set out the ground rules for the partition of Africa based on what was termed 'effective occupation' – whenever a European power occupied a parcel of land it could legitimately integrate that territory into its empire. There was no regard for the multiplicity of ethnic peoples of Africa. Professor Boahen summarises the main rules agreed upon at the conference as follows:

> The first was that before any power claimed an area, it should inform the other signatory powers so that any who deemed it necessary could make a counterclaim. The second was that annexation and effective occupation should follow all such claims before they could be accepted as valid. The third was that treaties signed with African rulers were to be considered as legitimate titles to sovereignty. The fourth rule was that each power could extend its coastal possessions

inland to some extent and claim spheres of influence. Finally, it was agreed that there was to be freedom of navigation on the Congo and the Niger rivers.[38]

Furthermore, the interested powers settled their individual claims in the lobbies and divided the territories concerned among themselves. For example, in the treaty they decreed an international free trade regime, and in the bilateral settlements they partitioned the area politically into exclusive spheres of influence which implied economic monopoly.

At this point, we can have no doubt about the importance of the foregoing narrative to us. The 'scramble for Africa', was prompted by a mix of economic and political motives among competing European powers and was facilitated by the Berlin Conference. The Acts of the Conference, adopted without any African input, proved disastrous for Africa because they led to the arbitrary carving up of the continent without consideration of indigenous factors, and consequently led to the production of a post-colonial continent of unstable, artificial and relatively meaningless state entities.[39] In Berlin, the European powers disregarded everything but their own acquisitions and the need for a balance in Europe. So, at independence, most African states inherited the borders left by the colonial powers. Thus, all state boundaries in Africa are of recent colonial creation,[40] and do not therefore coincide with nations, as they do in Europe.

Despite the time constraints experienced by African countries in their formation, these very fragmented 'quasi-states', to use Robert Jackson's terminology, were embraced into the community of nations, with its own rules, conventions and codes. In this way nothing much can be blamed on the Africans themselves. International law is the offspring of European diplomatic history and has been adopted to bind the new members of the club of nation-states, Africa included.[41] And one real cause of problems in most of Africa today began with the creation of the nation-state that has remained fractured. Major consequences have been a crisis of identity on the one hand, and one of authority and control on the other. African countries assumed equal representation in the international system without having consolidated enough required institutions for governing society, thus creating problems, which Professor Ali Mazrui has rightly pointed out: 'the crisis of identity in Africa is a crisis whose main theatre is the nation, while that of authority and control is a crisis whose main theatre is the state'.[42] From here, we can turn to examine the concepts of the 'nation' and the 'state' in African politics.

Conceptions of 'nation' and 'state' in Africa

What is 'the nation'? What is 'the state'? These are the kinds of question that must be addressed before any analysis of their function in African politics. Unfortunately, 'state' and 'nation' are the types of concept that have continued to defy attempts at technical definition in the social sciences. According to the *Penguin Dictionary of Politics*, 'the "state", though a very commonly-used word in the political vocabulary, is surprisingly opaque. Even the derivation of the term is obscure, and in many cultures (including early medieval European society, to take one example) it would be hard to specify what word should be translated as "state"'.[43] Defining the concept of 'nation' is no less difficult.

In International Relations (IR) the state is given one specific definition: *the national-territorial totality*. For example, Hedley Bull defined the state as a political community.[44] Kenneth Waltz said it is in practice coextensive with the nation.[45] F. S. Northedge used it to refer to a territorial association of people recognised for purposes of law and diplomacy as legally equal members of the system of states.[46] And Allan James straightforwardly uses 'state' to comprise 'territory, people, and a government'.[47]

Unlike the case in International Relations literature, sociological writings on the state do not take into account the social-territorial totality, but rather a specific set of coercive and administrative institutions, distinct from the broader political, social and national context in which the state finds itself. For example, Theda Skocpol defines the state as a set of administrative, policing and military organisations headed, and more or less well co-ordinated, by an authority.[48] Within the sociological approach alone, one finds many alternative definitions of the state. The history of the state, as Max Weber, Barrington Moore, Charles Tilly and others have shown, is of the imposition of administration and coercion on territories and population by competing groups of rulers, for their own purposes, with appropriate myths of justification. Thus Weber's precise definition of state embodies four major elements: '(1) a differentiated set of institutions and personnel, embodying (2) centrality, in the sense that political relations radiate outwards from a centre to cover a (3) territorially demarcated area, over which it exercises (4) a monopoly of authoritative binding rule-making, backed by a monopoly of the means of physical violence'.[49]

As far as traditional thinking in political philosophy is concerned, the 'state' is often regarded as an essential element of democracy. For a long time, under European conditions, democracy only applies to a state. The social contract theory – as proposed by Hugo Grotius, Samuel von Pufendorf, Jean Barbeyrac, Burlamqui, Thomas Hobbes and John Locke, and even Jean Jacques Rousseau – believes that the state was the outcome of a covenant or agreement among men. The purpose of the state became the protection of those people to which it owed its being, and the same theorists also agreed that the sovereign must have enough power to provide such protection. A state, or 'civitas', is a civil partnership – 'civilis societas'. This most pregnant term naturally translates as 'civil society'. In Roman law, 'societas' is a partnership, implying free contractual agreement of the partners. This concept, as applied to the state, connotes a civil partnership constituted by the free contract of citizens, and the terms of their contract are the laws of the state, without which the state cannot exist.[50]

Unlike the state, defining and conceptualising the 'nation' is much more difficult, because the essence of a nation is intangible. According to Walker Connor, this essence is a psychological bond that joins a people and differentiates it, in the subconscious conviction of its members, from all other people in a most vital way.[51] The nature of that bond and its well-being remain shadowy and elusive, and the consequent difficulty of defining a nation is usually acknowledged by those who attempt this task.

The term 'nation' often refers to a single inclusive group whose members – or the majority of them – share common traditions, history and ethnic identity.[52] When defined broadly, a nation encompasses both subjective and objective indicators. Objective indicators include: language, history, territory, culture and political organisation. Subjective indicators include: a common sense of identity, and commitment or loyalty to the group.[53] For example, a nation in its original connotation refers to the Igbo or Yoruba in Nigeria; Kikuyu or Luo in Kenya; Baganda or Acholi in Uganda; Dinka, Lotuko, Nuer or Zande in South Sudan; Shona and Ndebele in Zimbabwe; or Hutu and Tutsi in Burundi and Rwanda. Unlike in many European societies, where the crystallisation of the structures of authority followed the sense of national identity, colonial arrangements brought the very opposite to most of Africa. Newly independent countries in Africa reversed the European sequence and instead conflated the use of the term 'nation' to mean 'the people of a territory united under a single government, country or state'. Thus, authority and sovereignty evolved ahead of self-conscious national identity and cultural integration. No contract or consent was sought from the African peoples in Hobbesian or Lockean terms. For this reason, some countries were wise enough to introduce one language such as in former British East Africa, where Kishwahili became the lingua franca.[54] To this extent, Mostafa Rejai and Cynthia Enloe were right to point out that whereas Europe produced nation-states, Africa and Asia produced state-nations.[55] As a result, the concept of 'nation' came to mean in East Africa, Kenya, Tanzania or Uganda, and not Kikuyu, Baganda or Sukuma.

In African politics, the concept of the state has been dealt with at length in plentiful published sources.[56] And the major task in this has been the desire to establish a coherent theory of the state in sub-Saharan Africa, but with less success.[57] The obvious failure in every effort has been the proliferation of terms that have been devised to characterise African states. They have been described as 'patrimonial' and 'neopatrimonial';[58] 'underdeveloped';[59] 'prebendal';[60] 'patrimonial administrative';[61] 'fictitious';[62] 'juridical' and 'quasi-states'.[63] Thus notwithstanding the fact that the examination of the concept of the state is often a starting point in the analysis of post-colonial African politics.[64] Yet, in order for us to fully understand the post-colonial state in Africa, it is imperative that we examine briefly what the colonial state itself looked like.

The colonial state

Patrick Chabal describes the colonial state as follows:

> The colonial state was...the legal and political superstructure invented to control and manage the colonial territories acquired through conquest; derived essentially from the nature of the imperial state and from the nature of its objectives in Africa. All meant to establish imperial sovereignty on the conquered territories; legitimate their rule and to ensure their subjects' allegiance; set up the administration and infrastructure needed to rule colonies at minimal (financial and coercive) cost to the empire. All were charged with exploiting the resources of the colonies; all attempted to 'civilise' their colonial subjects in their own image. As a conquest state, it embodied the tensions of being both an outpost of the empire and an autonomous state.[65]

In other words, the colonial state needed local collaborators in order to rule – collaboration is always cheaper and infinitely preferable to force.[66] Because it attempted to invent a new political community to suit its imperial designs, the colonial state rested on force, however much it appeared to rule by consent.[67] The colonial state was also the architect of the political community. Thus it defined the boundaries of the community, created its political infrastructure and invented the rules of the game, rules which could always be changed arbitrarily to suit the situation at hand. The colonial state dominated the economic sector and created a currency, levied taxes, developed markets, codified the uses of labour, introduced new crops, controlled all sources of production, internal trade and export, and brought in foreign labourers or encouraged settlers. Above all, the colonial state sought to integrate the economies of the colonies into the imperial economy and in so doing it was at once the arbiter and the main agent of economic activity.[68] The colonial state was also a bureaucratic state, in the sense defined by Weber.[69] In short, the colonial state transformed indigenous African traditional structures arbitrarily to suit the crucial interests of the mother country, whether that was Great Britain, France, Portugal, Spain or Italy.

In short, the colonial state left a mixed legacy to the African people and their leaders. The most destructive legacies are those of centralised and coercive governance inherited by post-colonial African leaders. The legitimacy of centralised governance depended solely on its ability to control and manage the political community it had created rather than on enabling representations of its constituent parts. However, this does not mean that a centralised state lacks local structures of government but one in which local government is accountable to central government rather than to the citizens of the locality. The state was never defined in terms of, or in relation to, its constitutent parts. Rather, the constituent parts were defined in relation to the state. Local government was the transmission belt of central government, however sophisticated, consultative or 'representative' councils appeared to be, or however 'indirect' colonial rule was claimed to be.[70] The colonial state used the external political power to coerce the political community, as the colonial secretary was not accountable to his subjects but to the imperial government. Thus the colonial state derived its power from legally sanctioned coercion unaccountable to the subjects of the state, a legacy that has continued to inhibit the smooth development of the African state up to the present time.

Finally, the rule of law and the use of force were, in the end, legitimated only by the colonial 'civilising' mission.[71] Generally, the concept of the post-colonial state is at heart relational rather than structural. It contains the notion of the new dialectical relationship between state and civil society which was brought about by the rupture in political accountability caused by independence. According to Patrick Chabal, the state in Africa cannot simply be understood as a political 'entity', but rather it must be seen as the focal point of the drive for political and economic hegemony.[72] It is the drive for hegemony, the political contest for supremacy between state and civil society, that is the hallmark of contemporary African politics. As to whether the state has succeeded in fulfilling its hegemonic ambitions, this has largely been determined by the politics of civil society, a concept we now also briefly examine in the concluding part of the chapter.

Bringing an end to the dilemma: the future of Africa in the new millennium

This chapter has attempted to analyse a divide that has persisted in studies of post-colonial African politics. The divide has been sensitive to the legacies of colonialism. Either way, there have been genuine arguments for those scholars who are sympathetic to colonialism (on the defensive) and those who insist that the post-colonial state must be absolved of all the mistakes that have occurred (on the offensive). The opinion of this chapter is that Jackson and Clapham seem better placed on the defensive side, for the simple reason that they tend to emphasise the collapse of 'Third-World' states while excluding the history of colonial domination, whose legacy has also had contributory effects on the mismanagement of the post-colonial political structures. Those on the offensive are numerous, and in the opinion of this chapter include the writings of such scholars as Walter Rodney, Samir Amin, the younger Mazrui, Claude Ake and others (both African and Africanists). Many fears have arisen that have in turn sustained the divide. For one, Western scholars may be afraid of the strength of the anti-colonial thesis which points out the mistakes of colonial history and has raised new demands for reparation. The strongest anti-colonial analysis widely cited is that by Edward Said. There are also fears that pillars of Western thought may collapse because such pillars have been besieged sporadically by new approaches in the social sciences in general. The new approaches emphasise inclusion rather than the exclusive orthodoxy that previously backed the colonial tradition. There is also an attempt to avoid interpretations that may point out that conflicts in the continent should not be viewed simply as side-shows of ethnic antagonisms or of regional instability, but as having their roots back in half a century of European colonialism. The best example is often the Hutu/Tutsi rivalry that is widely believed to have begun with the Belgian colonial administration in what used to be Rwanda-Urundi. The Belgians favoured the Tutsi, educated them and made them dominate the military, while undermining the Hutu. Similarly, there are also those African scholars who resent what is often termed 'Eurocentric views', and wholly blame any mistakes in the post-colonial African political order on colonialism.

This chapter has attempted to adjust such perspectives by apportioning the blame of the failure of the African states and their governments on both the colonial superstructure and the post-colonial structure. It has argued that the European colonial system bears some responsibility for all the ills that have befallen the African continent, be it on political, social or economic grounds. Similarly, the Africans themselves must swallow the bitter pill and accept that their leaders also contributed to the mistakes. Corruption, mismanagement of the economy, widespread ethnic animosities and so on are some of the major anomalies that have inhibited the post-colonial state in Africa. Some of the negative aspects of colonial rule have been pointed out. For example, one aspect of colonialism that exerted widespread negative effects on the post-colonial state in Africa is the transfer of power. This was often accelerated in the hope of installing new successor governments of 'immoderate' nationalists loyal to the new representative institutions planted by the mother country (the metropole), sympathetic to the mixed economy of private and state capitalism, enthusiastic for economic development (along approved Western lines), and eager to remain part of the post-imperial associations of influence devised by Paris and London – the French Community and the British Commonwealth.[73] Colonialism also turned post-independence Africa into a battleground where the Soviet East and the West contended for primacy, often through sponsorship of revolutionary movements (as in Ethiopia and Angola) during the Cold War, or through military or other kinds of authoritarian regime. This was a negative contribution because it militarised African societies. We also pointed out that post-colonial African governments themselves contributed to the deterioration of the African states. For example, the African states belied their early promise of political and economic progress and instead gradually relapsed into one-party rule, military dictatorships and economic mismanagement. All these count as major reasons that have kept the continent in an increasingly peripheral position in the international system.[74]

This chapter also embraces the idea that if Africa is to provide the necessary protection to the budding democratic process, state structures must loosen to allow civil associations room for manoeuvre in the interests of transforming society. Thus, this chapter argues that civil associations are a potential integrating element for the continent in the new millennium.

Notes and References

*　This chapter was first presented as a paper at the ECPR/ISA joint Conference in Vienna, Austria in September 1998 but has been extensively edited for the purpose of publication. I would like to thank Keith Webb for having organised a panel on ethno-national conflict, where this chapter was presented. I would also like to thank Stephen Chan, Andrew Williams, Makumi Mwagiru and Soforonio Efuk for having read drafts of this chapter.

1　See Naomi Chazan *et al.* (1992) *Politics and Society in Contemporary Africa* (Boulder, Col.: Lynne Rienner), pp. 14–21.

2　These are well articulated in the seminal work of the late Professor Claude Ake, which has won admiration in the analysis of African politics. See his (1996) *Democracy and Development in Africa* (Washington, DC: The Brookings Institution), pp. 1–17.

3　R. Robinson expressed the vital importance of local collaboration in his 'The Non-European Foundations of European Rule: Sketch for a Theory of Collaboration' in R. Owen and B. Sutcliffe (eds) (1972) *Studies in the Theory of Imperialism* (London: Longman).

4　See David Robertson, (1990) *The Penguin Dictionary of Politics* (Harmondsworth: Penguin), p. 440.

5　See their seminal works: Robert H. Jackson (1990) *Quasi-States: Sovereignty, International Relations, and the Third World* (Cambridge: Cambridge University Press); Robert H. Jackson (1986), 'Negative Sovereignty in Sub-Saharan Africa', *Review of International Studies*, vol. 12, no. 4, October, pp. 247–64; Christopher Clapham (1996), *Africa and the International System: The Politics of State Survival* (Cambridge: Cambridge University Press); and Christopher Clapham (1998), 'Degrees of Statehood', *Review of International Studies*, vol. 24, no. 2, April, pp. 143–57.

6　See Clapham, 'Degrees of Statehood', p. 143.

7　See F. Halliday (1994) *Rethinking International Relations* (London: Macmillan), pp. 3–4.

8　I refer here mainly to three particular books: Jean-François Bayart (1989) *The State in Africa: The Politics of Belly* (London: Longman); Robert H. Jackson (1990) *Quasi-States: Sovereignty, International Relations and the Third World* (Cambridge: Cambridge University Press); Christopher Clapham (1996) *Africa and the International System: The Politics of State Survival* (Cambridge: Cambridge University Press).

9　Schuman, Frederick L. (1958) *International Politics: The Western State System and the World Community* (New York, Toronto & London: McGraw-Hill), pp. 55–6.

10　For details on this, refer to the following literature on the origins of states: J. H. Shennan (1974) *The Origins of the Modern European State, 1450–1725* (London: Hutchinson); Elman Rogers Service (1975) *Origins of the State and Civilization: The Process of Cultural Evolution*, (New York: Norton); Ronald Cohen and Elman R. Service (eds) (1978) *Origins of the State: The Anthropology of Political Evolution* (Philadelphia, Pa.: Institute of the Study of Human

Issues); Ralph Pettman (1979) *State and Class: A Sociology of International Affairs* (New York: St Martin's Press), pp. 108–12.

11 See K. J. Holsti (1992) *International Politics: A Framework for Analysis*, 6th edn (Englewood Cliffs, NJ: Prentice-Hall), pp. 82–114, esp. 'The Purposes of States: Foreign Policy Goals and Strategies'.

12 See Hedley Bull (1977) *The Anarchical Society: A Study of Order in World Politics* (London: Macmillan).

13 See Frederick L. Schuman *International Politics*, pp. 66–72.

14 Records show that by about 1500, Portugal alone had taken some 700 tons of gold out of Africa. See Hosea Jaffe (1985) *A History of Africa* (London: Zed Books), esp. pp. 43–64; also Georges Nzongola-Ntalaja (1937) *Revolution and Counter-Revolution in Africa*, (London: Institute for African Alternatives) p. 5; and Paul Cammack, David Pool and William Tordoff (1988) *Third World Politics: A Comparative Introduction* (London: Macmillan), pp. 13ff.

15 See Basil Davidson (1994) *Modern Africa: A Social and Political History* (London and New York: Longman), p. 4.

16 The circumstances that led to the 'scramble for Africa' and its partition have been discussed at length in numerous published works. See, for example, A. Adu Boahen (1987) *African Perspectives on Colonialism*, (London: James Currey), pp. 26–57; A. Adu Boahen (ed.) (1985), *General History of Africa, vol. VII*, (London: Longman); J. Schumpeter (1955) *Imperialism and Social Classes*, (Cleveland: World Publishing Company); R. E. Robinson and J. Gallaghar (1961) *Africa and the Victorians* (London: Macmillan); J. A. Hobson (1965) *Imperialism: A Study* (Ann Arbor, Mich.: University of Michigan Press); V. I. Lenin, (1983) *Imperialism: The Highest Stage of Capitalism* (Moscow: Progress Publishers); J. S. Keltie (1983), *The Partition of Africa* (London: E. Stanford); G. N. Uzoigwe (1974) *Britain and the Conquest of Africa* (Ann Arbor, Mich.: University of Michigan Press); B. Sutcliffe and R. Owen (eds) (1972) *Studies in the Theory of Imperialism* (London: Longman); Walter Rodney (1972), *How Europe Underdeveloped Africa* (Dar es Salaam: Tanzania Publishing House); and Claude Ake, *A Political Economy of Africa*, pp. 26–9.

17 In these two useful major publications on the history of Africa, various scholars have contributed massive accounts of events. See *The Cambridge History of Africa*, 8 vols, (Cambridge: Cambridge University Press), 1976; and *UNESCO General History of Africa*, 8 vols, (Paris: UNESCO), 1985.

18 See Adu Boahen *African Perspectives on Colonialism*, op. cit., pp. 1–26.

19 See Robert O. Collins (1971) *Europeans in Africa* (New York: Alfred A. Knopf), pp. 71–7.

20 These are dealt with well in a number of scholarly sources such as Raymond F. Betts (ed.) (1972) *The Scramble for Africa: Causes and Dimensions of Empire* (London: D. C. Heath); G. N. Sanderson (1986) 'The European Partition of Africa: Origins and Dynamics' in J. D. Fage and R. Oliver (eds) *The Cambridge History of Africa* (Cambridge, New York: Cambridge University Press) pp. 96–158; G. N. Sanderson (1974) 'The European Partition of Africa: Coincidence or Conjuncture?', *Journal of Imperial and Commonwealth History*, vol. 3, no. 1, October; and a number of articles in both the Cambridge and the UNESCO histories of Africa series cited in note 17 above.

21 See Robert O. Collins, *Europeans in Africa*, p. 71.

22 Ibid.

23 According to Claude Ake, *Democracy and Development in Africa*, p. 29, within a few years after King Leopold II had triggered off the scramble for Africa in 1876, the continent was divided among the European powers and subsequently colonised. See also the chapter on 'Central Africa and Europe' by Thomas Pakenham (1991) *The Scramble for Africa: 1876–1912* (London: Weidenfeld & Nicolson), pp. 11–23.

24 See M. E., Chamberlain (1974) *The Scramble for Africa* (London: Longman), pp. 19–20.

25 See Robin Hallet (ed.) (1964) *Records of the African Association, 1788–1831,* (London: Nelson).

26 In 'Saving the Bey' and 'Saving the Khedive', see Thomas Pakenham, *The Scramble for Africa*, pp. 109–122 and 123–140.

27 See Robert O. Collins *Europeans in Africa*, p. 72.

28 Ibid., pp. 99–137.

29 See H. S. Wilson (1977) *The Imperial Experience in Sub-Saharan Africa Since 1870* (Minneapolis, Minn.: University of Minnesota Press), pp. 24–30; and A. Nutting (1994) *The Scramble for Africa: The Great Trek to the Boer War* (London: Constable 1994).

30 A counter-argument has been advanced that, while African-based imperialism took place, that process was already concluded by the time the European partition began, and to ignore that fact would be to discount significant elements of European purposiveness, premeditation and aggression. See H. S. Wilson, *The Imperial Experience in Sub-Saharan Africa*, p. 50; and Makumi Mwagiru (1994) *The International Management of Internal Conflict in Africa: The Uganda Mediation* (PhD thesis, University of Kent at Canterbury 1994), pp. 99–100.

31 See A. Adu Boahen *African Perspectives on Colonialism*, pp. 1–26; Dorothy Dodge (1996) *African Politics in Perspective* (Princeton, NJ: Van Nastrand) pp. 15ff; and Paul Cammack, David Pool and William Tordoff, *Third-World Politics*, pp. 12–20.

32 See Albert Adu Boahen (1990) 'Africa and the Colonial Challenge' in A. Adu Boahen (ed.), *UNESCO General History of Africa*, vol. VII, '*Africa Under Colonial Domination 1880–1935*', (London: James Currey), p. 1.

33 See Thomas Pakenham *The Scramble for Africa*, p. xv.

34 See A. I. Asiwaju, chapter presented at the Nigerian National Open University, quoted by A. Adu Boahen (1937) *African Perspectives of Colonialism*, p. 28.

35 See Z. Ergas (ed.) *The African State in Transition* (Macmillan); and Adrian Leftwich (1993) 'States of Underdevelopment: The Third World State in Theoretical Perspective', *Journal of Theoretical Politics*, vol. 6, no. 1, pp. 55–74 and 63–70.

36 I have no intention of discussing Westphalia here, but the impact of its legacy has been mentioned by a number of scholars. See, in particular, Ali A. Mazrui and Michael Tidy (1934), *Nationalism and New States in Africa* (Nairobi and London: Heinemann) pp. 373–5; Frederick L. Schuman, *International Politics*, and William C. Olson, *International relations then and now: Origins and trends in Interpretations* (London: Routledge) and A. J. R. Groom (1991); also K. J. Holsti, *International Politics*, pp. 15–44.

37 See Basil Davidson, *Modern Africa*, p. 5.

38   See John D. Hargreaves 'The Berlin Conference, West African Boundaries, and the Eventual Partition' in S. Forster, W. J. Mommsen and R. Robinson (1988) *Bismark, Europe and Africa: the Berlin Africa Conference 1884–1885 and the onset of partition (Oxford: Oxford University Press), pp. 313–14.*

39   See Robert H. Jackson, *Quasi-States*, and Stephen Wright (1992), 'The Foreign Policy of Africa', in Roy C. Macridis (ed.), *Foreign Policy in World Politics* (Englewood Cliffs, NJ: Prentice-Hall), pp. 330–56 and 332.

40   See, for example, Mohammed Ayoob (1995) *The Third World Security Predicament: State-Making, Regional Conflict, and the System International* (Boulder, Col.: Lynne Rienner).

41   See Hedley Bull and Adam Watson, *The Expansion of International Society,* (Oxford: Clarendon), 1984.

42   See Ali A. Mazrui (1983) 'Africa: The Political Culture of Nationhood and the Political Economy of the State', *Millennium*, vol. 12, no. 3, Autumn, pp. 201–10.

43   See Raymond Duvall and John R. Freeman (1981) 'The State and Dependent Capitalism', *International Studies Quarterly*, vol. 25, no. 1, p. 106; and David Robertson, *The Penguin Dictionary of Politics*, p. 444.

44   See Hedley Bull (1977) *The Anarchical Society: A Study of Order in World Politics* (London: Macmillan), p. 8.

45   See Kenneth Waltz (1959) *Man, the State and War: A Theoretical Analysis* (New York: Columbia University Press), pp. 172–8.

46   See F. S. Northedge (1976) *The International Political System* (London: Faber & Faber), p. 15.

47   See Allen James (1986) *Sovereign Statehood* (London: Allen & Unwin), p. 13.

48   See Theda Skocpol (1979) *States and Social Revolutions* (Cambridge: Cambridge University Press), p. 29; and Charles Tilly (1985) 'War making and State Making as Organised Crime' in Peter Evans *et al.* (eds) *Bringing the State Back In* (Cambridge: Cambridge University Press); and in Charles Tilly (ed.) (1975) *The Formation of National States in Europe* (Princeton, NJ: Princeton University Press).

49   See M. O. Hardimon (1994), *Hegel's Social Philosophy: The Project of Reconciliation* (Cambridge: Cambridge University Press).

50   See M. Salamonio (1955) *De Principatu* (Milan: Giuffre Editore), quoted by Michael Lesnoff (1986), *Social Contract: Issues in Political Theory* (London: Macmillan), pp. 26–7.

51   See Walker Connor (1972) 'Nation-Building or Nation-Destroying?', *World Politics*, vol. 24, April, pp. 319–55; and Walker Connor (1978) 'A Nation is a Nation, is a State, is an Ethnic Group, is a . . .', *Ethnic and Racial Studies*, vol. 1, no. 4, October, pp. 377–400.

52   See M. G. Smith (1971) 'Institutional and Political Conditions of Pluralism', in L. Kuper and M. G. Smith (eds), *Pluralism in Africa* (Los Angeles: University of California Press), p. 32.

53   See J. Isawa, Elaigwu (1993) 'Nation-Building and Changing Political Structures', in Ali A. Mazrui and C. Wondji (eds), *UNESCO General History of Africa. vol. III: Africa Since 1935*, (Oxford: Heinemann).

54   See the works of Mwalimu Julius Nyerere. Mzee Jomo Kenyatta, *Harambee: The Prime Minister of Kenya's Speeches, 1963–1964*, also published by Oxford University Press (n. d.), is a better illustration of post-colonial nation-building in Africa.

55 Mostafa Rejai and Cynthia Enloe, 'Nation-States and State-Nations', *International Studies Quarterly*, Vol. 13, No.2, June 1969, p. 140; Connor, Walker, 'A Nation is a Nation, is a State, is an Ethnic Group, is a...', p. 382.

56 A wide range of literature associates the concept of the state with the political analysis of Africa. See Patrick Chabal (1992) *Power in Africa*, pp. 68–81; Naomi Chazan *et al.*, *Politics and Society in contemporary Africa*, pp. 38–46; Jean-François Bayart (1989) *L'Etat en Afrique* (Paris: Fayard); J. Lonsdale (1981) 'States and Social Processes in Africa', *African Studies Review*, vol. 24, no. 2–3; these two offer most useful discussions of state in Africa. And for a review of the concept of the state, see J. P. Nettl (1968), 'The State as a Conceptual Variable', *World Politics*, vol. 20, no. 4, pp. 559–92; Stephen D. Krasner (1984), 'Approaches to the State: Alternative Conceptions and Historical Dynamics', *Comparative Politics*, vol. 16, no. 2, pp. 223–45; Peter Anyang' Gnawing' (1983), 'The Economic Foundations of the State in Contemporary Africa', *Presence Africaine*, No. 127/128, p. 195; Claude Ake (1981), *A Political Economy of Africa* (London: Longman); Peter Evans *et al.* (eds) (1985) *Bringing the State Back In* (Cambridge: Cambridge University Press); Theda Skocpol (1980) *The State and Social Revolutions* (Cambridge: Cambridge University Press); and more.

57 See Z. Ergas (ed.), *The African State*.

58 See Aristide Zolberg (1966) *Creating Political Order: The Party States of West Africa* (Chicago: Rand McNally); G. Roth (1968) 'Personal Rulership, Patrimonialism and Empire-Building in the New States', *World Politics*, vol. 20, pp. 195–206; and R. Sandbrook (1985) *The Politics of Africa's Economic Stagnation* (Cambridge: Cambridge University Press).

59 See J. F. Medard (1982) 'The Underdeveloped State in Tropical Africa: Political Clientism or Neopatrimonialism', in Christopher Clapham (ed.), *Private Patronage and Public Power* (London: Pinter).

60 See R. A. Joseph (1983) 'Class, State and Prebendal Politics in Nigeria', *Journal of Commonwealth and Comparative Politics*, vol. 21, pp. 21–38; R. A. Joseph (1987) Democracy and Prebendal Politics in Nigeria: (Cambridge: Cambridge University Press).

61 See T. M. Callaghy 'The State as a Tame Leviathan: The Patrimonial Administrative State in Africa' in Z. Ergas (ed.), *The African State in Transition*, pp. 87–116.

62 See again R. Sandbrook, *Politics of Africa's Economic Stagnation*, pp. 319–32.

63 See Robert H. Jackson and C. G. Roseberg (1986), 'Why Africa's Weak States Persist', in A. Kohli (ed.), *The State and Development in the Third World* (Princeton, NJ: Princeton University Press), pp. 259–82; and Robert H. Jackson, *Quasi-States*.

64 It should be noted from now onwards that in African politics, the term 'nation' is often synonymously used to mean 'state'.

65 See Patrick Chabal (1992) *Power in Africa*, (London: Macmillan), pp. 74–6.

66 See also Ronald Robinson (1972) 'Non-European Foundations of European Imperialism', in R. Owen and B. Sutcliffe (eds), *Studies in the Theories of Imperialism* (London: Longman).

67 See J. Gallagher *et al.* (1973) *Locality, Province and Nation: Essays on Indian Politics, 1870 to 1940* (Cambridge: Cambridge University Press).

68 Quoted from G. Kitching (1980) *Class and Economic Change in Kenya* (New Haven, Conn.: Yale University Press).
69 For an argument on the overdevelopment of the colony, see Hamza Alavi (1972) 'The State in Post-Colonial Societies: Pakistan and Bangladesh', *New Left Review*, vol. 74, p. 61.
70 For a better example, see J. Iliffe (1979) *A Modern History of Tanganyika* (Cambridge: Cambridge University Press).
71 See Patrick Chabal (ed.) (1986) *Political Domination in Africa* (Cambridge University Press), p. 146.
72 See Chabal part IV, pp. 200–16.
73 Ibid., pp. 204–5.
74 See John, Darwin (1996) 'Africa and World Politics Since 1945: Theories of Decolonisation', in Ngaire Woods (ed.), *Explaining International Relations Since 1945* (Oxford: Oxford University Press), pp. 199–218 and 201–2.

6
Progress towards Democracy in Africa: Uganda as a Case Study*

Oliver Furley

In recent years there has been considerable progress made by many African states towards more democratic systems of government. This is partly because of international pressure, where foreign aid, whether it is from the World Bank or IMF, or from donor states, is often made conditional upon 'good governance', which is measured by, among other things, progress towards democracy and the better observance of human rights. This progress also, results from internal pressures within African countries, especially where technology has vastly improved knowledge and information about world-wide movements towards democracy. Examples of 'people power' in Eastern Europe, the Philippines or Indonesia, and scenes of mass protest in many countries have increased African awareness of the power of these movements. The mainspring of African aspirations for democracy, however, comes from Africans themselves, tired of the dictatorial and corrupt regimes of the decades since the 1960s, and determined to force a change. Many of the old leaders have gone, some having been swept away by revolution or civil war, a recent example being President Mobutu of Zaire. In other countries, where leaders cling to the older oligarchic or elitist forms of rule, as in Kenya under President Moi or Zimbabwe under President Mugabe, patience is wearing thin and protest is mounting in favour of more democratic systems. It is noteworthy that President Kabila of the Democratic Republic of Congo (DRC), formerly Zaire, made promises of a new constitution to be framed by a constituent assembly and followed by a freely elected Parliament after he came to power through a victorious rebel movement; but as he has shown few signs of carrying out these measures, and appears to be more a leader of the old school, he has been faced with a rebellion against his own regime. The neighbouring states that had previously supported him, and which have been dubbed by international observers the 'new leaders' of a more liberal and demo-cratic Africa, namely Uganda, Rwanda, Ethiopia and Eritrea, have sig-nificantly dropped their support for him. The remaining involvement of Ugandan and Rwandan troops in the DRC appears to be mainly for security reasons regarding their own borders.[1] The Paris conference of November 1998, which involved all the leaders in the crisis of the Great Lakes region, demonstrated yet again that pressure for democratisation is applied continually and is regarded as one of the most urgent needs.

Uganda has been hailed as an example of hope for Africa in this respect, under President Yoweri Museveni, who took power in 1986 after a long guerrilla campaign against Milton Obote's regime. It is the purpose of this chapter to investigate the origins and elements of this new beginning for democracy in Uganda and to evaluate what has been achieved so far.

Uganda has had only a short experience of democracy in its history. Colonial rule was authoritarian, with power emanating from the top down. It was only in the last few years before independence in 1962 that elements of democracy began to appear, and were indeed encouraged by the government as independence was seen to be approaching. National political parties began to emerge in the mid-1950s, especially the Uganda People's Congress (UPC) and the Democratic Party (DP). The trouble was that these parties did not have truly national support based on political programmes or ideological goals; instead, they were rooted in religious and regional loyalties, which meant that the verdicts of national elections were unlikely to be accepted in a democratic spirit. For this reason, Museveni has many times expressed his dislike of pol-itical parties, which he regards as 'sectarian and divisive', a view to which we shall return.

At independence, however, hopes were high. Uganda had a new con-stitution which ushered in full parliamentary democracy; it had a two-party political system in which Obote's UPC began with a clear majority. Unfortunately, this honeymoon period lasted only a few years. By 1966, Obote had replaced this constitution with another one, the so-called 'pigeon-hole constitution', which Members of Parliament found copies of in their pigeon-holes and were prevented from discussing or amend-ing. This was followed by the 1967 Constitution which was debated, but the UPC-dominated house allowed the president to extend his executive powers greatly. The result was the emergence of virtually a one-party state and an autocratic regime that caused much unrest. When General Idi Amin carried out his military coup in 1971, it was therefore welcomed by many in Uganda as the lesser of two evils. Sadly, this was not the case and Uganda then had to suffer fifteen years of tyranny, chaos and violations of human rights. Obote was re-elected as president in 1980 but the election was widely condemned as fraudulent, and a civil war followed in which Museveni's National Resistance Movement (NRM) triumphed in 1986.[2] It was this allegedly rigged election of 1980 and the consequent bloody civil war which stamped itself on people's minds as a great lesson to be learned. In the future, there must be a fully democratic constitution, drawn up with the people's consent, capable of securing the rule of law and the rights of its citizens.

This was indeed the aim of Museveni's NRM during its long guerrilla campaign. At an early stage the guerillas declared their aim of establishing a truly democratic Uganda so that dictatorship could never return again, and this was to be achieved through constitutionalism – either a thorough revision of the existing 1967 Constitution or the drafting of a completely new one, which it was hoped would be a panacea to solve all the problems that had arisen in the past. It was almost inevitable that the latter option was chosen, as Museveni was very keen to show that his 'Movement' was an entirely new phenomenon which constituted a revolution in itself. It was to win the hearts and minds of the people through democratic processes and regard for the rights of individuals. Thus the training and discipline of his army (the NRA – National Resistance Army) was of a high standard, and during the war breaches in this code of behaviour towards the civilian population were severely punished. As it progressed through the country, taking more territory under its command, a system of 'grassroots democracy' was built up, with a hierarchy of local councils or 'resistance councils' of elected civilians who were given some administrative duties to perform. These were popular and have remained one of the key elements of democracy in Uganda today.[3]

Museveni, however, was not in a hurry to establish the mechanisms for the process of constitution-building. It is acknowledged that first he had to defeat the last elements of military opposition, driving out the ex-Obote and ex-Amin soldiers into the extreme north of the country and across the border into Sudan. This was a long process and indeed had not been fully achieved in the late 1990s. The government has to face rebel groups such as the Lord's Resistance Army (LRA) in the north, the West Nile Liberation Front (WNLF) in the north-west, and the Allied Democratic Forces (ADF) in the west. In the north there has been almost continuous guerrilla warfare which has kept the NRA very busy and has inflicted grievous losses and hardship on the civilian population. In the west also, the raids have been more sporadic but at times they have been serious, especially in the region of Bundibugyo. A tragic event recently was the burning down by the ADF of Kichwamba Technical College, in which at least sixty students lost their lives and many were abducted. There were also some bomb attacks in Kampala itself, in which lives were lost. In some respects these attacks increase the urgency of the need to establish a fully democratic political system which is acceptable to and supported by the vast majority of the population. On the other hand, the security situation raises ever-present issues about the behaviour and discipline of the NRA, an army that was much expanded after 1986, and also about the human rights of the civilian population who suffer at the hands of the security forces. Museveni has enjoyed widespread popular support because he brought peace and security to the country, or the major part of it at least. He has to cling on to this primary task because it is the main basis of his power. Therefore his approach to political reform has been cautious and the slow pace of the constitution-making process in particular has been criticised, both in Uganda and internationally.

Consulting the people: the Constitutional Commission

Before coming to power, Museveni had set out his aims in his Ten-Point Programme, which made a clear commitment to introduce democratic rule.[4] Two years after he took power, his National Resistance Council, the legislative body at the top of the Resistance Council's pyramid, passed the Uganda Constitutional Commission Act of 1988. This step itself was very significant, as it showed that a thorough consultation and debate was intended before any constitution was drawn up, and that the constitution was likely to be a more deeply thought-out and carefully crafted document than previous ones had been. Inevitably, too, it signalled that the process would be a long one. This had its dangers, because the longer the process took, the more likely it was that Museveni would be accused of prevaricating and clinging to power. The Commission was to have twenty one members appointed by the minister for constitutional affairs and the president, and its task was to propose a new constitution with all the attributes of a fully democratic system. It was to seek wide consultations with the public through meetings, seminars and workshops throughout the country. If the people participated in this way, it was envisaged that the eventual document would secure the acceptance and respect of all.

It was to take two years for this task to be completed, and longer could be allowed if necessary. This proved to be the case, and the work was in fact extended for a further two years – a length of time that many judged to be far too long and simply a device for prolonging the period in power of Museveni and his colleagues of the NRA and NRM. Furthermore, the fact that it was purely a government-appointed body, and that there appeared to be no provisions laid down for the promulgation and approval of the constitution, raised questions. Who was to do this? Many alleged that it would be an NRM-drafted constitution, approved by the NRC, and the Constitutional Commission was just a smoke-screen.

There were also questions raised about the Commission's methods of procedure. They were to 'educate the public' concerning the issues involved in drafting a new constitution, as well as discovering the views of the people. The Commission toured the country and held seminars and consultations with large numbers of people; indeed, the seminars proved to be very popular and people came in overwhelming numbers to some of them – a meeting of 600 people or more could hardly be called a seminar. Instead, some discussions deteriorated into political slanging matches with noisy hecklers, and it was soon perceived that preparatory literature was needed. This took the form of *Guidelines on Constitutional Issues*, seeking to 'guide people further on the major constitutional issues to which the people should address their minds in contributing their views on the new Constitution'.[5] The guidelines thus concerned issues such as citizenship, human rights, political parties, the forms of central and local government, the electoral system, the legislature, executive and judiciary, the civil service and so on. Critics of the Commission raised suspicions that this was a case of the government attempting to state its terms on which the discussions were to proceed, even though the document stated that these did not represent official views nor were they the Commission's preliminary proposals. But the *Guidelines* were accompanied by another document called *Guiding Questions on Constitutional Issues*, which listed no fewer than 253 questions, intended to assist groups and individuals in preparing their memoranda for submission to the Commission.[6] These instructions were no doubt well-intentioned, and assurances were given that the questions were not 'slanted' but couched in neutral terms; nevertheless they were a hostage to fortune in that critics could accuse the government of trying to bend the public view in particular directions. For example, those questions referring to the form of government, the position of the traditional rulers (because Uganda up to 1966 had no fewer than four separate kingdoms within the nation-state) and the political parties, which were still banned from party political activities, were bound to raise the tempo as these were the most contentious matters. Furthermore, answers to these questions were to be submitted by the Local Resistance Council Executives to the next higher councils, the Sub-County Resistance Councils, for presentation to the commissioners as they toured around the country. This would have the effect of filtering the views of the public before they reached the commissioners – a process in which anti-NRM views might be toned down. Members of the 'traditional' political parties, the UPC and DP, were especially critical of these devices, and Cecilia Ogwal, the assistant secretary-general of the UPC, questioned how far the process was democratic and how far the people could participate and freely express their views.[7] Yet it cannot be denied that the exercise was a remarkable experiment in throwing open the debate about a new constitution. The public did flock to the meetings and the records in the Constitutional Commission's interim and final reports show how vigorously some of the issues were discussed. The commission's archives, housed in a special building in Kampala, also bear testimony to the extraordinary activity it inspired, with reports, memoranda from all kinds of groups and institutions, and even thousands of essays by schoolchildren. If the constitution was not 'their' constitution, it was not for want of trying.

The Constituent Assembly

During these discussions it emerged that distrust of the process was still strong. It was feared that the government would in the end impose its own version of a new constitution, no matter what the public might say. Although it had not been envisaged at the start of the Commission's work, the idea of an elected constituent assembly to debate and approve the draft was strongly supported, especially with pressure from the UPC and other political parties. The massive public consultation by itself was not enough: if the constitution was to have the desired credibility and public support, then the draft itself would have to be scrutinised and finalised by an elected assembly. Whatever the suspicions were that the NRM government was a self-perpetuating body, this much is clear: it was determined to obtain the strongest support it could for the regime under a new constitution. Hence the announcement that elections to a constituent assembly would take place in 1994.[8]

President Museveni, however, was taking a risk in calling these elections. His movement, the NRM, still firmly adhered to the notion that 'no-party democracy' was best for Uganda, at least for some time to come, given the legacy of chaos and civil war that had followed the end of a multi-party system. This issue had been discussed widely in the public meetings organised by the Constitutional Commission, and the no-party system had received wide support, but similarly the multi-partyists had found their voice, especially in the north. The elections would be a further test of the legitimacy of the no-party government. The rule was laid down that candidates were to stand on a no-party basis, but of course in practice the voters knew when a candidate was a party supporter as they knew his or her background, and at some of the election gatherings party loyalties were barely disguised.

Second, the purpose and function of a Constituent Assembly was new to the people of Uganda. It was to meet and discuss the draft constitution, pass amendments to it if agreed; it had no legislative powers and was not a 'parliament'. It followed therefore that the electioneering campaign was intended to focus exclusively on the constitutional issues, but both candidates and voters tended to disregard this. Candidates often made promises of aid and development for their regions which they had no power to secure, while voters similarly supported influential candidates who might be in a position to procure such benefits. There was also the hope that a member of the Constituent Assembly could well follow up his or her electoral victory with a second one when a National Assembly or Parliament was called, as it surely would be, in which case he or she could then, it was hoped, fulfil his/her promises.

These ambitions were part of the reason for another feature of the elections to the Constituent Assembly, namely the large expenditure by candidates on their campaigns, and the use of widespread bribery of the voters. One of the causes of this was the 'open voting' system. Instead of a secret ballot, which had been used in previous elections and had occasionally been tampered with, the NRC, debating about the procedures for these elections, asked voters to line up behind their preferred candidates. This made them visible to all and meant that if a candidate bribed voters, he or she could expect them to act accordingly, or they might afterwards suffer victimisation. Further, no limit was imposed on the amount of money candidates could spend on their campaigns, and since party affiliations were not allowed to be paraded, they sought to win votes by lavish hospitality and ostentatious displays of wealth. It was alleged that many members of the government and the NRC used official funds and cars in their campaigns, so the advantages of incumbency were clear. President Museveni stopped the use of government vehicles and resources during the campaign but this was not until 24 February 1994, rather late in the proceedings.[9] In some cases, ministers and officials used their positions to make donations or bring other benefits to their localities.[10] This was in contrast to a very few really poor candidates who conducted their campaigns on bicycles and had no funds to offer. The elections were thus not entirely 'free and fair', to use UN terminology.

Another query about the democratic nature of the process can be raised regarding the composition of the assembly. The existing NRC, the embryo Parliament consisting of elected and nominated members, many of them officials or NRA officers, had at first been suggested as the Constituent Assembly. Both the NRC and the NRA Council were billed to participate in the discussion, adoption and promulgation of the constitution.[11] Events overtook this plan, however, and the political parties in particular made objections, insisting that the assembly must be a new, elected body. After a fierce debate in the NRC, a new bill was passed which gave the assembly its eventual shape, but the government succeeded in retaining in it some of the undemocratic characteristics of the NRC. Thus the house was not entirely elective: thirty-nine women members were to be indirectly elected through various bodies; ten delegates were to be nominated by the president; ten by the NRA; two by the trade unions; eight by the political parties (two each); four by the National Youth Council; and one by the National Union of Disabled People of Uganda.[12] The rest were to be elected directly by the electorate in the 214 constituencies of the country. These special features of seats for women, youth and so on were typical of Museveni's regime, through which he wanted to respect groups who previously had been somewhat excluded from political processes. He always argued, for example, that his NRA in the field was a young army, and he wished to acknowledge the support of the youth of the country. Nevertheless, the composition of the assembly disappointed the political parties, who forecast, correctly, that the assembly would be dominated by NRM supporters.

The elections themselves passed off reasonably well, although there were some disputes about the demarcation of constituencies.[13] It was also acknowledged that the election commission's task of the 'civic education' of electors, many of whom had little experience of democratic elections, was almost impossible in the time available, even though the commission shared the task with the Uganda Joint Christian Council. Similarly, the preparation of an accurate voters' register proved to be difficult and the time allocated had to be extended, as voters were slow to register, until the local resistance councils were requested to encourage them.[14] The Constituent Assembly Statute laid down that 'elections for delegates shall be non-partisan' – that is, on non-party lines – and that every candidate shall stand on 'personal merit'. Yet it was difficult to conceal party loyalties and some candidates did not try very hard to do so; while during the campaign it was clear that some of the burning issues now raised, such as the movement versus party politics and a unitary state versus a federal form, would inevitably give birth to new types of political caucuses when the assembly met.[15] Candidates had very little opportunity to describe at length to voters their views on these issues. The statute laid down that government officials had to arrange candidates' meetings at which all the candidates were to meet collectively. Each candidate was only allowed a short speech and a limited time to answer questions. All kinds of devices were used by the candidates to undermine the effectiveness of their rivals' speeches.[16]

This lack of opportunity to campaign politically caused many candidates to resort heavily to bribery, gifts and drinks for the voters in the run-up to polling day.[17] On the other hand, there was an astonishing number of candidates: 1122 candidates in 211 constituencies out of 214 (three candidates were returned unopposed). When the elections took place on 28 March 1994 after the 'official' election meetings in February and March, there was tremendous popular enthusiasm, and very little violence was reported; the international observers who had been invited duly reported the elections to be 'free and fair', with few reservations.

The election results show that, broadly speaking, Buganda and western Uganda were in favour of the movement as a political system, while eastern and northern Uganda were for multi-partyism and a return of the traditional political parties. The question of a federal or unitary form of state took second place to this, and it was clear that the assembly would have a strong majority of members who still supported the movement. It was this that caused Museveni to declare after the elections, 'we won'. This somewhat rash remark of course gave rise to further accusations that, no matter what protestations might be made to the contrary, the movement system was very close to a one-party state.

When the Constituent Assembly met, it proved to be a lively body, and the debates were vigorous, with every issue freely argued. Its duration was supposed to be only seven months by the statute, from May to December 1994, but this had to be extended twice. One reason for this was the strong position taken up by rival groups in defence of the movement, or of multi-partyism, or the role of Buganda. Another was the long and detailed examination given to such matters as human rights in the new constitution.[18] Regarding the Buganda question, Museveni's government had introduced a clever counter-move to take some of the steam out of this issue by a policy of decentralisation, which devolved more powers to local government centres from the central government; indeed, this had been seen by some as a feature of democratisation in Uganda at least equal in importance to the constitution-making process.[19] Nevertheless, the debate on 'federo' was one of the hottest in the assembly, before it was rejected by a strong majority. Decisions were carried by acclaim – 'aye' or 'no' – which was quicker than counting votes, if less accurate.[20] Much of the work of the assembly was carried out in five main committees, because it was decided wisely that all the chapters in the draft constitution could not be debated in plenary session as this would take up an inordinate length of time. The last major debate, on the question of the movement type of government or a multi-party system, was predictably very acrimonious, but it ended in the approval of the proposal in the draft constitution, that the movement system should continue for another five years from the promulgation of the new constitution, when the issue should be decided by the people in a referendum. This was a remarkable victory for the movementists, considering the vigour of the multi-partyists' attack, and the mounting pressure from the international community, which was expressing unease at the continued banning of political party activity.

The presidential and parliamentary elections

In the end, the assembly approved the draft constitution with few substantial changes. The proposal for a council of state was rejected, but otherwise one could say that, broadly speaking, the Constitutional Commission, with behind it the backing and influence of the NRM government, had carried the day. It was said that 80 per cent of Ugandans could agree with 80 per cent of the constitution, though of course the remaining 20 per cent contained some serious issues, not least of which was whether, or when, multi-partyism should return, and this was to be decided by the referendum. The government had therefore succeeded in prolonging its period of power for another five years, as did Museveni himself, who was duly elected president for five years under the new constitution. This is not the place for a detailed examination of the Constitution itself – which is an unusually long one – but it is sufficient to say that it embraced most of the features of modern parliamentary democracies. For example, it limited the powers of the president and the length and number of his terms of office; it ensured due separation of the executive, judiciary and legislature, and it safeguarded the rights of the citizen, except for the issue noted above.[21] The fact that Museveni won 72.4 per cent of the votes cast in the presidential election shows the solid support of the people for the present political system, for the time being at least. It was only in the north of Uganda, which was still suffering under the guerrilla campaign of the LRA that he lost to the rival candidates. His victory bore fruit in the strong support still given to him by the major donor states in the international community. They judged – fairly or unfairly – that this brand of democracy was what Uganda needed at the time, and strong financial backing was forthcoming. Indeed, it may be questioned as to how far Museveni could have gone with his very strong hold on the political progress of the country if he had not had this important asset – that he was able to draw on the goodwill of the international community who were still willing to back his rule with plentiful funding.

The parliamentary elections followed in June 1996, and it was clear that the NRM government still intended to control the electoral process tightly. A task force was appointed to oversee the campaign and to identify names of the election officials to the electoral commission. This task force was headed by Haji Moses Kigongo, the NRM vice-chairman, and many government ministers were part of it.[22] Partly political activity was still banned, and parliamentary candidates were again to stand on 'individual merit'. The main political parties were, in fact, grouped together in the Inter-Party Co-operative, but they rashly decided to boycott the elections in protest and so eliminated an important test of the support for multi-partyism. The seats for the special interest groups – women, youth, workers and so on – were retained, and this, of course, meant that Museveni could rely on their support for the movement.[23] About three-quarters of the new Parliament were reckoned to be movement supporters.[24] Though the Commonwealth Observers' Group pronounced the elections to be free and fair, interestingly there was a low turn-out of voters, because many thought that the presidential election was the more important one, and this gave Museveni and the movement an overwhelming vote of confidence.[25]

A lively parliament

Museveni announced that his government was to consist of a more 'balanced' cabinet in future, so he increased the number of ministers from forty-two to sixty-one, representing all the regions of the country, to emphasise its broad-based character, though his own region in the west was still heavily represented.[26] Parliament was not overawed and soon showed that members were prepared to be strongly critical of the government and to make ministers accountable for their misdoings.

Their attack was specially focused on corruption. A parliamentary select committee was appointed to enquire into alleged corruption in the Uganda Railways Corporation and to report back to Parliament. The parliamentary sessional committee on finance and economic planning criticised the minister of finance, Mr Mayanja-Nkangi, because of the large deficit of Sh. 7.4 billion in the budget, and they blocked a government amendment to the finance bill. They threatened him with a vote of censure for incompetence and called for his resignation.[27] Mr Kirunda Kivejinja came under attack for allegedly drawing quantities of fuel for private use from Uganda Railways Corporation when he was minister of works, transport and communications. He was removed from office but was further attacked when MPs heard that he was still drawing his salary and using an official car. This underlined one of the unsatisfactory features of the practice of accountability as far as this Parliament could exercise it: they could pass votes of censure and call for resignations, but appropriate action did not necessarily follow. However, a more significant attack was made against Brigadier Jim Muhwezi, minister of state for primary education and a former member of Museveni's guerrilla force. He and Brigadier Moses Ali were accused of renting out the Customs House for an exorbitant sum to a private company in which the former had an interest, and for diverting Sh. 300 million from the Uganda Wildlife Authority. In the same week, Parliament attacked officials of the Uganda Railways Corporation, and Samuel Apedel wrote in the *Sunday Vision* newspaper that this was a time when the voter was king and the leaders were servants.[28] A record number of 136 MPs signed the petition for a motion of censure against Muhwezi. Professor T. B. Kabwegyere wrote that, in passing the motion of censure, in accordance with Article 118 of the Constitution, Parliament was exercising its supremacy over the executive.[29] It should be noted, however, that the minister was not dismissed immediately, but was dropped in a cabinet reshuffle in June 1998. Furthermore, Ugandan politicians have a tradition of bouncing back, and the *New Vision* newspaper noted at the end of the year that Muhwezi was staging a political come-back when he won a seat on the powerful parliamentary standing committee on rules, privileges and discipline. Among other tasks, it noted, it draws up a set of rules for the censure of ministers.[30] Parliament maintained a lengthy attack against corruption in the privatisation process being carried out in accordance with government policy. They passed a resolution calling for the government to suspend the process, citing corruption as the reason. They set up a fifteen-member select committee to investigate this corruption, and this indeed achieved some results, because Major-

General Salim Saleh, Museveni's brother, had to resign from his post as senior adviser to the president on security, and Mathew Rukikaire, minister for privatisation, also resigned, saying he took political responsibility for mistakes in the divestiture process, but denied wrong-doing or being corrupt. Other ministers also came under attack.[31] Turning its attention to military matters, Parliament pressed for the government to hold talks with the LRA rebels in the north, to try to find a peaceful solution as the NRA (now called the Uganda People's Defence Force – UPDF) seemed to be unable to bring the war to a conclusion. This was turned down by Museveni, however, who said he refused to talk to 'terrorists'. Further, MPs complained that Parliament had not been consulted when Museveni sent UPDF troops into the Congo civil war, but while enthusiasm for Uganda's involvement in this was clearly lacking, it continued on the grounds that Uganda needed to guard security on its borders.

Last, one may question how much longer the movement can continue to enjoy wide popular acceptance in lieu of a multi-party system. The Movement Act of 1997 confirmed a new structure for it, and it continued to be in theory all-embracing, with every shade of political opinion included. However, many regard it as still being biased towards the south-west, and support for it varies according to region, and according to other alignments such as the idea of federalism. Within such a large movement, it is possible that new political groups may spring up, which might overtake loyalties to the older traditional parties such as the UPC and the DP, which have been in some disarray. The New Movement is one such group; there are also the Young Parliamentarians; a Free Movement, led by law lecturers at Makerere University,[32] and the Young Democrats. The referendum, due by the year 2000 as laid down in the Constitution, on whether to restore multi-party democracy, is beginning to loom like the Sword of Damocles over the existing system. In the local government elections of November 1997, although the movement still won with a big majority, there were signs that multi-partyism was gaining a hold. It is possible therefore that by the end of 2000 the political scene in Uganda may be considerably different, and this writer has, in fact, heard many varying forecasts from Ugandans of the outcome of the referendum.

Conclusion

In conclusion, it is clear that Uganda's political system is still held together largely by the charisma of President Yoweri Museveni. He has maintained political control through the movement, which in spite of his protestations has to be seen as fairly closely resembling a one-party state. Nevertheless, his popularity and the peace and security he has brought to most parts of Uganda – the exceptions being the war in the north by the LRA and guerrilla raids in the west – after more than fifteen years of civil war and anarchy, would appear to ensure his continued control for some time to come. A very important element in this is the strong backing and financial support Uganda receives from the international community, although even in these circles there is growing disquiet about the continued banning of party activity.[33] Parliament, however, in its short life so far, has shown itself to be a lively, critical body, not intimidated or overawed. It has shown teeth in attacking corruption and has succeeded in forcing the resignation of some ministers. The principle of accountability is acted upon, and the government has been made to show more transparency in its actions. The public is acquiring education in the language of democracy through a vigorous free press. The exercise in public consultation and debate carried out by the constitutional commission was a remarkable achievement, even though the government framed the debate and steered the results in the directions it desired. Uganda has a very modern-style Constitution, most of which has been agreed by, and has the commitment of, the bulk of the population. Those points of difference that still remain can be settled by democratic means as the machinery is there to enable this to happen. The poverty of the mass of the population who are rural peasants remains a serious problem, because democracy needs a reasonably prosperous society in which to flourish. Uganda has had a good record of economic growth in recent years but prosperity is confined to a small upper class. Spreading the benefits of the improved record will be important politically as well as economically – and this has not yet happened.[34] In short, Uganda does indeed provide an example of progress in democracy since 1986, which many African countries could follow, and those shortcomings that have been described are capable of solution, given the conditions of peace and stability.

Notes and References

* My thanks are due to Dr J. Katalikawe, of the Law Faculty, Makerere University, Kampala, who has collaborated with me on other publications in this area.

1 At the Paris Peace Conference in November 1998, Uganda and Rwanda took part in discussions over a cease-fire but 'demanded guarantees and commitments on security at their borders'. President Kabila made commitments regarding democratisation, openness and dialogue, while earlier he had

announced that political parties would be legalised in two months' time. Panafrican News Agency, 28 November 1998, and IRIN Update, 20–26 November 1998.

For a general overview of the progress of democracy in Africa, see M. Ottaway (ed.) (1997) *Democracy in Africa: The Hard Road Ahead* (Boulder, Col.; London: Lynne Rienner); M. Bratton and N. van de Walle (1997) *Democratic Experiments in Africa* (Cambridge: Cambridge University Press); J. Widner (ed.) (1994) *Economic Change and Political Liberalisation, in Sub-Saharan Africa* (Baltimore, Md.; London: Johns Hopkins University Press); and J. Wiseman (ed.) (1995) *Democracy and Political Change in Sub-Saharan Africa* (London: Routledge).

2 For the events of these years, see Phares and Mutibwa (1992) *Uganda Since Independence* (London: Hurst & Co.); G. Kanyeihamba (1975) *Constitutional Law and Government in Uganda*, (Nairobi: East African Literature Bureau); A. G. Gingyera-Pinycwa (1978) *Milton Obote and His Times*, (New York; London: NOK Publishers); F. A. Bwengye (1985) *The Agony of Uganda from Idi Amin to Obote* (London; New York: Regency Press).

3 See O. W. Furley (1992) 'Uganda: The Second-Phase Bid for Legitimacy under International Security', in K. Rupesinghe (ed.), *Internal Conflict and Governance* (London: Macmillan); (n.d.) 'Towards a Free and Democratic Uganda: The Basic Principles and Policies of the National Resistance Movement (NRM)' (Kampala).

4 Museveni, Y. (1985) *The Ten-Point Programme*, NRM Publications.

5 *Guidelines on Constitutional Issues* (Kampala: Government Printer) 1990.

6 *Guiding Questions on Constitutional Issues* (Kampala: Government Printer) 1990.

7 Ogwal, Cecilia, letter to the Minister of Constitutional Affairs, 5.6.94.

8 For a general survey of the process, see H. B. Hansen and M. Twaddle (eds) (1994) *From Chaos to Order: The Politics of Constitution-Making in Uganda* (London: James Currey); and for a detailed study of the Constituent Assembly, see G. Sabiti-Makara, B. Tukahebwa and F. Byarugaba (eds) (1996) *Politics, Constitutionalism and Electioneering in Uganda. A Study of the 1994 Constituent Assembly Elections* (Kampala: Makerere University Press).

9 *New Vision* (Newspaper), 26 February 1994.

10 *New Vision* (Newspaper), 3 September 1993, 18 October 1993 and 30 December 1993.

11 Legal Notice No. 1 of 1986, amended by Statute No. 1 of 1989. I am indebted to Dr J. Katalikawe for this reference.

12 *New Vision* (Newspaper), 3 August 1993. These proportions represent a climb-down by the NRC, which had previously considered themselves a sufficiently democratic body to discuss and adopt a draft constitution. It was Major General Mugisha Muntu, Commander of the NRA, who persuaded them that the Constituent Assembly should be very largely a newly-elected body. See Ondoga ori Amaza (1998) *Museveni's Long March, from Guerrilla to Statesman* (Kampala: Fountain Publishers), pp. 178–80.

13 *The Monitor* (Newspaper), 4 October 1993.

14 *New Vision* (Newspaper), 22 December 1993.

15 See Ondoga ori Amaza, *Museveni's Long March*, pp. 180–8.

16 See O. W. Furley and J. Katalikawe (2000) *No-Party Democracy: Uganda's Elections to the Constituent Assembly* (Kampala: Kampala Centre for Basic Research).

17 *New Vision* (Newspaper), 3 September 1993 and 18 October 1993.

18 The writer was privileged to attend some of these debates, and the determination to ensure that the terrible violations of human rights that Uganda has suffered in the past were not to be repeated, was most impressive.

19 See S. Villadsen and F. Lubanga (eds) (1996) *Democratic Decentralisation in Uganda: A New Approach to Local Governance* (Kampala: Fountain Publishers).

20 See Ondoga ori Amaza, *Museveni's Long March*, pp. 189–94, for a detailed account of this debate.

21 Republic of Uganda, Constitution of the Republic of Uganda, 1995. It is 196 pages long.

22 *The People* (Newspaper), 13–20 December 1995; and *New Vision* (Newspaper), 13 December 1995.

23 *The East African*, 1–7 July 1996.

24 Interview with Dr J. Katalikawe and Mr J. Byamugisha, Coventry, 15 October 1997.

25 *The East African*, 1–7 July 1996.

26 *African Research Bulletin*, 1–31 July 1996; and the *Monitor* (Newspaper), 2 May 1996.

27 *New Vision* (Newspaper), 30.10.97, and the *Monitor* (Newspaper), 29 November 1997.

28 *The Sunday Vision* (Newspaper), 9 November 1997.

29 Professor T. B. Kabweguere, 'The Lessons from Jim Muhwezi's Censure', *The Sunday Vision* (Newspaper), 28 March 1998.

30 *New Vision* (Newspaper), 23 December 1997. 'Are they serious about corruption?', was a rhetorical question put to me by Dr J. Katalikawe, Kampala, 23 July 1998.

31 *New Vision* (Newspaper), 1 September 1998, 16 December 1998; and *Guardian Weekly*, Special Report on Uganda, 'Corruption Haunts Economic Success', 23 December 1998.

32 *The Monitor*, 2 June 1998; and interview with Mr George Baitera Maiteki, MP, Kampala, 12 May 1998.

33 'Donors' Darling Losing Its Allure' was the headline in the *Financial Times*, 9 December 1998 (though this was chiefly regarding economic performance). The *Guardian*, however, wrote of Museveni: 'His no-party system is beginning to look suspiciously like a one-party state. There are growing complaints that by stifling opposition, he is encouraging disaffected Ugandans to turn to rebel groups in the northern and western areas', *Guardian Weekly*, Special Report on Uganda, 23 December 1998.

34 The 'Human Development Index' for developing countries ranks Uganda 160th out of 174 countries, and the 'Human Poverty Index' ranks it 57th out of 77: United Nations Development Programme, *Human Development Report*, Oxford University Press, 1998, pp. 21 and 26. President Museveni admits in his book that 'the main issue facing Uganda now is the underdevelopment of the rural economy': Y. Museveni (1997) *Sowing the Mustard Seed. The Struggle for Freedom and Democracy in Uganda* (London: Macmillan), p. 214.

7

State Collapse, Post-conflict Peace-building and Sustainable Democracy in Africa

Timothy Murithi

Introduction

At the dawn of decolonization in 1963, Frantz Fanon predicted that 'this ethnicisation of the central authority, it is certain encourages regionalist ideas and separatism. All the decentralising tendencies spring up again and triumph, and the nation falls to pieces, broken to bits'.[1] The target of his observation was the post-colonial African state and his prognosis was to prove insightful. The scenario is not unfamiliar to Africa. Over-centralisation and the consolidation of authoritarian power at the centre has presided over the emergence and growth of sub-national ethnic mobilisation against the state. The self-destructive tendency of the centralised predatory state is increasingly coming to the fore. There has been a decline of constitutionalism in the post-colonial era and the increasing prominence of institutionalised repression in Africa. This in turn instigates the gradual delegitimisation of the state and fuels intense competition to capture the state. The African continent unfortunately is becoming familiar with the phenomenon of disintegrating states. This study will assess this phenomenon and the difficult challenge this poses for post-conflict peace-building with regard to democratisation.

In recent times we have witnessed African states simply ceasing to exist as central sovereign organisations. Somalia remains in a state of fragmentation, while Liberia and Sierra Leone have undergone periods of fragmentation. Congo-Kinshasa remains an unwieldy entity perpetually on the brink of disintegration. A whole host of other states are confronted by a fragile instability – for example, Sudan, Rwanda, Burundi, Algeria, Western Sahara and Guinea Bissau. At the start of the twenty-first century a significant number of countries on the continent are having to contend with sub-national actors defying their central authorities.

These events raise some crucial questions as far as conflict resolution and the transition to democracy is concerned. Too often there is a desire to see democracy implemented in these war-torn societies without questioning whether or not the democratic institutions that are put in place are sustainable in the medium to long term. In contributing towards the advancement of a mature agenda for stability and development in Africa, this chapter will attempt to bridge the conceptual gap between the process of conflict resolution, which seeks to address ethnic disputes once activated, and the process of democratisation, which seeks to manage the transition towards legitimate governance in post-conflict situations. In particular, this study will highlight the significant parallels that exist between conflict resolution and democratisation. The question that needs to be asked, in this case, is whether we should be considering conflict resolution itself as a process of democratisation. With this in mind, what are the implications devising institutions for post-conflict peace-building? This chapter will ultimately seek to highlight the importance of democratic institutions and, more specifically, electoral systems, which can foster sustainable political arrangements by encouraging ethnic groups to feel that their sociocultural survival and security will be safeguarded in the aftermath of conflict. The study will conclude by exploring the proposition that genuine proportionality in national legislatures and government goes a long way towards assuaging the fears of marginalisation that ethnic groups were subjected to in erstwhile over-centralised post-colonial states.

The post-colonial state in Africa: charting the decline of constitutionalism

In pre-colonial Africa a wide variety of political organizations in the form of villages, city-states, kingdoms and empires rose and fell. So in one respect the events we are witnessing at the present time in the form of state collapse are not as unique as has often been thought. During decolonisation, the diversity of Africa's political heritage was sidelined as the African nationalists took over power in nation-states that were defined politically and geographically by their European colonisers. Indeed, as Jeffrey Herbst notes, it was quite ironic that even as African nationalists such as Kwame Nkrumah, Julius Nyerere, Jomo Kenyatta and Sekou Toure were vigorously proclaiming their break with Europe and the West they uniformly adopted that most Western of political organizations, the nation-state, to rule over their people.[2]

In the name of building national unity, constitutional frameworks designed to uphold democracy were gradually replaced by the institutionalisation of authoritarianism.[3] As Jackson and Rosenberg observe, 'once sovereignty had been transferred and the colonial authority had departed, the independence constitution of the new African governments was usually either amended, ignored or discarded by those in power. Through military coups the constitution was further undermined or violated by those seeking power'.[4] Constitutional democracies were transformed rapidly into regimes of personal rule.[5] With the militarisation of African politics the *coup d'état* became a common means of changing governments.[6]

The rise of authoritarianism and the de-legitimatisation of the state

The majority of Africa's post-colonial leaders inherited the apparatus of the colonial state and used it decisively for their own ends. The state machinery and ill-fitting borders were put into the hands of leaders who went on to develop authoritarian tendencies. The combination of an authoritarian leadership intent on personal rule and the colonial inheritance of a centralised state – complete with its coercive instruments – turned out to be a volatile one indeed, and many African states are still contending with this legacy. At the end of the 1980s, the single-party system was dominant in most African states with the exception of a few countries such as Senegal and Botswana. In several countries military dictatorships had replaced civil regimes, suspending constitutions and outlawing all political activity. The African state, which was also facing an economic crisis, was essential a system of institutionalised repression – the hypocritical arguments for nation-building were weakened by the force of their contradictions.

What we are confronted with at the beginning of the new millennium is the legacy of a centralised authoritarian state institution which has gradually been delegitimated by the overwhelming majority of its African constituents. The majority of these people do not identify with these states and have in fact become victims of the policies that some of these states implement. As a consequence, in several African countries, more or less organised armed groups are in open conflict with the central government. The authoritarian state defined by the centralisation of power enabled a small group of actors to establish a *de facto* rule over vast tracts of land and a multitude of different ethnic groups. When this small group of people comes from one ethnic group, or a coalition of ethnic groups, then such a group is capable of establishing its political dominance through the institutions of the state and thereby securing its identity and cultural survival, as witnessed in Rwanda. The inevitable consequence of this is the decline in the perception by other ethnic groups of their sense of security.

When the domination of one ethnic group by another in effect became institutionalised through the state apparatus, far from being a nation-state, such an entity effectively becomes an 'ethnicised' state. The privileging of one ethnic group in this type of situation negates the possibility of legitimate governance, and genuine democracy is compromised. As Claude Ake suggests, politics in Africa has been shaped by this character of the African state.[7] It is mainly about access to state power, and the goals of political struggle are the capture of an all-powerful state. Politics becomes a case of who can get the state first. Therefore, in Africa, as in other parts of the world, the resulting inflexibility and exclusivity of these events spawns sub-national groups, and politicises ethnic identities, who feel compelled to challenge the institutionalised system of ethnic dominance, which leads ultimately in a significant number of cases to the ignition of conflict. Some of these conflicts, such as the one in South Sudan and Western Sahara, have been raging since the 1970s; more recently, sub-national upheavals were witnessed in Congo-Kinshasa, Congo-Brazzaville and Guinea Bissau. Protracted ethnic conflicts, past and present, remain highly destructive and signal the loss of authority, and the eventual breakdown of the governing institutions of a nation-state becomes a reality. When access to state power becomes the precondition for human welfare, and where such access is not equally available to all groups, then the state becomes the object of conflict as well as the means through which the conflict is waged. In the end, the level of tension created, particularly in weaker states, leads ultimately to disintegration. When the centre collapses, the peripheral structure it upheld collapses with it.

State collapse and the challenge to conflict resolution initiatives

The loss of control over socioeconomic and political space means, in effect, that the state has become dysfunctional:

In the case of collapse, the basic functions of the state are no longer performed. As the decision making centre of government the state is paralysed and inoperative. National laws are not made, order is not preserved and societal cohesion is not enhanced. As a symbol of identity it has lost its power of conferring a name on its people and a meaning to their social activity. As a territory it is no longer assured security and provisionment by a central sovereign organisation.[8]

Such fragmentation constitutes a violent form of rejection of the state by sections of the population. Yet these same populations find themselves with an even greater sense of uncertainty, insecurity and anarchy. There is no guarantee that these polities will restructure themselves around the organising principle of statehood. Yet the international community remains conceptually bound to the idea of putting-the-state-back-together-again. Less emphasis is placed on implementing post-national forms of political community that reduce the intensity of competition for the state and engender institutions that are more sensitive to the needs of ethnic minorities for guarantees of participation in political life. The case of Somalia is informative in this respect: opposition against the state was organised on a clan and sub-clan basis against the dominance of three clans allied to the autocracy of President Siad Barre. With the collapse of the state, power at the centre was claimed by the United Somali Congress, but a centralised authority was rejected by other clans, to the extent that the northern-based Somali National Movement decided to declare *de facto* an independent republic in the form of Somaliland. The uniqueness of this situation and the ensuing confusion has meant that the African and international community at large are lacking a coherent approach to dealing with the problem of a collapsed state.

The challenges for any initiative aimed at fostering conflict resolution are monumental. If the 'state' is to be reconstituted after collapse (even though this should not be viewed as being either inevitable or essential in the short-run, though for medium- and long-term socioeconomic regeneration of the region it may be necessary) then we need to raise questions about how sustainable democracy can be constructed. By sustainable democracy here the allusion is to the ability of the African state to govern its people effectively and equitably, based on a post-national model which encourages the legitimate representation of all sections of the population – which means institutional provisions for the inclusion of the political will of the various ethnic groups within it.

State collapse raises questions about legitimate governance in African societies and should make us reflect on the authoritarianism still present in some African states at the start of the new millennium. In the 'failure' of the state we are witnessing the legacy of the forces of authoritarianism which Fanon identified as being susceptible to political manipulation. Conflict resolution in these collapsed states is unlikely to be effective in the long-run if disputing parties do not feel that they can safeguard their interests, cultural survival and security within established political arrangements. In one sense, then, most of these conflicts, which are essentially a manifestation of competition for the state, can only be settled when sub-national groups are granted greater political control over their social and cultural lives. This would, in effect, mean relocating it away from a heavily centralised, overbearing and authoritarian state.

From conflict resolution to sustainable democracy: electoral systems and the management of ethnic cleavages

The concern therefore needs to be with the kind of democratic institutions that can sustain a political arrangement in which communal groups do not feel the need to resort to extreme forms of resistance to offset the encroaching power of the state. The conflict resolution process, by definition, is geared towards encouraging co-operation between groups rather than competition. Yet there are instances where models of democracy in African societies, essentially fragmented along ethnic lines, are based on competitive winner-takes-all electoral systems. This is an inherently contradictory position that needs to be highlighted and addressed.

In war-torn areas the post-conflict resolution process fails in its objectives if it does not at the same time lay the foundations for sustainable democracy. Thus conflict resolution is synonymous with democratisation. The principles of co-operation that function during the conflict resolution process are the same ones that should underpin the post-conflict democratic institutions if sustainability is the objective. Too often there tends to be a strenuous effort to see so-called 'democracy' implemented in these war-torn societies without a basic recognition that some forms of democracy are more democratic than others; and further, that some models of democracy can be unstable and may actually perpetuate the delegitimation of the government rather than reduce it. Decision-makers, researchers and democratic activists alike need to question whether or not the democratic institutions to which they appeal to remove the violence from politics are sustainable in the medium to long term. Given that the conflict resolution process is geared towards fostering reconciliation through co-operation, it is also necessary to place an emphasis on democratic institutions which sustain reconciliation through co-operation. The issue here is one of the role that electoral mechanisms can play in managing ethnic conflicts that may contribute to state collapse.

Comparing majoritarian and proportional electoral systems

Can the electoral system have an impact on the sustainability of a peace agreement? Given the fact that much of the political energy in Africa has been focused on putting pressure on intransigent autocratic regimes to commit themselves to democratic reform, this is a question that has remained largely unaddressed. As David Quintal noted in his pioneering study, the electoral system 'authoritatively prescribes the manner in which political preferences of a community are to be expressed and ordered'.[9] Therefore electoral systems need to be considered as a central issue in the peace-building process rather than as mere details that do not merit much attention. It is appropriate therefore to address the above question by comparing two electoral models – the majoritarian system and the proportional electoral system.[10]

The majority rule electoral system refers to a first-past-the-post framework of democratic competition. Also known as the winner-takes-all system, it constitutionally centralises the exercise of political power. The proportional representation (PR) system, on the other hand, with its provisions for power-sharing, is based on including communal groups in constitutionally decentralised decision-making institutions. In reductionistic terms, the majoritarian system leaves decisions about governance in the hands of the majority that wins the state elections. The majority takes over a hierarchical form of government in which sub-national units are strictly subordinated to the national governments' policy-making power. In this sense, majoritarian frameworks increase the stakes of competition and they also increase the intensity of competitiveness and decrease direct access by sub-national groups to political institutions.[11] The proportional representation system, on the other hand, combined with the notion of power-sharing, places an emphasis on the constitutional division of political power between the national government and sub-national units of government. National and sub-national governments have defined responsibilities which come from constitutionally guaranteed spheres of power, putting in place a checks-

and-balances framework for governance. Thus proportional regimes are sensitive to proportions, while majoritarian regimes are sensitive to majorities. They decrease the stakes of competition as well as decreasing the intensity of competition by increasing direct access to political institutions.[12]

In the case of failed, or even failing, states, it is necessary to take into account the fact that once ethnic identities become activated, then the tendency from that point is for power to be mobilised around an ethnic base. In this case, ethnicity becomes politicised and a politicised ethnicity is by its very nature entrenched in its goal of achieving some form of control over its sociocultural destiny. Democratic institutions which do not acknowledge or try to suppress such a politicised ethnicity only serve to increase the level of tension within the state and to foment an even more entrenched resistance to centralised national government.

In states that are communally diverse democratic institutions operating on the principle of a majoritarian winner-takes-all framework are hard-pressed to contend with politicised ethnicity. As the studies carried out by Arend Lijphart demonstrate, the surest way to kill the idea of democracy in a society in which ethnicity has become activated is to adopt an electoral system based on the winner-takes-all system.[13] The largest coalition of politicised ethnicities can effectively 'capture' the state, leaving other ethnicities under their rule. Without proportionality and some power-sharing arrangement, the majority rule system fosters the 'ethnicisation of the state'. It becomes increasingly evident that in failed, and failing, states, conflict resolution and democratic consolidation cannot be effected by majoritarian institutions. They only seem capable, when confronted with politicised ethnicity, of instituting a fragile ethnocentric democratic regime which institutionalises the dominance of the largest coalition of ethnic groups.

Ethnic conflict and the majoritarian framework of electoral competition in Sudan and Angola

Events in Africa have borne witness to electoral systems designed to sustain an ethnic conflict resolution process, ultimately subverting the process and exacerbating divisions. In Sudan, where conflict continues between the Muslim north and non-Muslim south, efforts to establish a democratic constitution, after the overthrow of Colonel Gaafar Mohammed Numeri in 1985, led to democratic elections in 1986. However, politicised ethnicity derailed the process when political parties became identified with the major religious groupings. Failure to believe that the other parties were not bent on total domination led to the collapse of a dialogue between the northern and southern parties, and a renewal of conflict. The Angolan experience is more telling, in that the ceasefire was secured between the two main disputing groups, namely Jose Eduardo dos Santos' People's Liberation Movement of Angola (MPLA) and Jonas Savimbi's National Union for the Total Independence of Angola (UNITA).[14] This included an agreement to hold multi-party elections in September 1992. Under the majoritarian electoral system the results of the election emerged with neither side receiving a clear majority in the presidential elections, which under the electoral laws meant submitting to a run-off election. Yet Savimbi cut his losses and subsequently declined to take part in the run-off, fearing defeat and removal from power. He subsequently rejected the election results. In the run-up to the election, Savimbi had campaigned on an ethnic platform with UNITA, being primarily an Ovimbundu organisation. After rejecting the electoral outcome he appealed to ethno-nationalism and fuelled the fears of domination by the MPLA. This enabled him to command the loyalty of his UNITA forces, culminating in the re-ignition of violent conflict in January 1993. A sense of alienation in the aftermath of ethnic conflict does not facilitate post-conflict peace-building. Institutionalised exclusion through the logic of 'winner-takes-all' electoral systems further politicises ethnicity. Many commentators now believe that the only option open in Angola is for some form of power-sharing based on proportionality. The question remains of whether electoral laws can be designed and negotiated so as to reduce the intensity of ethnic rivalry. Given the power that resides in electoral systems, all the disputing parties should take part in deliberations about the types of electoral law that will determine how their various polities can be represented in a fair and equitable manner. Thus electoral systems need to become subject to negotiation if they are to serve effectively as extensions of the conflict resolution initiative.

Sustaining democracy through proportional representation in Africa

On this issue, Frank Cohen makes the argument that proportional ethnic conflict management is more sustainable than majoritarian management because it has a relative respect for the integrity of ethnic cleavages within state boundaries.[15] Rather than brush aside the politicised ethnicities, the proportional system is explicit in recognising this reality. Effectively, it makes ethnic division a visible object of negotiation and democratic management efforts. It also institutionalises these ethnic divisions, not with the purpose of entrenching them but with the aim of accommodating them in order to offset the centrifugal tension they can generate. Majoritarian systems, which assume that it is possible to cross-cut political ethnic cleavages and make them irrelevant by suppressing them, fail to acknowledge the instrumental nature of ethnic identity once it becomes activated. Proportional democratic mechanisms predicated on an ethos of power-sharing seek to include disaffected ethnic groups into a system of governance. Thus, rather than suppressing ethnic cleavages they provide channels through which the communal will can be expressed. Politicised ethnicity can only gradually be depoliticised when ethnic groups do not feel that their socioeconomic and cultural survival is not under threat. With regard to Africa and the management of ethnic conflicts, any attempt to design PR systems will always be a highly contextual exercise that should be based on the will and participation of communal and national societies. Historically, potentially inclusive governments in Francophone Africa, elected on a PR system, were often undermined by a highly centralised and overbearing presidency. To a large extent, each situation must take into account the political traditions and the degree of civic and voter education that is essential to the effectiveness of a PR system. A post-conflict democratic arrangement emerged in Namibia, with elections being carried out under a system of proportional representation. An assessment of this process shows that the PR system was particularly advantageous to smaller political parties, which would have been excluded from the assemblies elected under most of the other types of electoral system. On this basis it is evident that the PR system has a significant role to play in African politics.

In the case of collapsed states, post-conflict peace-building means confronting the challenge posed by politicised ethnicities when constructing democratic institutions which give political representation to minorities. In the quest for sustainable democracy the concern has to be to prevent a repeat of the past by ensuring the protection of minorities from majoritarian tyranny and the distribution of political power to ensure minority participation; which means providing minority groups with an apparatus for sub-national governance. There will always be disputes to be settled between groups: that is the essential nature of the political process. The question is therefore one of how these disputes can be addressed, and genuine proportionalism[16] goes some way towards making this process less violent. Extreme forms of political violence emerge when human freedom is repressed. Majoritarian institutions of democracy can, and do, generate the tension which can lead ultimately to this kind of violence and cause state disintegration; a situation that can be witnessed in the Sudan and Congo-Kinshasa.

Recent events in Burundi and Sierra Leone have demonstrated how external pressure can be placed on countries to restore democratic government. In some respects, this points to the emergence of a new way of thinking in Africa, as in other parts of the world. We are witnessing what is, in effect, the 'transnationalisation of the democratic ethos'. Increasingly with regard to collapsed states, external support will be essential if the sub-national polities are to forge any form of sustainable coexistence based on proportionality and power-sharing. Thus a qualitative shift needs to be made away from the artificial isolationism in Africa fomented by the fictional states towards a new era of mature cross-border interdependency. As Francis Deng and others note, the emphasis has to be on a framework which no longer sees 'sovereignty' as a cloaking device ensuring protection against external interference in a state's internal affairs. Rather, the state, or the political arrangement that replaces it, must be held accountable to its domestic and external constituencies. Sovereignty needs to be viewed as a responsibility – the moral responsibility of the sovereign institution towards individuals and communal groups under its jurisdiction.[17]

Conclusion

The point that Frantz Fanon was trying to make in 1963 was that the legitimacy that is necessary to engender sustainable democracy in Africa can only be based on an acknowledgement of the debilitating effects of politicised ethnicity. This chapter has discussed how politicised ethnicity can lead to the delegitimisation of the state and ultimately foment state collapse. The fragmentation of the central sovereign organisation creates a difficult challenge for the conflict resolution process and ultimately for post-conflict democratisation. This study has argued that the principles of co-operation which underpin the conflict resolution process need also to guide the building of democratic institutions. In particular, with regard to electoral systems, there needs to be a recognition that frameworks that appeal to a majoritarian first-past-the-post electoral model can do more harm than good, on the grounds that it effectively institutes governance by the largest ethnic group or coalition of ethnic groups. By disenfranchising other communal groups this can further politicise ethnicity and ultimately undermine the integrity of the state. In contrast, proportional representation systems operating within the context of a power-sharing framework can accommodate politicised ethnicity and thus strengthen the political community between different groups.

For failing, and failed, states, if the objective is to restore sustainable democracy, then sovereignty has to become more responsible. Institutional arrangements in the post-national era need to foster trust and equality among the sub-national groups in a state. The centralised nation-state that remains cocooned in contemporary thinking, and unquestioned by an international system intent on privileging an increasingly outmoded form of sovereignty, is unlikely to achieve this. There is a civil and socioeconomic crisis still afflicting many parts of Africa as we go into the new millennium. What we have essentially are states in a condition of flux. Their destinies remain uncertain. A concern with sustainable democracy needs to become a priority; only then can a progressive and mature form of overall development also become a reality.

Notes and References

1 Frantz Fanon (1963) *The Wretched of the Earth* (New York: Grove Press), p. 147.
2 Jeffrey Herbst (1997) 'Responding to State Failure in Africa', in Michael Brown (ed.), *Nationalism and Ethnic Conflict* (Cambridge, Mass: MIT Press), pp. 347–98.
3 For a general discussion, see Julius Nyerere (1963) *Democracy and the Party System* (Dar es Salaam: Tanganyika Standard).
4 Robert Jackson and Carl Rosberg (1985), 'Democracy in Tropical Africa', *Journal of International Affairs*, vol. 38, no. 2.
5 For various debates see Robert Jackson and Carl Rosberg (1982) *Personal Rule in Black Africa* (Berkeley, California: University of California Press); John Cartwright (1983) *Political Leadership in Africa* (London: Croom Helm); and Samuel Decalo (1985) 'African Personal Dictatorships', *Journal of Modern African Studies*, vol. 23, no. 2, June.
6 Samuel Decalo (1976) *Coups and Army Rule in Africa* (New Haven, Conn.: Yale University Press).
7 Claude Ake (1995) 'The Democratization of Disempowerment in Africa', in Jochen Hippler (ed.) *The Democratization of Disempowerment: The Problem of Democracy in the Third World* (London: Pluto Press), p. 73.
8 I. William Zartman (1995) 'Introduction' in I. William Zartman (ed.), *Collapsed States: The Disintegration and Restoration of Legitimate Authority* (London: Lynne Rienner).
9 David Quintal (1970) 'The Theory of Electoral Systems', *Western Political Quarterly*, vol. 73.
10 A comprehensive analysis of the detailed characteristics of these electoral systems are beyond the scope of this chapter and will not be discussed here. For a further assessment, see T. Murithi (1998) 'Electoral Systems and the

Management of Ethnic Conflict in Africa', in Andrew Dobson and Jeff Stanyer (eds), *Contemporary Political Studies* (Nottingham: Political Studies Association), pp. 14–21; and A. Lijphart and B. Grofman (1984) *Choosing an Electoral System: Issues and Alternatives* (London: Praeger).

11   A more detailed discussion of the impact of these systems on the management of ethnic conflict can be found in Frank Cohen (1997), 'Proportional Versus Majoritarian Ethnic Conflict Management in Democracies', *Comparative Political Studies*, vol. 30, no. 5.

12   Ibid.

13   For a more detailed discussion on power-sharing and proportionality in what Lijphart also refers to as 'consociational democracy', see Arend Lijphart (1969), 'Consociational Democracy', *World Politics*, vol. 21, no. 4; Arend Lijphart (1977) *Democracy in Plural Societies: A Comparative Exploration* (New Haven, Conn.: Yale University Press).

14   Anthony Pereira (1994) 'The Neglected Tragedy: The Return to War in Angola, 1992–3', *Journal of Modern African Studies*, vol. 32, no. 1.

15   Cohen, 'Proportional Versus Majoritarian'.

16   Proportional representation has been functional in a number of Francophone African states. But with national legislatures ultimately subordinate to a powerful centralised executive presidency, the benefits that could have been accrued through genuine proportionality were negated and ethnicity still determined the political distribution of resources. Thus power-sharing between national and sub-national groups was not effectively in place.

17   Francis Deng, Sadikiel Kimaro, Terrence Lyons, Donald Rothchild and William Zartman (1996) *Sovereignty as Responsibility: Conflict Management in Africa* (Washington, DC: Brookings Institution).

8

ECOWAS and Liberia: Implications for Regional Intervention in Intra-state Conflicts

*Thomas Jaye**

Introduction

Between 1990 and 1997, the Economic Community of West African States (ECOWAS) was involved in peace-making and peace-keeping in Liberia, a West African country engulfed by internecine strife. For seven years the regional body tried to resolve the conflict, convening a number of peace meetings and brokering several peace accords, only to realise that the armed factions would renege on them. The UN and the OAU were brought in to provide legitimacy, but that was not sufficient to bring the war to an immediate end. It was not until the factions became exhausted militarily, coupled with internal and external pressures, that they finally agreed to resolve the crisis through a democratic process. By this time, the war had cost 250 000 lives out of a total of 2.5 million people, the death of more than thousand peace-keepers, and the destruction of the national infrastructure and the fragile economy. The general and presidential elections of 19 July 1997 resulted in a landslide victory for Charles Taylor, a leader of one of the main warring factions, and his National Patriotic Party (NPP). This effectively marked 'the end' of the war.

ECOWAS intervened in the Liberian imbroglio as a result of both internal and external circumstances. Internally, the Liberian state had collapsed and it was carved up between rival factions who established mini-states for themselves; foreign nationals from the region and elsewhere as well as ordinary Liberians were caught in the barbed-wire of the war without security; and peace initiatives by the Inter-Faith Mediation Committee (IFMC) failed to yield fruitful results. Externally, the UN and the USA were indifferent, being preoccupied at the time with the Gulf War. The OAU proved to be incapable of intervening because of its incapacity and institutional constraints. The task of intervention fell on the shoulders of ECOWAS, with Nigeria, the regional leader, to the fore. The main purpose of this chapter is to explore and analyse whether ECOWAS's intervention constitutes a precedent in state practice. Is this the future of regional responses to situations of violent, armed intra-state conflicts in sub-Saharan Africa? I shall focus on the following issues: legality and legitimacy as they relate to state sovereignty and the non-intervention norm; and the practical problems encountered by ECOWAS in the implementation of its peace plan.

This chapter argues that the ECOWAS intervention in the Liberian imbroglio offers lessons that could be useful for future regional interventions in conflicts in sub-Saharan Africa. It also argues that, while ethnicity can be used as an explanatory variable in discussing the origins of the crisis, it is part of a larger set of factors which shaped the war. Thus, it is not *the* explanation of the origins of the crisis. As will be discussed later in the chapter an explanation has to be sought in the lack of security, in the widest sense of the word, for the vast majority of Liberians.

The chapter is divided into three main parts. The first part examines the origins of the crisis and the immediate internal and external factors that motivated ECOWAS to intervene. The second part explores the peace-making and peace-keeping role of ECOWAS; and the third part analyses the issues arising from the role of ECOWAS as well as the lessons offered by its intervention.

Context for intervention

Origins of the crisis

A detailed historical account of the origins of the crisis cannot be provided within the limits of this chapter. In fact, much has been written elsewhere on this subject and thus what follows is a summary of what I consider to be the most persistent factors that shaped the Liberian crisis. In most of what has been written, allusion is made to the more than a century of rule by the Americo-Liberian ethnic group over the amalgam of various indigenous ethnic groups and the decade of rule by Samuel K. Doe and his Krahn ethnic group. In essence, ethnicity has been employed to explain the origins of the crisis. Without doubting the validity of these claims, ethnicity is only a facet of a wider complex of factors that shaped it. I assume that the crisis can be traced to the lack of security in the widest sense of the word for the vast majority of the people. What do I mean by this, and how has it manifested itself in the Liberian context?

Traditionally, security studies have focused on its military dimension and states, but Barry Buzan has broadened it to include five dimensions – societal, economic, political, environmental and military.[1] As Ken Booth points out, though states are traditionally the primary referent of security, they are by no means the only possible candidates as primary referents. Alternatives include nations, ethnic and kinship groups, and individual human beings – and ultimately the whole (potential) global community of humankind.[2] States have been viewed as being the primary referent of security 'because traditional political theory sees them as the guardians of "their peoples" security, from external and internal threat'.[3] As will be illustrated briefly later, the Liberian state, far from being the 'guardian angel' of the Liberian people, has from one regime to another, itself served as the source of insecurity. How has this manifested itself concretely?

Prior to the outbreak of the civil war, Liberia faced problems of economic mismanagement, political repression and exclusion, and a decline in living standards at one end of the social pyramid, with luxury and opulence at the other end. In essence, Liberians lacked internal security: the lack of broader political participation, lack of access to scarce resources, adequate health care, education, employment and other basic necessities. The wealth of the country was concentrated in the hands of a very tiny stratum of society.

Attempts by various regimes to address this imbalance failed to yield any fruitful results, perhaps because they were more interested in regime security than societal security. Since the declaration of independence on 26 July 1847, the dominant theme in Liberian politics has been the hegemony of the Americo-Liberian ethnic group in every sphere of Liberian life: social, economic, political and cultural. They controlled every institution of the state, denied citizenship rights to the indigenous Africans, and the main national symbols – seal, flag, national anthem and numerous others – incorporated only the ideas of one group and negated the concerns of others.[4] Though this issue was partially addressed when citizenship was granted to indigenous Liberians and a plan of indirect rule was formulated, it was under President William V. S. Tubman that the issue was given more serious attention.

Tubman made attempts to ameliorate this cleavage through a 'unification and integration policy'. Accordingly, amendments to the Constitution were made that gave indigenous ethnic groups and women the right to vote, provided that they owned real estate or other property.[5] In addition, he created four new counties (in addition to the original five) by an Act of Legislature in 1963 and thus effectively replacing indirect rule with an incorporation of the hinterland into the Liberian body politic. As laudable as these changes were, Tubman's twenty seven years of rule were marked by an obsession with regime security. Sycophancy permeated the fabric of Liberian officialdom to the extent that deductions were made on an annual basis to finance the birthday celebrations of the president. Opposition was not countenanced and a reign of terror was instituted to intimidate those opposed to his rule.

Tubman died in 1971 and was replaced by his vice-president, William R. Tolbert, Jr, in keeping with the terms of the Liberian constitution. The latter came to power at a time when the country was afflicted by serious social, economic and political problems. As E. Dunn and S. Byron Tarr point out, among the numerous national problems, Tolbert needed to address the issues of economic inequities between the haves and the have-nots, as well as dealing with the political pre-eminence of the core [Americo-Liberian elite].[6] Tolbert promised to raise the Liberian people from 'mats to mattresses', build a 'wholesome functioning society' and carry them to 'higher heights'. Furthermore, he reduced the numbers involved in the security network, but despite these efforts geared towards societal security, he also privileged regime security over societal security.

Perhaps a few examples would be useful here: first, when a newspaper criticised his brother Steve A. Tolbert (then finance minister) for unscrupulous business activities, the president banned the paper and harassed its editors. Second, when his government proposed an increase in the price of rice, it sparked a mass demonstration in Monrovia which was brutally crushed and left more than a hundred people dead and several others wounded. Third, he cancelled the Monrovia mayoral elections in which, for the first time in more than four decades, a True Whig Party (TWP) candidate was challenged by an opposition candidate.

On the economic front, he assumed power at a time of decline in the demand for the country's key export commodities – iron ore and rubber. Despite this, he pursued wasteful ventures and his administration was marred by mismanagement and corruption. Evidence of this is the fact that he spent more than $100 million to host the 16th Summit of the OAU. At the time of his rule, the disparity between rich and poor was high. It is estimated that about 4 per cent of the population controlled more than 65 per cent of the wealth. Similarly, the average annual income for urban dwellers was $600, while that of their rural counterparts was $75.[7] In a critique of Tolbert's claims to uphold societal security, Amos Sawyer argues that Tolbert was only committed to the protection of civil liberties and the promotion of an open society as long as his own actions and those of his relatives were not subjected to close scrutiny.[8]

These growing disparities did not only lead to pressure for more political participation and the call for social changes, but the content of Liberian politics changed. Sawyer points out that:

> the crucial question was not simply larger receipts from the distributive capabilities of the society. More importantly, it was a demand for a redefinition of the structure and process of decision-making governing society. In other words, what was being called into question in the 1970s was not just how the pie should be divided but also who should decide how the pie should be divided.[9]

As the democratic forces in Liberia tried to find a peaceful solution to this Liberian puzzle, seventeen enlisted military men led by Samuel K. Doe assassinated Tolbert on 12 April 1980 and overthrew the True Whig Party (TWP) regime. This made Doe the first indigenous leader of Liberia after 133 years of political independence.

The coup was welcomed by many because they thought that it would pave the way towards addressing the social, economic and political problems the country was facing. But the decade that followed proved to be even more difficult, brutal and disappointing. According to the new ruling People's Redemption Council (PRC), the coup was necessitated by corruption; abuse of power; unemployment; disregard for civil, human and constitutional rights of the ordinary citizens; illegal detention; illegal search; and others.[10] Significantly, a broad-based government was formed comprising both civilians and military officers. Despite the promise of a new era, the Doe regime, like its predecessors, reverted to regime security. A few cases will illustrate this.

First, barely a month and day after the coup (on 13 May 1980), thirteen officials of the previous regime were publicly executed before television cameras. Second, three soldiers were executed for looting and eight others sent to a maximum security prison – Belle Yella – for harassing citizens.[11] Third, in August 1981, five members of the PRC, including the vice head of state, Thomas Weh-Syen, were tried in a kangaroo court and summarily executed for allegedly plotting to overthrow the Doe regime. Fourth, on 22 August 1984, 200 soldiers marched on to the campus of the University of Liberia, attacked students, raping female students and employees. An unknown number of students died. The only crime committed by the students was a protest demonstration against the Doe regime for arresting and detaining university lecturers who were allegedly involved in a coup plot. Fifth, between 1981 and 1984 the regime clamped down on the press, closing down the *Daily Observer* newspaper four times and arresting its editor for writing antagonistic articles. Finally, after the general elections of October 1985, which Doe won, transforming himself from a military to a civilian leader, his erstwhile commanding general of the Army, Thomas Quiwonkpa, led an abortive invasion on 12 November 1985 from Sierra Leone. About 2000 Gio and Mano people were killed, and Quiwonkpa was beaten beyond recognition, castrated and dismembered.[12]

These events had wider implications for what was to occur later in Liberia. They did not only mark a departure from the promise to respect human, civil and constitutional rights of individuals, but they also served as triggers that shaped the origins of the seven-year-old civil war. Between 1980 and 1990, the regime declined into a state of security paranoia, removing real and imagined enemies. As Sam Amoo contends, while repression and violence existed in Liberia's political life before the advent of the military regime, Doe and his cabal took these to a pathological level. Murder, torture and incarceration became the predominant instruments of governance: it was not enough to kill political opponents, they also had to be tortured and quartered.[13]

The Doe years were also characterised by mismanagement, favouritism and the decline of the living standards of the vast majority of the people. Corruption became rampant even by Liberian standards, with much of the aid monies disappearing into the personal accounts of Doe and other members of his government.[14] Doe had a private jet to whisk him to his appointments.[15] One of those implicated in this act of national robbery was the Liberian president at the time of writing, Charles Taylor. He was arrested in May 1984 in the USA after having been charged with embezzling $1 million dollars.[16] All this was happening when government employees went for months at times without pay. A negative factor that affected the Doe era was the fact that, at the time of his rule, there was sharp decline in Liberia's export sector, the country could not meet its financial obligations internationally, which made credit difficult; and public expenditure was high. Even when the government reduced public employment and salaries of government employees by an average of 20 per cent in 1983, and 25 per cent across the board in 1985, the country still remained a shambles economically.[17]

Furthermore, because of Liberia's liberal investment incentives, in keeping with which 65 per cent of goods imported were duty-free, it is estimated that some $50 million was owed in tax arrears at the end of 1985; state enterprises faced mounting managerial and financial problems, and the collective indebtedness for which the government was responsible amounted to approximately $115 million in May 1985.[18] One should not forget the fact that many of Liberia's problems of the 1980s derived from the excesses of the Tolbert and even the Tubman eras, as well as from the drop in prices for the country's key export.[19]

The civil war and the collapse of the Liberian state

It is against the above lack of security that war broke out on 24 December 1989. Between that period and July 1990 the entire Liberian state collapsed, ordinary people – Liberians and non-Liberians alike – lacked physical security let alone other dimensions of security for their daily survival. They were at the mercy of the marauding armed factions and government troops. Doe, the beleaguered president, characterised the situation:

> in the suburbs of Monrovia thousands have been displaced by the NPFL forces, homes have been destroyed, hundreds slaughtered even before their dubious victory is achieved. I am therefore concerned that the fighting could accelerate in Monrovia and thus inflame the suffering of the people of Liberia.[20]

In addition, according to Martin Luwenkopf, by August, some fifty to sixty people were dying each day from disease and starvation.[21] Bodies littered the city as each side of the conflict targeted its real and perceived enemies.

By July 1990, all semblance of civil authority within Liberia had ceased to exist, with rebel forces (which by then had fractured into rival factions) holding the whole of Liberia except the capital, Monrovia.[22] As Martin Luwenkopf points out:

> in Liberia, not only is 'the state as a legitimate functioning order' absent, but society in general has been shattered, the nation fragmented, the population dispersed, and the economy ruined. In addition, in the absence of a state, neither order nor power nor legitimacy has devolved to local groups (although several existing organisations could evolve in that way). Both the reality and symbols of power are

up for grabs among several Liberian armed factions fighting one another.[23]

With the collapse of central authority in Liberia, the legislative, executive and judicial branches of government ceased to function. The rival armed factions carved up the state between themselves, creating kinds of mini-states and establishing their own laws. Liberian sovereignty was compromised because the state, territoriality and independence are associated with sovereignty. Sovereignty also refers to legal supremacy within a given territory. Turning to the state, according to John Agnew and Stuart Corbidge, the two aspects that define it are its exercise of power through a set of central institutions, and a clear spatial demarcation of a territory within which the state exercises its power.[24] All of this vanished under the heels of the civil war.

Externally, the eruption of the civil war in Liberia coincided with the collapse of Eastern Europe, the end of the Cold War, and the eruption of the Gulf War. The UN's initial attitude to Liberia's problems was one of indifference and according to W. Ofuatey-Kodjoe, the unwillingness of the UN to intervene was because of its preoccupation with the Gulf War, and later with conflicts in the former Yugoslavia and Somalia, and the perception that the Liberian situation was not a serious threat to general international peace and security.[25] Further, attempts to discuss the issue at the Security Council were blocked by African members of the body at the time, including the Ivory Coast, which was supportive of the NPFL. Perhaps these African states did not want to set a precedent that could apply to them in the future. It was on 19 November 1990 that the Security Council adopted Resolution 788, imposing an arms embargo and commending ECOWAS for its peace efforts. Thereafter, it established UN Observer Mission in Liberia (UNOMIL) and actively cooperated with the OAU and ECOWAS in peace making and peace keeping exercises.

OAU dignitaries attended all meetings of ECOWAS at which the Liberian crisis was discussed and in which decisions were made. However, the organisation was still locked into its fervent adherence to the principles of non-interference in internal matters. Nevertheless, it did not condemn the ECOWAS initiative; that it welcomed it clearly indicates that under changed international conditions, the organisation was prepared to adopt a flexible attitude to the non-intervention norm.

Given the so-called 'traditional ties' between the USA and Liberia, it was widely thought that the former would have used its leverage to bring the situation under control by bringing the parties to a negotiated settlement, if necessary by force. On the contrary, however, the USA sent in its marines to airlift its citizens and other nationals to nearby ships anchored off the shores of Monrovia.

From its inception, the Inter-Faith Mediation Committee – a consortium of Muslim and Christian leaders – tried to negotiate a settlement to the dispute, but their efforts proved fruitless. As the situation deteriorated inside Liberia to unimaginable anarchy, with great loss of life and ungovernability, refugees fled in droves into neighbouring countries. It was estimated that by March the figure had reached 60 000 in the Ivory Coast and 84 000 in Guinea with about 1000 people leaving Liberia on a weekly basis.[26] It was under these macabre internal conditions plus the indifference of the UN and the USA to the crisis that ECOWAS intervened.

ECOWAS's peace efforts in Liberia 1990–7

Between 1990 and 1997 ECOWAS, joined later by the UN and the OAU, employed both peacemaking and peacekeeping methods to resolve the Liberian conflict. This process went through three main stages, as follows: Standing Mediation Committee (SMC) period – May 1990–May 1991; Yamoussokro period, June 1991–June 1993; and Cotonou period, July 1993–July 1997. Given the limited length of this chapter, I shall briefly outline the features and key developments that characterised each period.

The SMC period, May 1990–May 1991

In the first period the following incidents occurred:

- The ECOWAS Monitoring Group (ECOMOG) was deployed amid opposition from Charles Taylor's NPFL and thus there were clashes between ECOMOG and the NPFL. ECOMOG was therefore, from the very first day, involved in enforcement action.
- The incumbent Liberian president, Samuel K. Doe, was captured at the ECOMOG headquarters by the rival Independent National Patriotic Front of Liberia (INPFL), a breakaway faction of the NPFL.
- An Interim Government of National Unity (IGNU) was formed in Banjul, The Gambia, headed by Amos C. Sawyer, much to the chagrin of Taylor.
- The first ever extraordinary session of ECOWAS was convened in Bamako, Mali, where the ECOWAS peace plan was adopted unan-

imously by member states in the presence of OAU and UN dignitaries, and the NPFL, the Armed Forces of Liberia (AFL) and INPFL
signed a ceasefire agreement to be monitored by ECOMOG.

Despite these developments, Taylor remained intransigent, with active
support from Burkina Faso. Taylor's intransigence stemmed partly from
a lack of trust in the Nigerian-led peacekeeping force and, more importantly, Taylor wanted nothing short of the presidency.

Yamoussokro period, June 1991–June 1993[27]

This period was ushered in against a background of continuing dissatis-
faction from some French-speaking countries, who expressed reservations about the operation. Consequently, President Felix Houphouet
Boigny, who was believed to be a supporter of Taylor, was brought in,
as a way of getting the French-speaking countries actively involved in
the peace process. The following developments occurred during this
period:

- The SMC was replaced by a Committee of Five headed by the Ivory
  Coast.
- Senegal contributed troops after they were induced by a financial
  package offered by the USA, including $15 million-worth of military
  equipment from the Pentagon and the forgiveness of Senegal's $42
  million public debt by the USA.[28]
- Taylor was forced personally to attend the peace meetings or risk
  losing the support of the Ivory Coast.
- The Carter Centre became involved in the peace process.
- The NPFL attacked Monrovia in 'Operation Octopus' in October 1992
  but was repulsed by the joint efforts of ECOMOG, the AFL, and the
  Black Berets.
- The new armed faction, the United Liberation Movement for Democracy in Liberia (ULIMO) emerged, challenging Taylor's military positions in south-western Liberia.

Cotonou period, July 1993–19 July 1997

This was the most decisive phase of the peace process, in which the
following events occurred:

- Given the continuous intransigence of the NPFL, the UN and the
  OAU were brought in to buttress the position of ECOWAS more
  actively.

- IGNU was replaced by Liberia National Transitional Governments I and i i, and the Council of State (COS), with Sawyer stepping aside for three successive interim leaders.
- New armed factions emerged, including the Liberia Peace Council (LPC), Central Revolutionary Council (CRC) – a breakaway faction of the NPFL, Lofa Defence Force (LDF), and ULIMO split into two camps – ULIMO(J) and ULIMO(K).
- The leaders of the armed faction became members of the ruling interim council of state in order to shoulder the responsibility of bringing peace to the country.
- General and presidential elections were convened, which brought Taylor, a leader of one of the armed factions, to power. Coupled with the lack of demobilisation and complete disarmament, this ushered in a fragile peace for Liberia.

ECOWAS intervention: an analysis

Rationales for the intervention

The ECOWAS intervention has been justified on two grounds: humanitarianism and regional security. It was argued that a state of anarchy and the total breakdown of law and order existed in Liberia. Further, that there was a government in Liberia that could not govern, and contending factions were holding the entire population hostage, depriving them of food, health facilities and other basic necessities of life. It was as a result of this that the heads of states and governments of the ECOWAS Standing Mediation Committee met in Banjul on 6–7 August 1990 and decided to assume the responsibility of ensuring that peace and stability was maintained within the sub-region and African continent, as they believed that the tragic situation in Liberia posed a threat to international peace and security.[29] But did these reasons constitute any justification for the ECOWAS intervention?

First, there is the issue of the humanitarian grounds for intervention. In the contemporary era, when state sovereignty has been challenged by concern for the protection of basic human rights, can one argue that there is a right for others to intervene in the internal affairs of a state that commits unbearable crimes against its subjects? Do states have the right to conduct genocide within their borders with impunity? This brings into focus issues of norms, ethics and morality in international relations. Since the end of the Cold War, the intervention of the allied forces in Northern Iraq to provide a 'safe haven' for the Kurds, and the US-led intervention into Somalia, have come under the rubric of humanitarian intervention. These may have set specific precedents in their own way but yet they do signify that such a right exists.

In the Liberian case, human lives were lost on a mass scale, bodies were littered around the capital, and there was gross abuse and violation of human rights. Furthermore, the fact that Doe, Taylor and Johnson did not have any effective control over Liberia made the humanitarian argument stronger. The prevailing anarchy and carnage provided moral grounds for the intervention. Buttressing the humanitarian argument put forward by ECOWAS is the fact that, on arrival, ECOMOG provided a buffer zone, performed relief work, and distributed food and medicines.[30] Moreover, there was an outflow of approximately 1.3 million refugees, who sought refuge in neighbouring countries.[31]

Second, there is the issue of regional security. Because ECOWAS did not define clearly what was meant by 'regional security', it posed more difficulties in justifying the intervention on that ground. But mention is made about the possible spill-over effects of the conflict. The number of refugees fleeing the country was huge, and this posed a threat to the already crumbling economies of the host countries. But arguably most, if not all, of the assistance provided to refugees came from the United Nations High Commission for Refugees (UNHCR) and humanitarian NGOs. Nonetheless, the involvement of nationals from other West African states in the NPFL operations was seen by ECOWAS as a conspiracy to destabilise the region.

This posed a threat to the regimes in the region because it set a precedent wherein civilians could take up arms against them. The role of Colonel Qadafi, President of Libya, further fuelled this fear. The initial cohort of NPFL rebels who invaded Liberia were trained in Libya. Confirming this spill-over fear is the fact that the Revolutionary United Front (RUF) backed by Taylor's NPFL invaded Sierra Leone in 1991. Moreover, soldiers who returned from ECOMOG operations in Liberia seized power in Sierra Leone and the Gambia. In January 1999 the RUF and the deposed junta forces of Johnny Koroma invaded Freetown, the capital of Sierra Leone, and this led to deaths and the destruction of property.[32] These long-term results could serve to justify the regional security fears expressed by ECOWAS.

Legality and legitimacy

The ECOWAS intervention has come under legal scrutiny. According to Anthony C. Ofodile, the intervention was illegal on three grounds: first, there is no right to humanitarian intervention, especially when state(s) act outside the auspices of the Security Council; second, the intervention exceeded purely humanitarian intervention and thus required the consent of the warring factions and prior UN authorisation, neither of which was obtained; and finally, the Community could not justify its action under the Protocol of Mutual Assistance on Defence (PMAD) because consensus was not obtained before the intervention.[33] Similarly, Kofi Oteng Kufuor argues that the 'intervention of ECOWAS was unlawful because it involved interference in the exercise of the functions of the sovereignty of the Liberian people' and that it is prohibited by the non-intervention principle.[34]

Without doubt, the legal issues raised by these authors are significant. However, they are raised out of context. Significantly, legal experts are divided over the permissibility of humanitarian intervention and as much as it is desired, state practice has yet to accept it. Clearly, Article 2(4) restrains state(s) from the threat or use of force against the 'territorial integrity or political independence' of any state, and Article 2(7) restrains intervention in 'matters that are essentially within the domestic jurisdiction of any state'. However, given the fact that the Liberian state had collapsed at the time of the intervention, it does not seem plausible to invoke these articles. Both the territorial integrity and independence of Liberia had been tampered with by the war. The country was carved up by the warlords and none of them seemed to have had any authority to rule the country. Similarly, though the matter was internal it manifested demonstrable transboundary repercussions. Thus, it could not be regarded as being essentially within the domestic jurisdiction of a state. After all, the very state had already collapsed as a result of the civil war. To reiterate a point raised earlier, a state exercises its power through central political institutions and a clear spatial demarcation of a territory within which the power is exercised.[35] At the height of the war, none of this existed. More importantly, part of ECOMOG's mission to Liberia was to restore the territorial integrity and political independence of Liberia, and not to violate it, as these critics would have us believe.

Moreover, while the intervention had no prior UN authorisation, the UN was not only informed regularly as required under Article 54, but the Security Council belatedly welcomed the peace efforts of ECOWAS. As Georg Nolte points out, the 'existence of a valid invitation (from the beleaguered President S. K. Doe) to ECOWAS served to avoid violations of both Article 2(4) of the Charter and the Principle of non-intervention. Even if an invitation alone would not suffice it may be possible to justify the intervention on the grounds that Taylor's rebellion was supported by other states'.[36] Under such conditions, Doe had the right to invite friendly state(s) to assist in repelling the externally backed invasion.

The problem with the applicability of the provisions of the PMAD had less do with the lack of consensus, as Ofodile implies, but with the fact that its provisions had never been implemented and there was no mechanism in place for this: there was no Allied Armed Forces of the Community (AAFC), as member states had not earmarked troops for it, and a Defence Council or Defence Commission did not exist at the time.[37] The PMAD clearly stipulates that ECOWAS member states shall take appropriate measures if it is found that an internal armed conflict within a member state is engineered or actively supported by external force(s), especially if such support constitutes a threat to the security and peace of the community. If community forces should decide to intervene, then, in keeping with Section II, Articles 7, 8, 9 and 13, a Defence Council comprising ministers of defence and foreign affairs will meet for the purpose of examining the situation. If need be, an Allied Armed Forces of the Community will be established. Unfortunately, none of these could be put in place and thus the SMC, and not the Authority of Heads of State of the Community, had to improvise. This gave birth to ECOMOG, which, as indicated earlier, was agreed upon by the extraordinary session of ECOWAS convened in Bamako, Mali in November 1990.

Given the reasons mentioned above, according to Abass Bundu (former Executive Secretary of ECOWAS), the legal mandate for the intervention had to be found outside the PMAD. Consequently, two grounds were advanced: (i) humanitarian intervention – rescue of ECOWAS citizens and other foreign nationals who were trapped in the conflict without security – and by the time of the intervention, the Doe Government's writ did not run beyond Monrovia; and (ii) once a cease-fire had been established (at Bamako in November 1990), ECOMOG was charged with responsibility for peace-keeping, restoration of law and order, and ensuring respect for the ceasefire.[38] Others could argue that ECOWAS could have evacuated their citizens and other foreign nationals (as the USA had done) and leave the resolution of the crisis to the Liberian people. Such an argument would be unfounded in every respect. Once they arrived in Liberia, the troops had a moral responsibility to help ordinary Liberians who lacked physical security in the midst of the anarchy and carnage. This explains why several thousand Liberians were evacuated to neighbouring West African countries while the peace process continued. Moreover, the signing of the ceasefire agreement by all the parties to the conflict meant that effectively they accepted the peacekeeping role of ECOMOG in Liberia.

Moreover, the fact that Libya, Burkina Faso and Ivory Coast, along with dissidents from the West African region, actively supported the NPFL invasion could provide legal grounds for the ECOWAS intervention in keeping with the provisions of the PMAD. Both the Ivory Coast and Burkina Faso had breached protocols by supporting, encouraging and condoning acts of aggression against a member state – Liberia.

As a regional organisation under Article 52 of the UN Charter, ECO-WAS had the right to take the initiative in maintaining peace and security in the region but with prior UN authorisation, which was given tacitly by its silence over the intervention and its subsequent approval. However, the OAU's moral support of the initiative could be counted as also legitimising the intervention. Salim A. Salim, argued that the

> most desirable thing would have been to have an agreement of all parties to the conflict and the convergence of views of all the members of ECOWAS. But to argue that there was no legal base for any intervention in Liberia is surprising. Should the countries in West Africa, should Africa just leave the Liberians to fight each other? Will that be more legitimate? Will that be more understandable? In my frank opinion the decision of the ECOWAS countries to despatch a peace-keeping force or a monitoring group was a timely and bold decision.[39]

On the one hand, Salim admits irregularities, but on the other he strongly supports the intervention. Added to the above is the fact that the decision to intervene was partly influenced by the Inter-Faith Mediation Committee and prominent Liberians. Even though the intervention was characterised by procedural irregularities, it can be justified legally under the ECOWAS protocols as well as on the grounds of humanitarianism and regional security, the two reasons advanced by ECOWAS for its intervention. In the situation ECOWAS faced, it was necessary to make decisions based on political necessity, rather than to be held down by the weight of procedural matters while thousands of people were dying and others fleeing the country. As Ademola Adeleke points out, to 'focus on legalism is to ignore the security and humanitarian problems which the civil war created for the states of the region and the Liberian people'.[40]

Problems of the ECOWAS intervention

The ECOWAS peace efforts faced enormous problems, but for the purposes of this chapter a mention of the most salient ones will suffice. The first major problem encountered by the peacekeeping forces was the fierce opposition by and intransigence of the NPFL. Later, when other armed factions emerged, not only was there distrust among them but their interests also became irreconcilable. The scope of the conflict widened and its dimension deepened. However getting the factions committed to the peace process was very difficult. Significantly, by the time of the intervention, the NPFL claimed more than 90 per cent of Liberian territory, but this balance changed after a year, when its position was challenged by ULIMO, and in later years by the LPC and other factions.[41] The peacekeeping forces became embroiled in the conflict by supporting different factions. For example, Nigeria was accused of supporting the LPC, while Guinea was accused of supporting ULIMO (K).

Another problem was that there was no consensus among the states of the region at the time of the intervention. Several francophone states opposed the deployment of ECOMOG while other states queried the criteria used to determine the choice of Liberia for a peacekeeping initiative. They felt that they had not been consulted sufficiently.[42] More specifically, Ivory Coast and Burkina Faso, which were believed to be supporters of the NPFL, vehemently opposed the initiative. This initial oversight of the lack of consensus was bound to haunt the operation throughout the peace efforts. Thus the Bamako extraordinary session referred to earlier did serve to put a lid on the cleavage.

Then there were command and control problems. For example, Sierra Leone had less peacekeeping experience, while for The Gambia, this was the army's first outside experience. Though Nigeria and Ghana had more experience, the latter favoured more traditional peace-keeping methods, while the Nigerians were interested in enforcement.[43] As Margaret Vogt points out, though Nigeria provided over 10 000 of the troops and provided 70 per cent of the funding, other troop-contributing states insisted that the use and deployment of their forces were authorised by them. The ECOWAS Secretariat exercised no control authority over ECOMOG, while the force commander received instructions from his home government.[44]

Closely tied in with this was the problem of logistics. As ECOWAS could not meet the logistics requirement of the troops adequately from a central fund, the burden fell on to the shoulders of the troop-contributing states, thus putting a strain on their already weak and fragile economies. As David Francis points out in Chapter 9 of this volume, the USA contributed to ECOMOG operations, including $31 million to Ugandan and Tanzanian peace-keepers sent to buttress ECOMOG's strength, and $75 million military assistance to individual ECOMOG countries. The impact of the lack of logistics on the operation was explained by General Olurin, fifth field commander of ECOMOG, who said:

> The lack of centralised logistics has inherent command and control problems for the Commander. Besides, it is bad for morale of troops who share the same accommodation or office or check points to have different standards of feeding and welfare amenities.[45]

It is this lack of logistics and sufficient funds that delayed the deployment of additional troops from Uganda, Tanzania and Zimbabwe. The African peace-keeping initiative in Chad in 1981–2 suffered a similar experience.

Conclusion

From the foregoing, the ECOWAS intervention has wider implications for regional peace-keeping in the post-cold war era. The intervention sets several precedents. First, as Robert Mortimer points out, it clearly sets 'a precedent for collective action, however tortuous its course in Liberia, has been set, and it may enable the region's states to navigate more surely in the post-Cold War waters'.[46] Second, it sets a precedent wherein regional organisations, without UN sanctions, can intervene forcibly in intrastate conflicts and yet acquire a belated endorsement. Third, it suggests that the UN can play second fiddle to regional bodies like ECOWAS. The indifference of the UN to the Liberian crisis could also reflect that state sovereignty and non-intervention are still strong within UN practice. Fourth, it challenges the principles and governing norms that the UN has adopted over the years, including non-intervention and the enforcement of international laws. Finally, though, Herbert Howe concludes that ECOMOG's efforts largely failed[47] and, similarly, Sam Amoo feels that the ECOMOG experience does not augur well for regional intervention in internal conflicts, and that a 'sub-region in turmoil should not be expected to monitor itself'[48], what are important are the lessons learned from ECOMOG and their implications for regional intervention in intra-state armed violent conflicts in sub-Saharan Africa. On the significance of the ECOWAS intervention, James Mayall writes:

politically ECOWAS has survived and has provided the required cloak of legitimacy for a regional peacekeeping force in the Liberian civil war. This operation may not have been an unqualified success, but at a time when neither the OAU nor the United Nations were willing to get involved, it has at least bought some time in which to check the slide into barbarism and anarchy and, optimistically, work out a viable political solution.[49]

The intervention has brought to the fore a vital problem in African geopolitics – the issue of consensus. If a consensus is not reached among member states of regional bodies, as was the case with ECOWAS, regional intervention can lead to inter-state rifts. This has the potential of weakening the prospects for regional solidarity. In the specific Liberian case, some francophone West African states disagreed about the intervention. Two of these states – the Ivory Coast and Burkina Faso – were supportive of the NPFL rebels, whereas the remaining states were committed to the ECOWAS Peace plan. Consequently, the effective implementation of the peace plan and peace efforts was hamstrung by the rivalry and thereby helped to prolong the war.

On the one hand, the Liberian experience indicates that if the agreement of parties to a conflict is not fully solicited before intervention, it can have long-term negative effects. In Somalia, the UN faced similar embarrassment when Mohammed Aideed was earmarked out for opposition. In the Liberian case, Taylor and his NPFL were singled out, thus placing the neutrality of the peace-keeping forces in question. If intervening forces are not careful, they can be drawn into a war as partisans rather than mediators or concilators. One accusation against ECOWAS is that it was partisan to the war in Liberia. Nevertheless, the fact that peace-keeping is a political action means that such accusations should always be expected no matter how neutral a peace-keeping force tries to be.

On the other hand, the Liberian case also proves that, with a strong political will buttressed by justified motives, regional organisations such as ECOWAS can intervene in internal disputes even without the consent of the armed factions. This involves risks, but as the Liberian case has proved, if the ordinary people, who are also key actors in any civil war, welcome the intervening force, that can help to consolidate its position and lead to some success.

In conclusion, as the book is about Africa in the new millennium, perhaps it would be good to make the point that despite the problems mentioned above, the ECOWAS experience provides lessons that can be useful for future regional intervention in Africa. The intervention can be justified within the context of the external and internal historical conditions in which it occurred. There was international indifference to the conflict, and, internally, there was general anarchy, ungovernability in the country as evidenced by the fact that neither Doe nor Taylor nor Johnson could establish effective authority and control over the country. The Liberian state and government had collapsed and thousands of people were starving, dying and suffering without anyone to provide security for them. Regional humanitarian intervention was the desirable and preferred action in a desperate situation for the thousands of innocent and ordinary Liberians and non-Liberian caught in the war. Significantly, the future of regional intervention, to a large extent, depends on the creation of a secure community which, among other things, will take into cognisance the establishment of the necessary institutional and preventive mechanisms for conflict management and resolution. This means that at both regional and national levels, societal and human security should be taken seriously or regional bodies will need to spend much-needed resources on managing intra-state conflicts. As laudable as the ECOMOG experience is, its hard lessons reveal that the process can be frustrating, it can drain fragile national economies, threaten regional security, and cost human lives.

Notes and References

*   Thomas Jaye is a doctoral candidate at the Dept of International Politics, University of Wales, Aberystwyth. This is a revised version of a work originally presented at the 'Seminar on Internal Conflict Management and International Relations Theory after the Cold War' organised by the Centre for Peace and Conflict Research, Copenhagen, Denmark, 15 March 1996. It draws on data contained in his PhD thesis.

1   See B. Buzan (1983) *People, States and Fear* (Brighton: Harvester Wheatsheaf).

2   K. Booth (1993) 'A Security Regime in Southern Africa: Theoretical Considerations', Paper presented at the conference on 'Security, Development and Co-operation in Southern Africa' organised by the Foundation for Development and Peace (Bonn), the Peace Research Institute (Frankfurt) and the Centre for Southern African Studies (Cape Town), held at Midgard, Namibia, 23–27 May, p. 6.

3   Ibid.

4   George Klay Kieh, Jr. (1992) 'Liberia: The Search for Democracy', Unpublished keynote speech delivered on the occasion of the 145th independence celebration of the Republic of Liberia and the second installation programme of the Conference of Liberian Organisations in the Southwest United States, held on 25 July in Tulsa, Oklahoma, p. 8.

5   Earl Conteh-Morgan and Shireen E. Kadivar (1995) 'Ethnopolitical Violence in the Liberian Civil War', *Journal of Conflict Studies*, Spring, p. 37.

6   E. Dunn and S. Byron Tarr (1988) *Liberia: National Polity in Transition* (Metuchen, NJ: Scarecrow Press), p. 75.

7   George K. Kieh Jr. (1992) 'Combatants, Patrons, Peacemakers, and the Liberian Civil Conflict', *Studies in Conflict and Terrorism*, vol. xv, no. 2, April–June, p. 128.

8   A. Sawyer (1992) *The Emergence of Autocracy in Liberia: Tragedy and Challenge* (San Francisco, California: Institute of Contemporary Studies Press), p. 291.

9   A. Sawyer (1987) *Effective Immediately, Dictatorship in Liberia 1980–1986: A Personal Perspective*, Liberian Working Group Paper No. 5, Bremen, p. 2.

10   Samuel K. Doe (1986) 'First Nationwide Broadcast, 14 April 1980', in Willie A. Givens (ed.), *Liberia: The Road to Democracy* (Abbotsbrook, Bourne End, Bucks: Kensal Press), p. 16.

11   J. Gus Liebenow (1987) *Liberia: The Quest for Democracy* (Bloomington and Indianapolis, Indiana: Indiana University Press), p. 192.

12   William O'Neil (1993) 'Liberia: Avoidable Tragedy', *Current History*, May, p. 214.

13   Sam G. Amoo (1993), 'ECOWAS in Liberia: The Challenges and Prospects for African Peacekeeping', Paper prepared for presentation at a conference of the Defence Intelligence College at Alconbury Royal Air Force Base, Cambridge, England, 6–7 May.

14   O'Neil 'Liberia: Avoidable Tragedy', p. 214.

15   *Best Friends: Human Rights Violations in Liberia, America's Closest Ally in Africa*, A Fund For Free Expression Report (New York: Fund For Free Expression), May 1986, p. 11.

16   See Keesing's Report vol. xxx, June 1984, p. 32898. Taylor was then Director General of the General Services Agency (GSA), the sole purchaser of government equipment and materials.

17   United Nations Development Programme, Fourth Country Programme for Liberia. 8 October 1986, in Marc Weller (ed.) (1994) *Regional Peace-Keeping and International Enforcement: The Liberian Crisis* (Cambridge: Cambridge University Press), pp. 26–7.

18   Ibid., pp. 25–6.

19   Liebenow, *The Quest for Democracy* p. 211.

20   Letter dated 14 July 1990 addressed by President Samuel K. Doe to the Chairman and Members of the Ministerial Meeting of the ECOWAS Standing Mediation Committee, Official Journal of the ECOWAS, vol. 21, November 1991, p. 6.

21   Martin Luwenkopf (1995) 'Liberia', in I William Zartman (ed.) *Collapsed States: The Distintegration and Restoration of Legitimate Authority* (Boulder, Col.: London: Lynne Rienner), p. 95.

22   D. Whippman (1993) 'Enforcing the Peace: ECOWAS and the Liberian Civil War', in Lori Fisler Damrosch (ed.), *Enforcing Restraint. Collective Intervention in Internal Conflicts* (New York: Council on Foreign Relations Press), p. 158.

23   Luwenkopf 'Liberia' p. 95.

24   J. Agnew and Stuart Corbidge (1995) *Mastering Space: Hegemony, Territory and International Political Economy* (New York: Routledge), p. 78.

25   W. Ofuatey-Kodjoe (1994) 'Regional Organisations and the Resolution of Internal Conflict: The ECOWAS Intervention in Liberia', *International Peacekeeping*, vol. 1 no. 3, Autumn, p. 270.

26 *West Africa*, 12–18 March 1990, p. 407.
27 For all practical purposes, by June 1992 the Yamoussokro period had come to an end but because no major peace effort occurred between that date and June 1993, I have decided to stretch the Yamoussokro period further.
28 Robert A. Mortimer (1996) 'ECOMOG, Liberia, and Regional Security in West Africa', in Edmond J. Keller and Donald Rothchild (eds), *Africa in the New International Order. Rethinking State Sovereignty and Regional Security* (London; Boulder, Col.: Lynne Rienner), p. 155.
29 Final communiqué of the First Session of the Community Standing Mediation Committee, Banjul, The Gambia, 6–7 August 1990, Official Journal of the ECOWAS, vol. 21, November 1991, p. 42.
30 *West Africa*, 8–14 October, 1990, p. 2631.
31 D. Sarroshi (1993) *Humanitarian Intervention and International Humanitarian Assistance: Law and Practice*, Wilton Park Paper No. 86 (London: HMSO), p. 12.
32 Details of the Sierra Leonean case has been provided in this chapter by David Francis.
33 See Anthony Chukwuka Ofodile (1994) 'The Legality of ECOWAS Intervention in Liberia', *Columbia Journal of Transnational Law*, vol. 32, no. 2.
34 Kofi Oteng Kufuor (1993) 'The Legality of the Intervention in the Liberian Civil War by the Economic Community of West African States', *African Journal of International and Comparative Law*, vol. 5, no. 3, pp. 550–1.
35 See Agnew and Corbidge, *Mastering Space*, p. 78.
36 Georg Nolte (1993) 'Restoring Peace by Regional Action: International Legal Aspects of the Liberian Conflict', *Zeitscherift Fur Auslandisches Offentliches Recht Und Volkerrecht*, vol. 53, no. 3, p. 627.
37 Abass Bundu (1997) 'ECOWAS: Conflict Management in Liberia and Sierra Leone', Unpublished paper delivered to the Aberystwyth Forum on Humanitarian Affairs, University of Wales, Aberystwyth, 20 November, p. 2.
38 Ibid., p. 3.
39 Salim A. Salim (1990) Interview *West Africa*, 22–28 October p. 2691.
40 Ademola Adeleke Ademola (1995), 'The Politics and Diplomacy of Peacekeeping in West Africa: The ECOWAS Operation in Liberia', *The Journal of Modern African Studies*, vol. 33, no. 4, p. 587 (emphasis added).
41 For details on this problem and the factors that shaped it, see George Klay Kieh Jr., (1994) 'The Obstacles to the Peaceful Resolution of the Liberian Conflict', *Studies in Conflict and Terrorism*, vol. 17; D. Elwood Dunn (1998) 'Liberia's Internal Responses to ECOMOG's Interventionist Efforts', in Karl P. Magyar and Earl Conteh-Morgan (eds), *Peacekeeping in Africa: ECOMOG in Liberia* (London: Macmillan). Other articles in this book will also be useful.
42 Margaret Aderinsola Vogt, (1996) 'The Involvement of ECOWAS in Liberia's Peacekeeping', in Edmond J. Keller and Donald Rothchild (eds), *Africa in the New International Order. Rethinking State Sovereignty and Regional Security* (Boulder, Col.; London: Lynne Rienner), p. 169.
43 For details on this, see Funmi Olonisakin (1997) 'African "Home" – made Peacekeeping Initiatives', *Armed Forces and Society*, vol. 23, no. 3, Spring, p. 363.
44 Vogt 'The Involvement of ECOWAS', p. 177.
45 Cited in Olonisakin 'African "Home" – made Peacekeeping Initiatives' p. 365.

46   Robert A. Mortimer (1996) 'ECOMOG, Liberia and Regional Security in West Africa', in Edmond J. Keller and Donald Rothchild (eds), *Africa in the New International Order. Rethinking State Sovereignty and Regional Security* (Boulder, Col.; London: Lynne Reinner), p. 162.
47   Herbert Howe (1996/7) 'Lessons of Liberia. ECOMOG and Regional Peace-keeping', *International Security*, vol. 21, no. 3, p. 176.
48   Sam G. Amoo (1993) 'ECOWAS in Liberia: The Challenges and Prospects for African Peacekeeping', Paper prepared for presentation at a Conference of the Defence Intelligence College at Alconbury, Royal Air Force Base, Cambridge, England, 6–7 May, p. 27.
49   James Mayall (1995) 'National Identity and the Revival of Regionalism', in Louise Fawcett and Andrew Hurrell (eds), *Regionalism in World Politics. Regional Organization and International Order* (Oxford: Oxford University Press), p. 185.

9
ECOMOG: A New Security Agenda in World Politics

David Francis

Introduction

This chapter seeks to examine critically the role and contribution of a regional economic integration grouping to the understanding of the security problems of Third-World regions in the post-Cold War era and its implications for contemporary world politics. In general, it is located within the current International Relations debate concerning the role that regional organisations can play in maintaining international peace and security. The multipolar nature of the post-Cold War period and its constraints on unilateral intervention of major powers in domestic conflicts, the diversity and multiplicity of the new agendas of the so-called new world order, and the growth of globalisation have all contributed to reawaken policy and academic interest in security regionalism. At the international level, a variety of proposals have been put forward as solutions to address conflict situations in Africa, such as the American-sponsored African Crisis Response Initiative, and mercenary intervention as alternative models for international security. At the continental level a variety of home-grown strategies have been established to help resolve conflict situations in Africa. One such initiative is that of the ECOWAS Cease-fire Monitoring Group (ECOMOG).

West Africa in the post-Cold War era is of limited geo-strategic and politico-economic significance to Western governments. In reaction to this international neglect, West African states were able to 'fashion their own response to an internal conflict, a response that was more complete and, at least until the collective intervention in Somalia, more effective than the response of the larger international community to most other contemporary internal conflicts'.[1] The role of ECOMOG in the Liberian and Sierra Leone crises has been perceived by political analysts and media commentators as providing a foundation upon which a permanent and sustainable regional security mechanism for Africa can be built. ECOMOG intervention in West African conflicts is not a peculiar phenomenon in international politics. Though the OAU Inter-African Force intervened in the Chad conflict in 1981, ECOMOG is the first intra-African intervention force to successfully, (albeit in a qualified way) manage and settle two African conflicts. Those who support the use of regional organisations for conflict management and resolution argue that the political and military advantages are numerous in that the regional multinational forces presumably understand the conflict better, they are more politically acceptable by warring factions, and their proximity makes it easier for troop deployment and logistics.[2] Herbert Howe and others posit that 'an inadequate peacekeeping force may instead prolong a war and weaken regional stability. The lessons of ECOMOG, generally negative, are important for any future subregional force'.[3] In this same light, Samuel Huntington and Robert Kaplan predict a rather apocalyptic or 'generalised chaos' for the future of much of Africa as a result of a complex combination of political, cultural, socio-economic and environmental factors, both domestic and international.[4] However, events in the late 1990s have not played out the predictions of these 'messiahs of doom'. Rather, they have generated novel initiatives from within the continent, of Africans taking control of their own destiny. This 'reawakening' of a conflict-ridden continent has been referred to optimistically as the so-called 'African renaissance'.

From ECOWAS to ECOMOG

The Economic Community of West African States (ECOWAS) was originally chartered in 1975 as an economic integration arrangement with common market objectives such as trade liberalisation, harmonisation of economic policies, free movement of the factors of production, and sectoral development programmes. It has uniquely taken on regional security responsibility with the formation of the ECOWAS Cease-fire Monitoring Group (ECOMOG). It was the Liberian civil war that led to the creation of ECOMOG as a peace-keeping force to help to resolve the conflict. Nearly ten years of President Samuel Doe's tyrannical rule was shattered by the rebel invasion of Charles Taylor, leader of the National Patriotic Front of Liberia (NPFL) on 24 December 1989. Samuel Doe, himself a Master-Sergeant, whose bloody coup in 1980 annihilated President Tolbert and his entire cabinet, presided over a government that was infamous for its gross human rights violations, political chicanery and economic mismanagement. Less than a year after Taylor's invasion, he succeeded in controlling 90 per cent of the country – that is, twelve out of the thirteen counties – which he later called 'Greater Liberia'. Charles Taylor's rebellion, for a variety of personal interests and political considerations was supported by Burkina Faso, Côte d'Ivoire (both ECOWAS members), and Colonel Muammar Qadhafi of Libya, in terms of arms, finances, logistics and even fighting forces. Within six months, Liberia had effectively degenerated into chaos and anarchy, and the authority of the president did not extend beyond the executive mansion where he was besieged. He was subsequently captured and killed by the rival Independent National Patriotic Front of Liberia (INPFL) led by Prince Johnson, while on an 'official mission' at the ECOMOG head-quarters. During this period, the level of human carnage and destruction provoked the world's revulsion. According to a US State Department Report on human rights in Liberia in 1990, 'All combatants routinely engage in indiscriminate killing and abuse of civilians, looting and ethnically based executions, with one of the worst single episodes occur-ring in July when AFL soldiers killed approximately 600 persons taking refuge in the courtyard of St. Peter's Church.' This led to a huge refugee influx into neighbouring countries.

Against this background, numerous calls for US and UN intervention in Liberia went unheeded. The USA in particular had a special relation-ship with Liberia, and by the mid-1980s it was the largest per capita recipient of US aid in sub-Saharan Africa, estimated at $500 million between 1980 and 1988. Foreign intervention was limited to the evacu-ation from Liberia of Western nationals by US Marines. West African nationals, mainly Nigerians, Sierra Leoneans and Guineans, were also targeted by the warring factions. The nature of Taylor's insurgent move-ment and the humanitarian crisis it provoked posed a serious threat to regional peace and security.

In the face of the unwillingness of the USA (primarily preoccupied with the Gulf War) and other international institutions such as the UN and OAU to intervene,[5] ECOWAS therefore assumed the role by default. President Babangida of Nigeria, the brain behind the creation of ECOMOG, at an impromptu briefing on the Liberian crisis in 1990 stated, 'When certain events occur in this sub-region, depend-ing on their intensity and magnitude, which are bound to affect Nigeria's politico-military and socio-economic environment, we should not stand by as helpless and hapless spectators'.[6] The ECOWAS Standing Mediation Committee was reconvened in an attempt to reach a negotiated settlement. After the meeting of 7 August 1990, the

ECOWAS Peace Plan for Liberia gave birth to ECOMOG. This plan was formulated to help the 'sick man of West Africa' but had far-reaching implications for ECOWAS. The mandate of ECOMOG was to serve as a ceasefire monitoring group that would create an atmosphere conducive to the establishment of a broad-based interim government and an eventual democratic election under international supervision, and the disarmament, demobilisation and encampment of the warring factions.

There is no precedent in the history of ECOWAS to prepare it for its military intervention in Liberia. Though a primarily economic community, regional peace and security considerations were never lost on member states. The 1975 treaty did not make any provision for co-operation on regional security matters. In an attempt to rectify this omission, a Protocol on Non-Aggression and a Protocol on Mutual Assistance in Defence were signed in 1978 and 1981, respectively, by Community members. It was a recognition that regional peace and security were necessary prerequisites for economic development and progress. These protocols generally enjoined member states to eschew the threat or use of force in their inter-state relations. They called for the peaceful settlement of inter-state disputes and the eventual establishment of a Standing Mediation Committee (SMC) in 1990. In particular, the Mutual Assistance protocol provided for permissible armed intervention by ECOWAS, but only in defence of member states against external aggression. It did not address the issue of intra-state conflicts, and the Community was militarily barred from intervening in any such conflicts. This, of course, was in conformity with the UN and OAU principles of non-intervention in the domestic affairs of states. The institutional mechanisms established by the 1981 Protocol, such as the Defence Council, Defence Commission, and the Allied Armed Forces of the Community (AAFC) were never implemented.[7] Therefore the ECOWAS response to the Liberian crisis was an *ad hoc* arrangement. The creation of ECOMOG can be compared with that of the UN's first peace-keeping operation during the Suez Crisis of 1956. The UN Emergency Force (UNEF) was largely improvisational, as the Charter did not provide for peacekeeping activities. Abass Bundu argues that, in the design of ECOMOG, the SMC drew great inspiration from the 1981 Protocol, thereby placing ECOMOG under a unified command and establishing procedures for supervising the implementation of the ECOWAS Peace Plan.[8] In financing ECOMOG operations, a special fund was established to which member states as well as external donors contributed voluntarily. Because of limited financial resources, each troop-contributing country was asked to take care of its own contingent without withdrawing from the central command and control structure.

ECOMOG's mandate embraced both peace-keeping and peace enforcement, which therefore gave it justification for military intervention. It was 'to conduct military operations for the purpose of monitoring the cease-fire, restore law and order'.[9] ECOMOG's 'Operation Liberty' landed in Monrovia on 24 August 1990 without the consent of the main protagonist, the NPFL. The multinational force[10] was thrust into the Liberian chaos and anarchy with no previous experience in peace-keeping. ECOMOG eventually became embroiled in the battle because a ceasefire had to be established by force before peace could be kept and monitored, and as such could not function as an inter-positionary force. The circumstances of ECOMOG's intervention and the complexity of the civil conflict forced it to move from peace-keeping to peace enforcement. This inevitably compromised its neutrality to the point that, in order to limit NPFL military superiority, it had occasionally to co-operate with, and even give logistical support to, other warring factions against NPFL, such as the United Liberation Movement of Liberians for Democracy (ULIMO); the Liberian Peace Council (LPC); and the Armed Forces of Liberia (AFL). Through UN co-operation, a United Nations Observer Mission (UNOMIL) was sent to Liberia to legitimise and facilitate the mandate of ECOMOG. Through diplomacy backed by force, the ECOWAS Peace Plan for Liberia succeeded in achieving its primary mandate. In July 1997, a democratic election was held in Liberia under the supervision of ECOMOG. Charles Taylor won the election, which was described by the international community as free and fair. ECOMOG, until March 1998, assisted the country in its transition from civil war to civil society in such areas as re-training the police force and reconstituting the national army.

On 23 March 1991, Sierra Leone saw the spill-over of the Liberian civil war into its territory when a rebel movement, the Revolutionary United Front (RUF), led by Corporal Foday Sankoh, invaded the eastern borders of the country. This confirmed fears about the threat to regional peace and security posed by the Liberian conflict. ECOWAS mandated that a buffer zone between Liberia and Sierra Leone be established, but it could not be implemented because of logistical and financial constraints. The Taylor-backed RUF rebel incursion made the state ungovernable and led to the overthrow of the APC government of President Momoh in 1992. On 25 May 1997, the military, in collaboration with the RUF rebel group, overthrew the democratically-elected government of President Ahmad Tejan Kabbah. This military coup posed a serious threat to regional security and further threatened the fragile peace in Liberia. An ECOWAS Peace Plan, supported by the OAU, the Commonwealth, the EU and UN Security Council Resolution 1132, saw the intervention of a Nigerian-led intervention force that overthrew the military junta of Major Johnny Paul Koroma in February 1998. ECOMOG has therefore come a long way from being a mere *ad hoc* arrangement to that of being a 'defender' of democracy and constitutional order. President Kabbah, after the restoration of his government, stated that 'by its professionalism and outstanding performance in the subregion, ECOMOG has demonstrated that it has the potential to become a regional peacekeeping and enforcement organisation on a par with any similar force anywhere in the world'.[11] The transformation of this economic community into a *de facto* security organisation is in itself a product of the interplay between economic development, regional security, democratisation and conflict management in Africa.[12]

State collapse and ECOMOG intervention

But what are the domestic and international imperatives that forced this economic integration grouping to assume regional security responsibility? The collapse of the state apparatus and the fragmentation of political authority in both Liberia and Sierra Leone made it possible for the NPFL and RUF to contest state hegemony. On the eve of ECOMOG intervention in both crises, the state, as the authoritative political institution, had lost its legitimacy and could no longer serve as security guarantor for its citizenry, nor could it control its territory or perform public welfare functions. State collapse in these West African polities had been caused by decades of patrimonial redistribution of state resources among the ruling elites and its supporters, thereby excluding the majority of the population from the political and socioeconomic processes. The repressive and exploitative Americo-Liberian rule of William Tubman and William Tolbert, and the civilianised military dictatorship of Samuel Doe provided the basis for state fragmentation.[13] In Sierra Leone, the APC one-party patrimonial authoritarianism under Siaka Stevens and Joseph Momoh established the foundations for state recession.[14] In several respects, Liberia and Sierra Leone are a reflection of the extended crisis of the patrimonial state in postcolonial Africa. The fragmentation of both Liberia and Sierra Leone as a result of the civil wars conferred on ECOWAS the surrogate state authority, particularly its ability to use force for the preservation of law and order.[15] Multilateral intervention to restore some semblance of law and order is part of the process of reconstituting these collapsed states. ECOMOG intervention in both crises is an attempt to uphold the status of the Westphalian state system bequeathed to post-independent African states. Ibrahim Gambari describes these as 'reconstructive interventions'.[16]

ECOMOG intervention, as part of the wider international response to the phenomenon of state collapse, is to focus on reconfiguring or resurrecting these failed states, not only as a means of halting the human tragedy, but also to satisfy both the public and private agendas of the Westphalian international system. Therefore, ECOMOG's peace-keeping efforts in Liberia helped to resolve almost nine years of bloody civil war and return the country to democratic governance. In Sierra Leone, the ECOMOG-led 'Operation Sand Storm' saw the restoration of constitutional rule. These spectacular conflict settlement efforts have earned ECOMOG 'the accolade of being Africa's first successful flagship in peacekeeping, peace-making and peace-building'.[17] Ernst Haas states that 'most observers agree that ECOWAS's first foray into collective security was a great improvement over the OAU's failures in these endeavours'.[18]

Nigeria: a benevolent hegemon?

A perennial problem that has bedevilled ECOMOG from birth to maturity is the regional political divisions between Anglophone and Francophone states and Nigeria's dominance in the politico-military and economic politics of West Africa. Nigeria's dominance in ECOMOG, and especially the restoration of democratic governance in Sierra Leone, have generated a lot of debate about Nigeria's democratic credentials. Ed O'Loughlin, writing in the *Independent*, opined that 'when forces acting in the name of democracy overthrow dictatorship, the international community is suppose to applaud. But when a Nigerian-led peacekeeping force chased Major Johnny Paul Koroma's military junta from Freetown, the world responded with only polite murmur... foreign diplomats in the region say their governments feel unable to congratulate Nigeria publicly'.[19] This is not surprising and, in fact, some political analysts and media commentators have been puzzled by the fact that the Nigerian leader, late General Sani Abacha, himself a military dictator and an epitome of anti-democratic forces, could champion such a cause. Ofuatey Kodjoe argues that 'the notion that a group of states headed by military dictatorships have the right to intervene in another state in order to establish a democratic regime is grotesque'.[20]

From a realist perspective, the resolution of the Liberian civil war and return of democratic rule in that country is a major boost for the domestic and international image of Nigeria's military government. Nigeria, under General Abacha, had been classed as a pariah state because of its gross human rights violations, especially after the execution of the human rights activist Ken Saro-Wiwa. According to Abacha's Machiavellian calculations, another military adventure in Sierra Leone to reinstate constitutional order would go a long way to silence his domestic and international critics who were instrumental in bringing about the suspension of Nigeria from the Commonwealth in 1995. The popular view expressed by pro-interventionists was that, if the USA could lead a UN intervention force to restore President Aristide in Haiti in 1994, then Nigeria could do the same in Sierra Leone. Some critics contend that Nigeria's posturing is simply part of a 'Pax-Nigeriana' designed to dominate the region, while others see it as a magnanimous gesture by a self-seeking dictator having nothing to do with the well-being of the ordinary Nigerian. Nigeria's former foreign minister, Professor Bolaji Akinyemi, posits that Nigeria's military regime, which subverted the democratic wishes of its own people in the 12 June 1993 elections, has no moral justification to lead a multinational force to restore democracy in Sierra Leone.

These charges of Nigeria's hegemonic ambitions and 'Pax-Nigeriana', however, play down the basic realities of the ECOWAS *sui generis* conflict settlement in Liberia and democratic intervention in Sierra Leone. Some have argued that Nigeria, as the hegemonic power, has regional responsibilities, the defence of which can be justified independently of whoever happens to be in power in that country.[21] The post-civil-war reassessment of Nigeria's foreign policy concluded that Africa must be the centrepiece of the country's diplomacy and the ECOWAS could serve as a bulwark to counter the destabilising influences of extra-regional actors such as France and other powerful economic blocs.[22] Nigeria, as the sub-regional leader, has the capacity and potential to provide regional security,[23] but most of the time has had to compromise 'on ECOMOG's goals and tactics in order to maintain a consensus within ECOWAS'.[24] Nigeria provides the supreme commander – that is, the field commander of ECOMOG. This arrangement is similar to that of NATO, where America provides the Supreme Allied Commander of Europe (SACEUR). The post-Cold War neglect of Africa shows that the UN and Western governments cannot and will not any longer police African problems. Nigeria has now filled this security void in West-Africa.

The crucial question is whether regional security is possible through the hegemonic role of Nigeria, a role that is increasingly being questioned. The analysis of Nigeria's dominant role in West Africa does not justify the lack of democracy in Nigeria. These unprecedented efforts have in several respects strengthened the case for the demilitarisation of Nigerian politics and a return to democratic governance. The post-oil boom in Nigeria has seen a considerable decline in other resources. This therefore brings into question the capability and willingness of Nigeria as the security provider in West Africa. It could be argued that intervention in West African crises is only an extension of Nigeria's foreign policy in pursuit of its national interests. In Liberia, after fighting with the NPFL for nearly seven years, it made a volte-face by supporting Taylor in the 1997 elections, with the hope that he would be amenable to the terms of Abuja. In Sierra Leone, it restored a puppet government, which had guaranteed Nigerian political and military elites a say in the exploitation of the country's diamond resources and further tied its political autonomy and national security to the 'apron strings' of Nigeria.

The role of Nigeria in ECOMOG has to be viewed within the broader perspective of the complex geopolitics of the region. The Liberian and Sierra Leone conflicts laid bare the divisive tensions inherent in the regional political and security co-operation. Some ECOWAS countries vehemently opposed the use of force to resolve both conflicts. In fact, this was only a front to hide their opposition to Nigeria's dominance in West Africa. Leaders in countries such as Benin, Togo, Burkina Faso and Ghana, who came to power through military coups, were faced with the dilemma of choosing between a familiar tradition and regional collective security. Though some perceive Nigeria's dominance in West Africa as one of 'benign' leadership, since it eschews an oppressive and coercive relationship with other Community partners, others, however, see the UN support for ECOMOG as 'a blue leaf and legitimacy' for Nigeria's gunboat diplomacy.[25] Robert Mortimer contends that 'the multilateral, but Nigerian-dominated force is more a classic study of competing national interests in the West African subregion than . . . a case study in regional peacekeeping'.[26] While Motimer's view can be justified to some extent, another plausible perspective is that this is a problem inherent in all multilateral coalitions for military intervention. A classic example is the American-led Gulf coalition against Iraq's aggression in 1990. The competing 'national interests' of the coalition partners were always a threat to the unity of the forces against Saddam Hussein. The primary concern was how the Iraqi invasion would affect their individual national interests, and not the territorial sovereignty of Kuwait. There is always going to be a willing regional leader, both financially and militarily, because it serves the country's interests to organise and lead a multilateral coalition against any perceived threat to international peace and security. Nigeria's role in West Africa and the competing national interests of ECOMOG countries is no different from that of the US Gulf coalition.

Alternative models for African security

Professor Norman Stone, writing in The *Observer*, argues that because of the bloody mess in Africa the empire must strike back and that 'only a programme of "enlightened re-imperialism" from Europe can put right the bloody mess made of its former colonies in Africa'.[27] Stone's view is in line with other Western proposals put forward to manage African conflicts. The two most popular alternative models for African security are mercenary intervention and the American-sponsored Africa Crisis Intervention Force.

Mercenary intervention: conflict stabilisation or economic exploitation?

Parallel to the regional intergovernmental collective security arrangements such as ECOMOG is the phenomenon of mercenary intervention in civil wars in the 1990s as an alternative framework for international security. The proliferation of violent intra-state conflicts in Africa at the end of the Cold War, often with debilitating consequences on lives, infrastructure and the collapse of state apparatus, have created market opportunities for mercenary companies privatising security to beleaguered African governments. The contemporary debate about mercenary or private military companies' intervention in African conflicts is based on their capability and military superiority to stabilise a conflict. The increasing usefulness of mercenary companies could be attributed to the reluctance of Western powers to intervene unilaterally in domestic conflicts in the post-Cold War era; the declining geo-strategic and political relevance of Africa; huge cuts in Western defence budgets and military forces reduction; the 'strategic over-stretch' of the UN; and public intolerance of casualties from national armies fighting abroad. Mercenary or private military companies such as Executive Outcomes (EO), Sandline International, Military Professional Resources Incorporated (MPRI) and others, do not operate covertly. According to Christopher Hird, these new breeds of mercenary are not the traditional 'Dogs of War': 'they are more of an advance army wanting to exploit the world's mineral resources...These mercenary companies are now multi-million pound business, with corporate videos, computer graphics and all the trimmings of a well financed multina-tional'.[28] These mercenary companies are hired not just for cash but also for diamond and oil concessions. It therefore establishes the link between low-intensity conflicts and strategic minerals. This kind of 'co-operative commerce' has been demonstrated in Angola (EO and MPRI); Sierra Leone (EO and Sandline International); and in Papua New Guinea (PNG) (Sandline International).

Based on their immediate strategic impact in stabilising domestic conflicts, mercenary interventions have been regarded as a viable altern-ative framework for international security, supported by both Western governments and international organisations such as the IMF and the World Bank. Those who argue in favour of the privatisation of security in Africa often cite the 'strategic impact on the political and security environment of the countries in which they operate', thereby stabilising a conflict and coercing a negotiated settlement.[29] The operations of EO in Sierra Leone tipped the military balance in favour of the government and forced the RUF to the negotiating table and the subsequent Abidjan Peace Accord of 1996. Sandline International, an affiliate of EO, assisted the Nigerian-led intervention force that overthrew Johnny Paul Koro-ma's military junta. In Angola, EO's direct military assistance to the MPLA government forced UNITA to sign the Lusaka Peace Accord. The military assistance of MPRI to Croatia against the Serbian army effected a considerable strategic balance in favour of the Croatian government.

However, mercenary companies, in the guise of providing security for collapsing but mineral-rich developing states, only accentuate their international exploitation and marginalisation. It is argued that corpor-ate mercenarism in search of strategic minerals represents the 'new face' of neo-colonialism, operating under the guise of neo-liberal market policies.[30] Hiring mercenaries amounts not only to a considerable ero-sion of political sovereignty, but also to the mortgaging of mineral resources and national security to a private corporation, as illustrated in Sierra Leone (diamonds), Angola (oil), and PNG (copper). Through this privatisation of security, mercenary companies therefore provide viable foreign policy proxies for Western governments in pur-suit of national interests. These considerations refute the emerging view that mercenary intervention could serve as a viable alternative for African security. The immediate strategic impact of mercenary interventions makes them mere short-term stabilisers of civil conflicts, a role that ECOMOG has demonstrated its capability to fulfil.

African crisis response initiative: another prescription for Africa

The American sponsored African Crisis Response Initiative (ACRI) illustrates that there is always something new being offered to Africa. The Clinton Administration in 1996 proposed a Western-sponsored Africa crisis intervention force with the objective of enhancing the conflict management capacity of African countries and contributing to peace-keeping efforts on the continent. Earlier, Presidential Decision Directive (PDD) 25 of 1994 stated that US support for peace-keeping operations should be contingent on a conflict's threat to international peace and security, or on 'a determination that the peace operation serves US interests'.[31] The killing of thirty US soldiers in Somalia was a defining moment that saw a return to the principles advanced by former defence secretary, Casper Weinberger, in 1984, which stated that the US should not enter a war unless doing so served its national interests and that the conflict could be won. Therefore, the basis for the USA's refusal to intervene in the Liberian conflict was its insistence that African conflicts required an African solution. This also partly explains the difficulty of getting the Liberian crisis on to the Security Council agenda in 1990 as the 'Council's members shared the US view that the problem should be solved by Africans'.[32] The American emphasis on African initiative might well have been a convenient excuse for inaction.

The American proposal contradicts its early support for African initiatives in resolving continental crises. The proposal was not only in direct opposition to the proposed OAU African Defence Force, but also a duplication of peace-keeping efforts on the continent. The proposal was therefore strongly criticised by the OAU on the grounds that the American initiative did not take into account the already existing OAU proposal, nor was there any broad consultation. There were also problems about the question of ownership of such a proposal. It is interesting to note that at the time when the American proposal was put forward, the Clinton Administration was busy cutting the budget deficit and making huge spending cuts. The restructured aid package for Africa included $990.4 million for sustainable development; $68.3 million for humanitarian assistance; $23.8 million for building democracy; and $5 million for promoting peace.[33] What becomes clear from this budget allocation is a half-hearted commitment to peace and security in Africa. Though the allocations for sustainable development, humanitarian assistance, and building democracy can be regarded as laudable, yet it could be argued that development and democracy are only possible in an environment of peace and security. Thus, it makes sense for a substantial allocation to promoting peace. Another plausible argument is that this half-hearted commitment is to ensure the perpetuation of African conflicts, hence the commercial survival of American and other Western arms industries. The international commercialisation of the civil wars in Liberia and Sierra Leone through warlord politics and Western multinational firms is reflected in 'arms for timber' and 'diamonds for arms'.[34] Therefore, peace and security remain permanently elusive as long as the arms keep on flowing. Ernst Haas forthrightly argues that 'without access to modern arms most third world countries would be unable to fight wars, civil and international'.[35]

It therefore becomes apparent that neither mercenary intervention nor the US-ACRI are not the solution to African civil conflicts. The role of ECOMOG in the resolution of West African crises suggests the legitimacy of such regional intergovernmental collective security organisations as conflict managers. Haas's seminal statement aptly describes the salience of this regional phenomenon in that 'multi-issue peacekeeping that is designed to make the introduction of democracy possible is the most important innovation in the field of conflict management in our time.'[36]

ECOWAS rescues the United Nations

When ECOMOG was established it was castigated by both media and academics as an example of how not to conduct peace-keeping operations outside the traditional UN framework. ECOMOG has confounded its critics and in the process rescued the United Nations in its management of international peace and security. What has emerged from this ECOWAS effort is a new kind of partnership for security and development between the regional body and the UN. The Liberian and Sierra Leone crises represent a good example of systematic co-operation between the United Nations and a regional organisation, as envisaged in Chapter VIII (Articles 52 & 53) of the Charter. In the words of the UN secretary-general, Kofi Annan, 'we developed a new form of co-operation which I am sure will serve as an important model of co-operation for the resolution of other conflicts, whether in Africa or elsewhere' (UN Special Representative Address, June 1997). UN Security Council Resolutions 788 (1992) (Liberia) and 1132 (1997) (Sierra Leone) legalised the peace-keeping and peace enforcement actions of ECOMOG in both countries. In addition, UNOMIL and UNOMSIL (United Nations

Observer Mission in Sierra Leone) complemented the mandate of ECO-MOG in the realisation of the ECOWAS Peace Plans for both states. The UN support for the ECOWAS Peace Plan for Liberia made it possible for the July 1993 Cotonou Agreement to provide for non-West African participation in the form of peace-keeping troops from Uganda, Tanzania and Zimbabwe.[37] The inclusion of other African troops 'de-Nigerianised' ECOMOG, a persistent demand by Taylor and other Francophone countries.

ECOWAS is therefore showing the way for other regional groupings such as the EU on how to conduct peacekeeping through UN partnership. The crisis in Kosovo and the inability of the EU to undertake enforcement actions in order to resolve the conflict further illustrates the impact of ECOMOG. The UN–ECOWAS partnership is important because the UN peace-keeping roles in the Gulf conflict, the former Yugoslavia and Somalia demonstrates the growing inability of the world body to respond adequately to the diverse crises faced by the international community. Against the background of the 'strategic over-stretch' of the UN, the general conclusion is that the world body is vastly overburdened. In the face of its inability to police trouble spots in the world, it has therefore turned to regional organisations for conflict management. Hence the salience of regional arrangements such as the NATO–UNPROFOR co-operation in Bosnia. What is new about the UN–ECOWAS partnership is that, unlike NATO, CSCE and ASEAN, ECOWAS was originally chartered as an economic grouping and not a security organisation and it has only taken on security responsibility by default. This partnership helps to deflect some of the pressures on the world body in assuming direct responsibility for every conflict situation in the world. Clement Adebi argues that the fact that 'the UN–ECOWAS partnership took place at all, given the circumstances of widespread fears of domination and mistrust, is indicative of progress in African diplomacy, in particular, and inter-institutional co-operation in general'.[38] The UN–ECOWAS partnership is predicated on the general assumption that UN co-operation or 'task-sharing' with regional security arrangements can contribute to the maintenance of international peace and security.[39]

However, UN support for ECOWAS initiatives in bringing about a peaceful settlement of both West African conflicts has brought UN impartiality into question, because ECOMOG's *modus operandi* has not complied consistently with international legal norms and in some instances has even acted in breach of UN regulations. For example, ECOMOG used force to enforce sanctions and an embargo against the military junta in Sierra Leone, and even conducted bombing raids in an attempt to reverse the coup before it was authorised officially by the Security Council. Abass Bundu vehemently criticises UN support for the Nigerian-led ECOMOG gunboat diplomacy against the military regime in Sierra Leone and thus concludes that 'it would be the greatest irony of the modern age for the United Nations to authorise no-one else but the military junta in Nigeria, a non-respector of human rights and democracy, to become the regional policeman for the enforcement of international morality, peace and democracy in West Africa'.[40] Adibe therefore suggests that 'the United Nations is obliged to ensure that those states and organisations that are authorised to mediate such conflicts are themselves free from the menace of despotism'. Though in principle it would be the rational thing to do, this is not only a tall order for the UN, given the dynamics of the political scenario in Africa, but it could also be viewed as unrealistic because the UN and regional states cannot entertain the luxury of finding the 'ideal' state or power willing to intervene, while the massacre of innocent civilians and destruction of property continue unabated.

The UN–ECOWAS partnership is a co-operative relationship beneficial to both. The UN is able to fulfil its primary responsibility of maintaining international peace and security, and as such does not assume direct responsibility for any potentially costly and protracted internal conflicts. The UN's moral authority and access to resources lends some semblance of international legitimacy to ECOWAS's conflict resolution efforts and in the process helps to revamp what has been a largely moribund economic community. Dick Leurdijk's description of the UN–NATO partnership in the former Yugoslavia aptly reflects the UN–ECOWAS partnership in that 'the experience of co-operation is relevant for a better understanding of the complex relationships within the UN's system of collective security as well as between the UN and regional organisations'.[41]

Rethinking Africa's international relations

ECOMOG interventions in Liberia and Sierra Leone have important implications for understanding the dynamics of African politics. Through these interventions the international community became involved under the aegis of ECOWAS, thereby making West Africa a testing ground for Africa's international diplomacy as far as conflict prevention, management and resolution are concerned. The transformation of this somewhat *ad hoc* arrangement into a credible peace-keeping and peace enforcement entity has been regarded positively as an alternative model for international security. Some even perceive it as a working model for a future all-African peace-keeping force.

The ECOMOG democratic intervention in Sierra Leone is the first example in the world to be undertaken by a regional economic grouping turned regional 'policeman'. Arguably, ECOWAS is setting a new security agenda in Africa – that is, as defender of democracy and constitutional order on the continent. This, in itself, is a major departure from the military-coup-prone public image of the political scenario in West Africa. What is important about this development is the fact that the 1990s saw the region become the new theatre of conflict and instability on the continent. The recognition has therefore dawned on the leaders that the domino effect of conflict in one member state has debilitating consequences for regional peace and stability. It could be argued that the intervention on behalf of democracy is an effort to lay the foundations for the proscription of *coups d'état* in West Africa. However, a post-mortem examination of the restoration of democracy in Sierra Leone seems to undermine the argument that the ECOMOG effort could be regarded as setting a new security agenda. Analyses reveal that the restoration was nothing more than a co-operative venture of all the parties concerned. Sandline International, which assisted ECOMOG by shipping 35 tons of Bulgarian arms, was only interested in exploiting the mineral resources of the country through mining concessions granted by the restored president. Nigeria was in the vanguard of this democratic intervention, for a variety of political and economic reasons. It therefore reinstated a government amenable to Abuja's terms. Britain, as a result of commercial and political considerations, co-operated with the Nigerian military government and Sandline in reinstating the ousted civilian regime. The restoration of democracy therefore became an instrument of foreign policy for Nigeria and Britain. However, ECOMOG provided the framework for regional inter-governmental collective security in West Africa. Arguably, the novelty of this democratic venture, in spite of the co-operative interests of the parties concerned, still remains relevant, and its implications for regional and continental politics should not be underestimated.

The intervention of ECOMOG effectively relegated to the sidelines the pristine UN and OAU principles of non-intervention in the internal affairs of member states. The OAU has adhered rigidly to this principle in order to prevent Africa from falling into a 'generalised chaos'. Its experience in Western Sahara and Chad clearly demonstrates the difficulty of forging and maintaining a common position and impartiality in internal conflicts. Though the principle of non-intervention formed the bedrock of ECOWAS, it seems to have approximated the concept of forcible humanitarian intervention largely as a result of the need to halt the potential humanitarian catastrophe, protect human rights and democratic regimes.[42] As such, the 'sanctity of the principle of non-intervention...is now under challenge'.[43] African states seem grudgingly to have accepted the obsolescence of their traditional revulsion to intervention in domestic affairs and recognised that 'internal human rights violations [are] a threat to international peace and security warranting the attention of outside states'.[44] This is not surprising, because most weak African states, lacking any real source of power, have zealously promoted the ideology of Westphalian sovereignty that legitimised their political authority. Christopher Clapham argues that the public goals of sovereignty were subverted to serve the private interests of the ruling elites in post-independent Africa.[45] The OAU, which has spent decades hiding behind the non-intervention principle, unequivocally supported the ECOMOG interventions. This endorsement amounts to what could be described as unthinkable in the pre-1990 period. Non-intervention is no longer a sacred area, as African states now have to demonstrate their capability to exercise both empirical and juridical sovereignty. Warlordism has changed the nature of politics in weak African states and inevitably brought into question the salience of internationally recognised sovereignty in fragmented states.[46]

However, the limitation of the principle permitting intervention in situations of state collapse as in Liberia and Sierra Leone is that it may possibly lead to abuse by powerful states. President Robert Mugabe of Zimbabwe argues that it might even impede legitimate efforts by oppressed peoples to overthrow tyrannical governments. Taking the opposite view, David Wippman posits that 'intervention that helps to restore the capacity of the affected people to re-establish order in a democratic fashion seems to promote, rather than to undermine the affected country's sovereignty'.[47]

ECOMOG therefore provides a prototype for an African peace-keeping force. This could be regarded as a step towards the realisation of Kwame Nkrumah's dream of an African High Command that will be permanently at the ready to scotch any attempt to derail development on the continent. The ECOMOG conflict resolution efforts have had a positive influence on the OAU's strategy for conflict prevention, management and resolution. At the 1995 OAU summit, a decision was reached to create a continental peace-keeping force to be deployed in African conflict situations. ECOWAS foreign ministers meeting in Abuja in October

1998 agreed to a draft treaty setting up ECOMOG as a permanent regional conflict-resolution mechanism with a military dimension. According to the director of information, the Treaty would solve the problem of ECOWAS intervention on an *ad hoc* basis as well as addressing the legality of ECOMOG's interventions.

Which way forward?

The ECOMOG project is a milestone in the development of ECOWAS, because it is 'the first time that the organisation has shifted its focus away from its primary objective of enhancing regional trade relations towards the uncharted waters of security integration'.[48] Most times, however, analysts and media commentators are often too quick to point out the failings of ECOMOG, with little appreciation of the complex difficulties faced by the regional body. Equally, they gloss over whatever contributions ECOMOG may have made in understanding the generalities of the post-Cold War debate on security regionalism. Thus, taking on security responsibility, in spite of the complex limitations, has enhanced the credibility of ECOWAS tremendously. It has placed the regional organisation on the map of political relevance, and in the process ECOMOG has now become part of the post-Cold War debate on security regionalism in world politics. The objective is not only to learn about the West African example, but also to take into consideration the valuable lessons learnt from Africa's first experiment in regional peace-making. As William Zartman puts it 'even in its misfortunes and malfunctions Africa has much to teach the world'.[49] ECOMOG's intervention in both crises helped to open the corridors for humanitarian relief supplies to reach the starving population. Faced with the crisis of state fragmentation, ECOMOG therefore assumed the status of surrogate state authority, particularly its ability to use force for the preservation of law and order. Despite the initial teething problems faced by ECOMOG, such as limited troop contribution from member states, ambiguity in interpreting its mandate as a peace-keeper or peace-enforcer, and enormous financial and logistical difficulties, it succeeded in halting the further decline of both states by enforcing a peace settlement and restoring democratic governance. ECOMOG's efforts, albeit rudimentary, are therefore an attempt to show that post-Cold War Africa is no longer content to be treated as an object of international politics. Herbert Howe, though critical of ECOMOG, accepts the fact that it is the 'first subregional military force in the third world since the end of the cold war, and the first subregional military force with which the United Nations agreed to work as a secondary partner. Liberia was one of the first conflicts where both the United Nations and the major regional organisation, the Organisation of African Unity (OAU), redefined traditional ideas of sovereignty in order to permit external intervention'.[50]

ECOMOG has added a new dynamic in understanding how civil war ends. In both conflicts, it effectively used coercive diplomacy – that is, a combination of diplomacy, economics, and the use of force to bring about political settlement. In the Liberian case, it first aligned itself with the anti-Taylor factions to tip the military balance in its favour, thereby forcing Taylor to the negotiating table. But realising that a total military victory will be impossible, it again aligned itself with the main protagonist – Taylor, with the tacit support of the regional leader, to end the civil war and hold democratic elections, which Taylor won. The downside to this is that it inevitably prolongs civil conflict.

ECOWAS's peace initiative in Liberia demonstrates a glaring lack of experience in the diplomacy of multilateral security. The improvised nature of ECOMOG's creation and its 'quick-fix objective' largely explains this. Herbert Howe therefore argues that 'The difficulties of ECOMOG's attempt at peace enforcement suggest strongly that states should not enter an on-going conflict without a clearly adequate force . . . The hastily assembled ECOMOG lacked the acceptance, knowledge and military capability to act as effective peace keepers or as peace enforcers . . . Temporary coalitions, especially of relatively poor states, should limit their mandate to that of peace keeping rather than peace enforcement'.[51] It becomes apparent that both ECOMOG interventions in Liberia and Sierra Leone were *ad hoc* arrangements designed specifically to respond to the peculiar circumstances prevailing in each situation at the relevant time. As such, though ECOMOG initially set out as a peace-keeping force, the complexity of the internal conflicts and regional imperatives were such that ECOMOG could not function as an inter-positionary force, but had to assume a peace enforcement role by default. Maintaining neutrality or passivity in the face of gross human rights violations and a potentially explosive internal conflict has its limitations. The experience of UN peace-keepers handcuffed to poles in the recent Bosnia conflict is all too familiar. These are valuable lessons learnt by ECOMOG. Its conflict settlement precedent set in Liberia was further strengthened by its democratic intervention in Sierra Leone. Considerable efforts were made to ensure that the Sierra Leone case would not be a repetition of the criticism of human rights violations and flagrant breaches of international law. Though not in all cases, its enforcement actions often received the authorisation of the UN Security Council, an impressive departure from its often 'Wild West' gunboat diplomacy. In contrast to Herbert Howe's conclusion that 'the precedent and record of ECOMOG might not discourage future insurgencies',[52] though this might be a possibility, the post-ECOMOG qualified success in both Liberia and Sierra Leone is now a major deterrent and a warning to insurgents waiting in the wings that any attempt to threaten regional peace and security will not go unchecked. This was demonstrated when a concerted ECOWAS effort led to the overthrowing of the military junta in Sierra Leone. As usual, peaceful negotiation of the conflict was the preferred option, but when the putschists started demonstrating the Taylor phenomenon of signing peace accords and breaking them the next day, ECOMOG had to resort to the use of force in order not to prolong the conflict. In addition, ECOWAS helped to broker the ceasefire in the conflict in Guinea-Bissau in 1998. At the time of writing, an ECOWAS Committee is working closely with the Lusophone members to bring about the political settlement of the conflict. The post-Liberian experience has seen increasing co-ordination of national units by ECOMOG chiefs of staff, standardisation of equipment, and co-operation in regional military training. The proposed treaty establishing ECOMOG as a permanent conflict-resolution mechanism will finally put to rest the debate about the legality of ECOMOG.

The legality of the use of force has been contested from both within and outside ECOWAS as being inconsistent with established rules prescribed by the UN and customary international law. The view is that ECOMOG landed in Monrovia without official ECOWAS approval and the same applied to the initial use of force against the military junta in Freetown. In both crises, ECOMOG did not intervene in the 'internal affairs' of a fully constituted state that demonstrated both domestic and external sovereignty. These states were fragmented, with the state apparatus virtually in collapse, and warring factions jostling to fill the gap created by state recession. Are we suggesting that every tenet of legality in such a complex situation had to be observed while a state of anarchy and lawlessness continue to fester with its corresponding debilitating effects on lives and property? In typical Machiavellian or realist fashion, the majority of West Africans – who in any case bear the brunt of these crises in blood and money – were more concerned with ends than with questions concerning the legality of the means. The international community's response to ECOMOG's intervention amounts to what David Wippman described as validating 'the result without formally validating the means'.[53] As a result of the ECOMOG experience, the international community appears to be willing to co-operate and support regional organisations to intervene in internal conflicts, particularly those of limited geopolitical and strategic value as a means of restoring law and order, and to create conditions for humanitarian relief operations. ECOMOG interventions therefore constitute what could be described as 'acceptable breaches' of international law for humanitarian ends.[54]

The *ad hoc* nature of this multilateral force is hindered by lack of sufficient logistical capabilities, an effective command structure, intelligence capabilities, and suitable training. The domestic sociopolitical and economic difficulties experienced by weak West African states deflects any meaningful financial support for ECOMOG. The USA is by far the largest financial contributor to ECOMOG's operations and relief efforts. In December 1993, it committed $31 million to finance the deployment of Ugandan and Tanzania peace-keepers.[55] In addition, the USA also handed out $75 million in military assistance to individual ECOMOG countries.[56] Logistical support also comes through the ECOMOG–US-based Pacific Area Engineers (PAE) co-operation. US support is not limited to humanitarian assistance, but extends to political and financial support for ECOWAS's peace negotiations. Financial and logistical support to ECOMOG in its democratic intervention came mainly from the USA, $3.9 million; the Netherlands, $4 million; Britain, $3.4 million; and Germany.[57] International financial, logistical and political support are therefore crucial to ECOMOG's success.

A valuable lesson learnt is that timely diplomatic intervention by the UN Security Council in low-intensity conflicts that threaten international peace and security will determine the speed with which the conflict is resolved and the extent of Western financial and logistical support. The Liberian UN Ambassador tried unsuccessfully in July 1990 to get the Security Council to consider the crisis. Its first comment on the civil war was in January 1991, thirteen months after the start of the war and five months after ECOMOG's intervention.[58] The UN's delayed involvement could be attributed to the reservation expressed by several states. Staunch supporters of the Taylor faction, such as Côte d'Ivoire, and the two African members of the Security Council, Ethiopia and Zaire, argued against UN involvement.[59] The UN's late diplomatic intervention and regional domestic politics in West Africa contributed to ECOMOG's failure as an effective intervention force.

In terms of political acceptance of ECOMOG, its compromised neutrality in the Liberian conflict, and the lawless and criminal behaviour (looting) of some of its forces gradually changed the perception of the contingent from a 'liberation army' to an army of occupation. This situation considerably improved in the Sierra Leone crisis, as most people commended the force for its professionalism. A learning process has definitely taken place since 1990. In both Liberia and Sierra Leone, it did not assume the sovereignty of the state, but supported the interim government of National Unity, and later Charles Taylor. In Sierra Leone, it propped up the civilian government of President Kabbah. Supporting the 'governments' in these war-torn countries was a convenient way of deflecting criticisms of assuming 'sovereign control of the state'.

ECOMOG involvement's in both Liberia and Sierra Leone show that an intervention force without a proper supervisory mechanism can prolong a war through international commercialisation of the conflict – another variant of the link between low-intensity conflicts and strategic minerals. These civil wars have become lucrative commercial enterprises as the nature and political economy of warlord politics criss-cross national boundaries. Corrupt ECOMOG officials have served as middlemen in this rather profitable parallel market of the collapsed states and insurgent movements' conflagration. It is alleged that ECOMOG officials actively prevent its forces from capturing the remaining 20 per cent of the territory controlled by RUF/AFCR rebels because of their involvement in the illicit diamond trade: the end of war means an end to profits from war.[60]

ECOMOG's new security agenda departs from the post-1990 tradition of favouring US-led UN interventions, for example, UNPROFOR's in Bosnia, Somalia and Haiti. Regional inter-governmental collective security organisations such as ECOMOG are the way forward for Africa as it marches into the new millennium. ECOMOG is a short-term security provider or stabiliser that helps to address the immediate problem of restoring law and order and reconstituting collapsed states. However, these kinds of multilateral interventions cannot by themselves establish sustainable security and credible peace. ECOMOG in both countries has shown that these organisations normally lack the potential and resources to put into place post-conflict reconciliation and reconstruction. Managing the 'triple transition' (that is, from war to peace; from dictatorship or authoritarian regimes to participatory democracy; and from centralised or mixed economies to liberal market economies) is the crucial basis for establishing the foundations of sustainable peace, economic development and a viable democratic order. It is here that international support is vital in terms of providing the necessary resources and political commitment that will make long-term sustainable political and economic development possible, and as an insurance policy against relapse into chaos and strengthening the fragile peace.

Conclusion

Contrary to popular views expressed about the inability of Africa to manage its own affairs in the post-Cold War international system, the example of ECOMOG shows the growing capacity of the continent in harnessing its natural and human resources into meaningful develop-ment. The so-called 'new African order' is, in effect, a neo-collective self-reliance strategy – a 'new spirit among Africans taking control of their destiny'. In future, the debate about post-Cold War security regionalism in world politics will be incomplete without the West African example. However, the qualified conflict settlement success of ECOMOG is only a regional phenomenon that has received international support. One should not be overtly optimistic about the replication of this West African experience in other parts of the continent, nor the immediate evolution of an all-African peacekeeping force. Nevertheless, ECOMOG has shown that it is a definite possibility. The UN Secretary-General's report, *The Causes of Conflict and the Promotion of Durable Peace and Sustainable Development in Africa* (18 April 1998) calls for the integration of some of the approaches and lessons learnt from ECOMOG conflict resolution efforts in Liberia and Sierra Leone into the standard opera-tions procedures and practices of future UN peace-keeping operations. Though a short-term conflict stabiliser, it is a more viable alternative framework for African security than the phenomenon of mercenary intervention and ACRI. ECOMOG's experience as a peace-keeping and peace enforcement organisation provided valuable lessons in terms of UN-regional organisations' co-operation in the resolution of internal conflicts, the legality and limitations of forcible humanitarian interven-tions, the use of coercive diplomacy in the resolution of civil conflicts, the difficulties in maintaining neutrality in complex domestic crises that threaten international peace and security, and the huddles involved in facilitating the process of transition from war to peace in post-conflict societies.

Notes and References

1 L. F. Damrosch (ed.) (1993) *Enforcing Restraint: Collective Intervention in Internal Conflicts* (New York: Council of Foreign Relations), p. 159.
2 G. Evans (1994) *Co-operating For Peace* (Canberra: Allen & Unwin).

3 H. Howe (1996/7) 'Lessons of Liberia: ECOMOG and Regional Peacekeeping', *International Security*, vol. 21, no. 3, Winter, pp. 145–6.

4 S. Huntington (1993) 'Clash of Civilizations', *Foreign Affairs*, vol. 72, no. 3, pp. 22–49; and R. Kaplan (1994) 'The Coming Anarchy', *Atlantic Monthly*, vol. 273, no. 2.

5 See Chapter 8 of this volume for a further discussion on the international neglect of the Liberian civil war.

6 Nwachukwu *et al.* (1991) *Nigeria and the ECOWAS Since 1985: Towards a Dynamic Regional Integration* (Nigeria: Fourth Dimension Publishing Co.), p. 104.

7 These omissions are now incorporated into the 1993 Revised ECOWAS Treaty which provides specifically for co-operation in political and regional security matters. It recognised the need to 'establish a regional peace and security observation system and peacekeeping forces' and 'assistance in the observation of democratic elections'. It addressed the issues of both inter-state and intra-state conflicts. See Chapter x, Articles 56 and 58 of the *Revised Treaty of ECOWAS*, ECOWAS Secretariat, Abuja, 1993.

8 A. Bundu (1998) 'Some Lessons of West Africa's First Experiments in Regional Security', Keynote address at BISA-Forum on Africa and International Relations Conference, London School of Economics, 20 June, p. 6.

9 ECOWAS Standing Mediation Committee, Decision A/DEC, 1 August 1990 on the ceasefire and the establishment of an ECOWAS Cease-fire Monitoring Group for Liberia, Banjul, The Gambia, 7 August 1990, ECOWAS Secretariat, Lagos.

10 ECOMOG's initial composition was made up of Nigeria, Sierra Leone, Guinea, Ghana and The Gambia. Senegal later contributed forced after $10 million US assitance, but was forced to withdraw its contingent after seven of its soldiers were killed, a political embarrassment that the Diof government could not afford in the run-up to the 1994 elections.

11 T. Kabbah, 'President's speech' available at http://www.sierra-leone.org/slnews.html.

12 J. Okolo and T. Shaw (eds) (1994) *The Political Economy of the Foreign Policy in ECOWAS* (New York: St. Martin's Press), p. 219.

13 W. Reno (1998) *Warlord Politics and African States* (London: Lynne Rienner).

14 P. Richard (1996) *Fighting for the Rain Forest: War Youth and Resources in Sierra Leone* (Oxford: Heinemann); W. Reno (1995) *Corruption and State Politics in Sierra Leone* (Cambridge: Cambridge University Press); and J. Kandeh (1992) 'Sierra Leone Contradictory Class Functionality of the "Soft" State,' *Review of African Political Economy*, vol. 55, pp. 30–43.

15 After the overthrow of the military regime in Sierra Leone, the ECOMOG Task Force entrusted with the responsibility of maintaining law and order prior to the official reinstatement of President Kabbah gave sweeping powers to the Task Force Commander, Col. Max Khobe, thereby assuming the status of *de facto* president.

16 Zartman, I. W. (ed.) (1995) *Collapsed States: The Disintegration and Restoration of Legitimate Authority* (London: Lynne Rienner), p. 223.

17 Bundu, 'Some Lessons of West Africa's First Experiments . . .'.

18 F. Kratochwil and E. Mansfield (1994) *International Organization: A Reader* (New York; London: HarperCollins), p. 246.

19 *Independent*, 2 March 1989.
20 W. O. Kodjoe (1994) 'Regional Organisations and the Resolution of Internal Conflicts: The ECOWAS Intervention in Liberia', *International Peacekeeping*, vol. 1, no. 3, p. 295.
21 *West Africa*, 1997, various issues.
22 O. Oju (1980) 'Nigeria and the Formation of ECOWAS', *International Organization*, vol. 34, no. 4.
23 General Abacha stated that ECOMOG's operations in Liberia in 1990–97 cost the government $3 billion. This is contested by other contributing countries, especially the Francophone states.
24 Damrosch, *Enforcing Restraint*, p. 193.
25 T. Weiss (ed.) (1998) *Beyond UN Subcontracting: Task Sharing with Regional Security Arrangements and Service-Providing NGOs* (London: Macmillan), p. xiii.
26 E. Keller and D. Rothchild (eds) (1996) *Africa in the New International Order: Rethinking State Sovereignty and Regional Security* (London: Lynne Rienner).
27 *Observer*, 18 August 1996. Norman Stone only perpetuates into the twenty-first century the tradition of some Oxford professors' views about Africa. In the 1920s, an Oxford professor described pre-colonial Africa as 'blank, uninteresting, brutal barbarism'; and in 1963, Hugh Trevor-Roper, a Regius Professor of History, talked of African history as 'no more than barbarous tribal gyrations' (quoted in Michael Brown (1995) *Africa's Choices: After Thirty Years of the World Bank*, Harmondsworth: Penguin, p. 15).
28 Channel 4 TV, *Dispatches – Business War*, 10 April 1998.
29 D. Shearer (1998) *Private Armies and Military Intervention*, Adelphi Paper 316 IISS (Oxford: Oxford University Press).
30 D. Francis (1999) 'Mercenary Intervention in Sierra Leone: Providing National Security or International Exploitation?', *Third World Quarterly*, vol. 20, no. 2.
31 Shearer, *Private Armies and Military Intervention*, p. 33.
32 Damrosch, *Enforcing Restraint*, p. 165.
33 Keller and Rothchild, *Africa in the New International Order*, p. 194.
34 Reno, *Warlord Politics and African States*, pp. 95–9.
35 Haas, Collective Conflict Management: Evidence for a New World Order in Kratochwil and Mansfield, *International Organisation*, p. 250.
36 Haas in Kratochwil and Mansfield, *International Organisation*, p. 252.
37 Zartman, *Collapsed States*, p. 92.
38 C. E. Adibe, 'The Liberian Conflict and the ECOWAS–UN Partnership', in Weiss, *Beyond UN Subcontracting*, p. 81.
39 Weiss, *Beyond UN Subcontracting*, p. 5.
40 A. Bundu (1997) *Letter to the Members of the United Nation Security Council*, Alliance for Peace and Democracy in Sierra Leone, September.
41 Weiss, *Beyond UN Subcontracting*, p. 49.
42 O. Ramsbotham (1997) 'Humanitarian Intervention 1990–5: A Need to Reconceptualise?', *Review of International Studies*, vol. 23, no. 4, October, pp. 445–68.
43 Weiss, *Beyond UN Subcontracting*, p. 15.
44 Damrosch, *Enforcing Restraint*, p. 160.

45   C. Clapham (1998) 'Westphalian Agendas in Tropical Africa', Paper presented at the 350th Anniversary of the Peace of Westphalia Conference, Twente University, Enschede, The Netherlands, 16–19 July.

46   Reno, *Warlord Politics and African States*.

47   Damrosch, *Enforcing Restraint*, p. 183.

48   Weiss, *Beyond UN Subcontracting*, p. 80.

49   Zartman, *Collapsed States*, p. 2.

50   Howe, 'Lessons of Liberia', p. 146.

51   Ibid., p. 174.

52   Ibid., p. 176.

53   Damrosch, *Enforcing Restraint*, p. 176.

54   Fonteyne, Jean-Pierre (1974) 'The Customary International Law of Humanitarian Intervention: Its Current Validity Under UN Charter', *California Western International Law Journal*, vol. 4.

55   Zartman, *Collapsed States*, p. 98.

56   Howe, 'Lessons of Liberia' p. 150.

57   Sierra Leone News Web, 10 October 1998, available at http://www.sierra-leone.org/slnews.html.

58   Howe, 'Lessons of Liberia', p. 151.

59   These African members of the Security Council feared that giving approval for UN intervention in what was perceived as an internal conflict would set a 'dangerous' precedent, which will inevitably affect them.

60   Sierra Leone News Web, 26 October 1998, see Note 57 above.

10

The Concept of Peoples' Rights in International Law, with Particular Reference to Africa[*]

Javaid Rehman

Introduction

The evolution of the concept of 'peoples' rights' has been extremely influential for the progressive development of international law. The rights of peoples – and in particular, the right to self-determination, has had a tremendous impact in reshaping the global political geography: colonialism has ended and new states have emerged under the banner of the right to self-determination. Notwithstanding this considerable impact on international law and international relations, the conceptualisation of the term 'peoples', particularly in the post-colonial context, remains problematic. Modern state practice also fails to provide a clear set of guidelines as to the rights that peoples may have in general international law.

This chapter, while having a focus on Africa, highlights a number of complexities surrounding the concept of 'peoples' rights'. As the chapter considers, African states have been the leading proponents of the concept of 'peoples' rights' in international law. African state practice, on the other hand, remains equivocal and uncertain; an acknowledgement of the existence of peoples has not led to any clearer definitions as to their constitution within post-colonial Africa. The *African Charter on Human and Peoples' Rights* (1981) remains the leading international and regional instrument dealing with the subject of peoples' rights. This chapter considers the provisions of the Charter and concludes with the view that, while it is not possible to come up with a definitive meaning of the term 'peoples', African state practice as well as the provisions of the Charter strongly condemn any view of self-determination that would negate the established principle of *uti posseditis juris*.

Peoples' rights and general international law

The term 'peoples' has been part of international relations ever since the American, French and the Russian Revolutions.[1] While the nationalists, politicians and revolutionaries relied on this term, often equating it to popular sovereignty and democratic governance, in international law the concept remained in embryonic form until the upheavals of the First World War. The term 'peoples' received a special international dimension when, at the end of the First World War, President Wilson of the United States invoked it in an effort to grant self-determination to various oppressed nationalities.[2] However, President Wilson's exhortations towards peoples' rights were unsuccessful, because no consensus could be achieved on the meaning or constitution of the term peoples'.[3]

The term was nevertheless deployed heavily during the inter-war years, and indeed provided potent ammunition to opposing camps during the Second World War. Self-determination and equality of all peoples was presented as one of the primary objectives for the allied forces in fighting the war against the Nazis. In view of the primacy accorded to peoples' right to self-determination, it is not surprising to note that the *United Nations Charter* (1945) makes express reference to this principle in its Articles 1 and 55.[4] Chapter xi of the Charter, which was subsequently to form the basis of the decolonisation movement, also implicitly recognises the rights of all peoples to self-determination.

Collective group rights was an issue which was not dealt with adequately by the *Universal Declaration on Human Rights* (1948).[5] The Declaration failed to make any reference to minorities or peoples' rights. However, subsequent developments in international law – reflected through the decolonisation movement and the emergence of new states in Asia and Africa – brought the subject of peoples' rights and self-determination to the forefront. The inertia generated through rapid decolonisation led to the establishment of the fundamental principle that the right to self-determination is an inalienable and primary right of all peoples, and that no derogation is permissible from the enjoyment of this right. The *International Covenant on Civil and Political Rights* (1966)[6] and the *International Covenant on Economic, Social and Cultural Rights* (1966),[7] the leading international treaties on human rights, confirm the supremacy of the right. Both the treaties in their common Article 1 forcefully assert the rights of peoples to self-determination.

Thus, according to the common Article 1:

1 All Peoples have the right of self-determination. By virtue of that right they freely determine their political status and freely pursue their economic, social and cultural development.
2 All Peoples may, for their own ends, freely dispose of their natural wealth and resources without prejudice to any obligations arising out of international economic co-operation, based upon the principle of mutual benefit, and international law.
3 The State Parties to the Present Covenant, including those having responsibility for the administration of Non-Self-Governing and Trust Territories, shall promote the realisation of the right of self-determination, and shall respect that right, in conformity with the provisions of the Charter of the United Nations.

Since the adoption of the Covenants in 1966, the term 'Peoples' has increasingly become a *lingua franca* of the modern international human rights instruments. The ILO Convention Concerning Indigenous and Tribal Peoples in Independent Countries (1989),[8] is a catalogue of the rights of indigenous and tribal peoples in international law. The *African Charter on Human and Peoples' Rights* (1981)[9] the most recent of regional human rights treaties, dedicates several articles to peoples' rights. This interest in peoples and their right to self-determination is also evident in the work of another organisation, the Organisation for Security and Co-operation in Europe (OSCE).[10] According to Article VIII of the Helsinki Final Act:

The Participating States will respect the equal rights of peoples and their right to self-determination...By virtue of the principle of equal rights and self-determination of peoples, all peoples always have the right, in full freedom, to determine, when as they wish, their internal and external politics, without external interference, and to pursue as they wish their political, economic, social and cultural development.

International Courts and Tribunals have consistently maintained support for the existence of peoples' rights. The point could be reinforced through a consideration of the jurisprudence of the World Court in the case of Namibia,[11] the Western Sahara case[12] and the Case Concerning East Timor (Portugal versus Australia).[13] In International Law, General Assembly Resolutions *per se* are non-binding, although they could provide evidence of state practice and may lead to the establishment of customary law. In this regard, the General Assembly Resolutions which make particular reference to the rights of peoples to self-determination, have been of substantial value and can be taken to represent international customary law. The primary example of such a Resolution is that of the Declaration on the Granting of Independence to Colonial Territories and Peoples (1960),[14] although there are a number of other resolutions that reaffirm the existence of the principle within general international law.[15]

Complexities in practice regarding 'peoples' rights' in international law

The existence of the concept of 'peoples' rights' and, in particular, the peoples' right to self-determination, is now firmly established in general international law. As noted earlier, the development of this concept of 'peoples' rights' has, however, been largely a consequence of the decolonisation process that became the primary concern of the United Nations at the height of the Cold War. The consensus built around the existence of peoples and their right to self-determination was directed towards the dismantling of colonialism, apartheid and racial oppression. During the decolonisation phase, the term 'peoples' was generally taken to mean the entire population of a colonial territory, and relying on the principle of *uti possidetis juris*, the colonial boundaries were maintained when states gained their independence.[16]

In many instances, the states that emerged from the rubble of colonisation were artificial, with populations consisting of various races with different languages and religions. Equally, in a number of cases the new governments within these states failed to legitimise their control through a popular mandate on the basis of adult universal franchise; and their often intolerant stance towards minorities and indigenous peoples led to further secessionist claims.[17] This is the story of such groups as the Tamils of Sri Lanka, the Baluchis of Pakistan, the Ogonis of Nigeria, and the Toruques of Mali. These collectivities continue to assert their existence as peoples claiming a right to self-determination. The governments of the states, on the other hand, remain reticent to acknowledge their claims to be peoples, fearing that their view of self-determination would ultimately lead to secession and fragmentation of the state itself. Amid these conflicts, general international law has failed to provide any clear answers to define the term 'peoples', or the scope of their rights.

While, as noted above, the International Covenants do acknowledge the rights of all peoples to self-determination, there is a failure to provide any guidelines as to the meaning of the term 'peoples' or that of 'the right to self-determination'. The International Covenant on Civil and Political Rights does have a distinct article which deals with rights of persons belonging to minorities, suggesting a difference between peoples' right to self-determination on the one hand and minorities' rights on the other.[18] This distinction has been maintained by the practice of the Human Rights Committee, the body responsible for implementing the Covenant. In a number of applications, where the petitioners have complained of the breach of the right to self-determination, the Committee has reinforced the distinction between minority rights *vis-à-vis* peoples' rights. Hence, claims put forward by individuals representing minority or indigenous groups have been unsuccessful under Article 1 of the Covenant.[19]

The approaches adopted by the states themselves, in particular the new states, have been neither satisfactory nor consistent. Some states have taken the view that the term 'peoples' only applies to those under colonial or foreign domination. A typical stance is represented by the position taken up by India. At the time of ratifying the International Covenant on Civil and Political Rights, India entered a reservation to Article 1, declaring that:

> with reference to article 1 . . . the Government of the Republic of India declares that the words 'the right of self-determination' appearing in this article apply only to the peoples under foreign domination and that these words do not apply to sovereign independent States or a section of a people or nation – which is the essence of national integrity.[20]

Some other states have maintained the orthodox position that 'peoples' means the entire population of a state, thereby denying minorities and indigenous peoples any independent claims to the right to self-determination. The failure to acknowledge the continuing existence of the right to self-determination in the post-colonial world, or an assertion that the term 'peoples' only applies to the entire population of a state has serious repercussions on the position of minorities and indigenous peoples – their aspirations to self-determination is consequently not accorded any recognition by the international community of states.

The meaning of peoples' rights as emergent from the practice of African states

The impact of the concept of a 'peoples' right to self-determination is nowhere more evident than in the African continent; and Africa has emancipated itself from the shackles of colonialism, racial oppression and apartheid through a reliance upon this concept. The term 'peoples' and 'the right to self-determination' therefore forms a vital element within the constitutional workings of independent African states as well as in the regional approach represented collectively.[21] A number of state constitutions support the principle of self-determination, and the regional approach is reflected through a wide range of treaties including the *Charter of the Organisation of Africa Unity* (1963)[22] and the *African Charter on Human and Peoples' Rights* (1981).[23]

The *Charter of the Organisation of Africa Unity* (1963) is the principal regional treaty representing the views of African states in international law. The preamble of the Charter reaffirms the 'inalienable right of all People to control their own destiny'.[24] The purposes of the Charter includes a commitment to intensify the collaboration of African states to achieve 'a better life for the Peoples of Africa'.[25] Even though the Charter supports the principles enshrined in the *United Nations Charter* (1945) and the *Universal Declaration on Human Rights* (1948), it does not have a particular vision on individual human rights or collective group rights.[26] The references to peoples are framed largely in the context of the right to sovereign state equality, and moves to eradicate colonialism.[27] There is no consideration of the right to self-determination apart from an emphasis on non-interference in the domestic affairs of states, and the guarantee for the 'respect for the sovereignty and territorial integrity of each State and its inalienable right to independent existence'.[28]

The latter provision is the reconfirmation of the *uti possiditis juris* principle – a principle that received complete support from the African heads of state at the time of the adoption of the *Charter of the Organisation of African Unity*. Indeed, at the inaugural session of the Treaty, the prime minister of Ethiopia, echoing the sentiments of other heads of government, commented: 'it is in the interest of all Africans now to respect the frontiers drawn on the maps, whether they are good or bad, by the former colonisers'.[29] Thus, while the *Charter of the Organisation of African Unity* fails to elaborate on the subject of peoples' rights to self-determination, it nevertheless affirms the African position on the inviolability and sanctity of boundaries inherited by the new states.

In contrast to the *Organisation of African Unity*, the *African Charter on Human and Peoples' Rights* (1981) has a much stronger focus on the subject of peoples' rights. As the rubric of the treaty reflects, there is a special position accorded to peoples' rights. Indeed, the Charter has the distinction of being the only international instrument to provide a detailed exposition of the rights of peoples. The peoples' rights, according to the Charter, are spelt out in Articles 19–24 of the Treaty. These are the right of all peoples to equality,[30] to existence and self-determination,[31] to dispose freely of wealth and natural resources,[32] to economic, social and cultural development,[33] to national and international peace and security,[34] and to 'a generally satisfactory environment'.[35]

Notwithstanding a detailed exposition of the rights of peoples, the drafters of the African Charter deliberately avoid the complex issue of the definition of the term 'peoples'. The only affirmative view that emerges from a close scrutiny of the provisions of the Charter is that there is no single uniform meaning that could be attributed to the term 'peoples'. The Charter presents a variable approach, depending on the issue in question. Thus, for example, on the subject of the disposal of wealth and natural resources in Article 21, the overlap between state and peoples is so strong that the terms could be used almost interchangeably. Similarly, according to Article 23(1), 'All Peoples shall have the right to national and international peace and security' – a right normally assigned to states.

On the other hand, the African Charter has provisions dealing with peoples' rights to equality and existence. In general international law, the right to equality and non-discrimination forms the basis of modern human rights.[36] The right to equality is an individual right, although it may also be applied to support particular group members *qua* individuals. In comparison to equality, the right to existence has a more direct application to groups within states. The right to existence is designed to protect 'national, ethnical or religious groups' from genocide and physical extermination.[37] Therefore, in the context of the right to equality and existence, the only permissible view that could be formed is that 'peoples' represent collectivities such as ethnic, national or religious minorities within independent states.

Article 20 of the African Charter, which provides for the right of existence, also accords peoples 'the unquestionable and inalienable right to self-determination'. The contrasting nature of the two rights and the manner of their proposed application, however, needs some analysis. The references to the right to self-determination are closely associated with colonialism and oppression. It is only colonised and oppressed peoples who have the 'right to free themselves from the bonds of domination'.[38] Although the term 'oppression' is not defined, the limitation of being under colonial or minority racist regimes is firmly engrained. It is certainly not permissible for minorities or indigenous peoples to seek foreign assistance to further any claims towards self-determination.

Conclusion

An inability to define terms such as 'peoples' is not necessarily synonymous with a questionable legal existence; many legal institutions have survived in the absence of specification and meticulousness. Quite the contrary, in fact, as the chapter has considered, the concept of 'peoples' rights remains of considerable significance for international law. Thus notwithstanding an end to colonialism, the terms 'peoples' and 'right to self-determination' have a continuing meaning both within general international law and in regional custom.

Through the *African Charter on Human and Peoples' Rights* (1981) the African States reaffirmed their commitment towards the rights of peoples. While the African Charter does not make any attempt to define the term 'peoples', a number of observations could be made. First, the term 'peoples' could in some instances be applied to national, ethnical, tribal or religious groups within independent states – the right to equality and existence is certainly designed to protect these groups. Second, in the light of the provisions of the African Charter as well as the existing African State Practice it seems clear that the claims put forward by minority groups to self-determination or secession would continue to remain impermissible. Therefore, in the context of self-determination, it could be argued that the term 'peoples' applies to the entirety of the population of the state.

Notes and References

* Dr Javid Rehman, Lecturer in International Law at the Department of Law, University of Leeds. This chapter is based on a presentation at Nottingham Trent University, November 1997.

1 For Commentaries on the subject, see M. Promerance (1982) *Self-Determination in Law and Practice: The New Doctrine in the United Nations* (The Hague: M. Nijhoff) A. Sureda (1973) *The Evolution of the Right to Self-Determination* (Leiden: Sijhoff).

2 In a statement before the Congress in 1916, President Wilson said, 'Every People has a right to choose the sovereignty under which they shall live', and in 1918 he was firmly of the belief that 'All well defined national aspirations

shall be accorded the utmost satisfaction that can be accorded them without introducing new or perpetuating old demands of discord and antagonism': cited in M. Shaw (1986) *Title to Territory in Africa*, (Oxford : Oxford University Press), pp. 60–1; of his famous fourteen points, Wilson's fifth point was 'A free, open-minded, and absolutely impartial adjustment of all colonial claims based upon a strict observance of the principle that in determining all such questions of sovereignty the interests of the populations concerned must have equal weight with the equitable claims of the government whose title is to be determined': cited in M. Nawaz (1965) 'The Meaning and Range of the Principle of Self-Determination', *Duke Law Journal*, vol. 82, pp. 82–101.

3 I. Claude Jr. (1955) *National Minorities: An International Problem* (Cambridge, Mass: Harvard University Press), p. 11; I. Jennings (1956) *The Approach to Self-Government*, (Cambridge: Cambridge University Press), p. 56.

4 According to Article 1(2), one of the purposes of the United Nations is to 'develop friendly relations among nations based on respect for equal rights and self-determination of all peoples and to take other appropriate measures to strengthen universal peace'. The other reference is made in Article 55, according to which 'with a view to the creation of conditions of stability and well-being which are necessary for peaceful and friendly relations among nations based on respect for the principle of equal rights and self-determination of peoples, the United Nations shall promote', followed by a number of objectives.

5 Adopted 10 December 1948, GA Resolution 217, UN Doc A/810, 71.

6 Adopted 16 December 1966, GA Resolution 2200 (xxi) 99 UNTS 171.

7 Adopted 16 December 1966, GA Resolution 2200 (xxi) 993 UNTS 3.

8 72 ILO Bull 59 (1989); 28 ILM (1989) 28 ILM (1989) 1382.

9 OAU Doc CAB/LEG/67/3 Rev 5; 27 Rev ICJ; 21 ILM 59.

10 See J. Wright (1996) 'The OSCE and the Protection of Minority Rights', *Human Rights Quarterly*, vol. 18, pp. 190–205; M. Koskenniemi (1994) 'National Self-Determination Today: Problems of Legal Theory and Practice', *International and Comparative Law Quarterly*, vol. 43, pp. 241–69.

11 See the Namibia case: 'the subsequent developments of international law in regard to non-self governing territories, as enunciated in the Charter of the United Nations, made the principle of self-determination applicable to all of them', ICJ Reports 1971, pp. 6, 31.

12 *Western Sahara Cases* ICJ Reports, 1975, pp. 12, 31–3; and Judge Dillard's celebrated opinion, especially at p. 122. For a succinct discussion see A. Cassese, 'The International Court of Justice and the Right of Peoples to Self- Determination' in V. Lowe and M. Fitzmaurice (eds.), *Fifty Years of the International Court of Justice: Essays in the Honour of Sir Robert Jennings* (Cambridge: Grotius Publications) 1996, pp. 351–363; J. Crawford, 'The General Assembly, the International Court and Self-Determination', Ibid., pp. 585–605.

13 ICJ Reports, 1995, p. 90; for commentaries on the case, see R. Kavanagh (1996) 'Oil in Troubled Waters: The International Court of Justice and East Timor, Case Concerning East Timor (Australia v Portugal)' 18, *Sydney Law Review*, pp. 87–96; M. Maffei (1993) 'The Case of East Timor before the International Court of Justice–Some Tentative Comments', *European Journal of International Law*, vol. 4, pp. 223–38; C. Chinkin (1993) 'East Timor Moves

into the World Court', *European Journal of International Law*, vol. 4, pp. 206–22; G. Simpson (1994) 'Judging the East Timor Dispute: Self-Determination at the International Court of Justice', *Hasting International and Comparative Law Review*, vol. 17, pp. 327–47.

14   General Assembly Resolution 1514 (xv).

15   See, for example, the Declaration of the Principles of International Law Concerning Friendly Relations and Co-operation Amongst States in Accordance with the Charter of the United Nations, GA Resolution 2625 (xxv) 1970.

16   See Article 3(3) of the *Charter of Organisation of African Unity*; Principle iii of the *Helsinki Final Act* 1975, 1975 ILM 1292; Article 62 2(2)(a) *Vienna Convention on the Law of the Treaties* 1969, 58 UKTS, 1980, Cmnd 7964; Article 2 of the Vienna Convention of State succession in respect of treaties 1978 17 ILM 1488, 72 *American Journal of International Law* 971. For judicial acknowledgement of the principles, see *Frontier Dispute case (Burkina Faso v Mali)* 1986 ICJ Reports 554; G. Naldi (1987) 'The Case Concerning the Frontier Dispute (Burkina Faso v Mali) *Uti Possidetis* in an African Perspective' 36 *International and Comparative Law Quarterly*, pp. 893–903; *Temple of Peach Vihar case (Merits) (Cambodia v Thailand)* 1962 ICJ Rep 6, pp. 16, 29; *Rann of Kutch Arbitration* 1968, 50 ILR 2, p. 408; *Guinea–Guinea Bissau Maritime Delimitation case* 77 ILR 1985, pp. 635, 637; *Arbitration Tribunal in Guinea-Bissau v Senegal*, 1990, 83 ILR 1, 35; *Land, Islands and Maritime Frontier case: El Salvador v Honduras (Nicaragua intervening)*, 1992 ICJ Rep pp. 351, 380; see also *Sovereignty Over Certain Frontiers (Belgium v The Netherlands)* ICJ Rep 1959, p. 209, in particular Judge Moeno Quitana's dissenting opinion, p. 252; *Avis Nos. 2 and 3 of the Arbitration Commission of the Yugoslavia Conference*, 31 ILM pp. 1497, 1499; *Taba Award (Egypt v Israel)* 80 ILR 1989, pp. 224, in particular arbitrator Lapidoth's dissenting opinion.

17   For the position in Africa, see O. Ojo and A. Sesay (1986) 'The OAU and Human Rights: Prospects for the 1980s and Beyond', *Human Rights Quarterly*, vol. 8, pp. 89–103; R. Howard (1984) 'Evaluating Human Rights in Africa: Some Problems of Implicit Comparisons', *Human Rights Quarterly*, vol. 6, pp. 160–79.

18   According to Article 27 of the *International Covenant on Civil and Political Rights*, 'In those States in which ethnic, religious or linguistic minorities exist, persons belonging to such minorities shall not be denied the right, in community with the other members of their group, to enjoy their own culture, to profess and practice their own religion, or to use their own language.'

19   See, for example, Communication No 167/1984, *Bernard Ominayak, Chief of the Lubican Lake Band v Canada*, Report of the Human Rights Committee, Volume ii GAOR 55th Session, Supplement No 40 (A/45/40), pp. 1–30.

20   United Nations Centre for Human Rights, *Human Rights: Status of International Instruments* (1987) 9 UN Sales NO E. 87. xiv. 2.

21   See R. Kiwanuka (1988) 'The Meaning of "Peoples" in the African Charter on Human and Peoples' Rights', *American Journal of International Law*, vol. 82, pp. 80–101.

22   For the text, see I. Brownlie (1981) *Basic Documents in International Law* (Oxford: Clarendon Press), p. 68.

23 OAU Doc CAB/LEG/67/3 Rev 5; 27 Rev ICJ; 21 ILM 59.

24 For the text, see I. Brownlie (1981) *Basic Documents in International Law* (Oxford: Clarendon Press), p. 68.

25 Article 2(1)(b).

26 Ojo and Sesay, 'The OAU and Human Rights', p. 89.

27 Article 2(1)(c) and (d).

28 Article 3(3).

29 Cited in J. Klabbers and R. Lefeber (1993), 'Africa: Lost between Self-Determination and Uti-Possidetis', in C. Brolmann, R. Lefeber and M. Zieck (eds), *Peoples and Minorities in International Law* (Dordrecht: M. Nijhoff), pp. 33–76, 57.

30 According to Article 19, 'All Peoples shall be equal; they shall enjoy the same respect and shall have the same rights. Nothing shall justify the domination of a people by another.'

31 According to Article 20:

   (1) All Peoples shall have the right to existence. They shall have the unquestionable and inalienable right to self-determination. They shall freely determine their political status and shall pursue their economic and social development according to the policy they have freely chosen.

   (2) Colonized and oppressed peoples shall have the right to free themselves from the bonds of domination by resorting to any means recognised by the international community.

   (3) All Peoples shall have the right to the assistance of the States Parties to the present Charter in their liberation struggle against foreign domination, be it political, economic or cultural.

32 According to Article 21 (1): 'All peoples shall freely dispose of their wealth and natural resources. This right shall be exercised in the exclusive interest of the people. In no case shall a people be deprived of it.'

33 According to Article 21(1): 'All peoples shall have the right to their economic, social and cultural development with due regard to their freedom and identity and in the equal enjoyment of the common heritage of mankind.'

34 Article 23 provides as follows:

   (1) All Peoples shall have the right to national and international peace and security. The principles of solidarity and friendly relations implicitly affirmed by the Charter of the United Nations and reaffirmed by that of the Organization of the African Unity shall govern relations between States.

   (2) For the purpose of strengthening peace, solidarity and friendly relations, States parties to the present Charter shall ensure that:

   (a) any individual enjoying the right of asylum under Article 12 of the present Charter shall not engage in subversive activities against his country of origin or any other State party to the present Charter;
   (b) their territories shall not be used as bases for subversive or terrorist activities against the peoples of any other State party to the present Charter.

35 Article 24.

36   See H. Lauterpacht (1945) *An International Bill of Rights of Man* (New York: Columbia University Press); B. Ramcharan (1981), 'Equality and Non-Discrimination', in L. Henkin (ed.), *The International Bill of Rights: The International Covenant on Civil and Political Rights* (New York: Columbia University Press), pp. 246–69.

37   See *Convention on the Prevention and Punishment of the Crime of Genocide* (1948) 78 UNTS 277; 58 UKTS 1970.

38   Article 20(2).

Part III

Towards an International Role in the Twenty-first Century

11

The United Nations and Africa: Redefining the UN's role in Africa for the Twenty-first Century

Malcolm Harper

Introduction

My relatively wide experience of sub-Saharan Africa has essentially been as a practitioner rather than an academic. I first sailed from Southampton to Africa in October 1961 in order to work for thirteen months as a lay personal assistant to Archbishop Joost de Blank of Cape Town. During that period I was able to witness, study and live under the horrendous system of apartheid but I also made many enduring friendships with people of all races who, in their different ways, were either living within the system or actively opposing it. The Archbishop was very much a leading mouthpiece of opposition, who did a great deal to make the Anglican Church in South Africa (of which he was the leader), other denominations and the Church overseas face the realities of what was, in essence, a neo-Nazi philosophy of racial domination by a minority who adopted over 200 Acts of Parliament in the essentially Whites-only legislature which were of a directly discriminatory nature.

It really was an appalling experience. My greatest 'triumph' – if that is the right word – was to entertain a Coloured girlfriend, Amy, to lunch at the (again Whites-only) Mount Nelson Hotel in Cape Town, to walk in and out of the building hand-in-hand with her, and to kiss her goodbye at the exit. All of which was, of course, illegal!

My return to Africa in 1968 was with the Oxford Committee for Famine Relief (OXFAM), when my wife, Ann, and I went to live in Kenya. I worked as OXFAM's regional field director for Eastern Africa for almost three years. There were twelve countries in my region: Burundi, Djibouti, Ethiopia, Kenya, Madagascar, Mauritius, Rwanda, the Seychelles, Somalia, Sudan, Tanzania and Uganda.

Since that assignment, I have made frequent trips to Africa – to a number of countries in the West of the continent; to Ethiopia for emergency work in the 1970s; to several conferences and consultations in East, Central, Southern and West Africa as Director of the (UK) United Nations Associations; and, latterly, as chairperson of the World Federation of United Nations Associations; and to undertake a refugee survey for the Windle Trust in the Horn of Africa, and evaluations for my Association of the UN's role in Somalia (1994) and the Great Lakes Region of Central Africa (1996). But enough of me. It is time now to talk about the United Nations.

The United Nations in Africa

In all recent UN estimates, such as the excellent annual *Human Development Reports* published by the United Nations Development Programme (UNDP); *The State of the World's Children*, produced annually by the UN International Children's Fund (UNICEF); reports from the International Bank for Reconstruction and Development – the World Bank – and many more, it is made quite clear that sub-Saharan Africa is the region of the world with the greatest levels of poverty and that it alone of all these regions is forecast to be *poorer* overall by 2010 than it is as the millennium begins. It was not by accident that, in 1995, the United Nations published a series of proposals for tackling poverty issues *and their root causes* in Africa under the banner of the 'Special Initiative for Africa'. There had been previous such initiatives and efforts to challenge the structural adjustment demands of such bodies as the International Monetary Fund (IMF) through such proposals from UNICEF as *Structural Adjustment with a Human Face*, published in the late 1980s.

The tremendous efforts of Africa itself, and of the wider international community, to diminish poverty levels through development programmes, especially since the great era of decolonisation in the early 1960s, have, of course, had a tremendous and positive impact on African society. These achievements should not be underestimated. Nevertheless, the appalling fact remains that millions of Africans, both rural and urban, live lives that are denied many of the basics largely taken for granted in the Northern industrialised countries of the world.

What are the major challenges still facing governments and civil society in Africa as the new millennium begins? And how should the United Nations redefine its role for Africa?

Governance

First, I believe, there must be a much more open assessment of the quality of governance in many parts of Africa. The considerable strengthening of the basic tenets of modern democracy and of civil society are major priorities. There is a persistent myth that very poor people – in Africa and elsewhere – have no time to become involved politically, since basic survival is their main priority. History must make us believe otherwise. See, for example, the mass movement in South Africa in the struggle against apartheid; the very high turnout to vote in the 1994 general election there; the widespread popularity of independence movements throughout the continent; or the 90 per cent or so of Nigerian voters who boycotted Sani Abacha's totally fraudulent election process in 1998.

The legacy of the Cold War is not yet fully behind us and old loyalties often die hard. The failure, for example, of the UN Security Council to deal fully and promptly with the gross misbehaviour of Jonas Savimbi, the leader of UNITA (the National Union for the Total Independence of Angola), especially after his party's defeat in the UN-sponsored and supervised elections of 1992 and as a result of his defiance of both the Bicesse Accord (1991) and the Lusaka Protocol (1994), beggars belief. Having been the key ally of the United States (especially under Presidents Reagan and Bush) and of the apartheid regime in South Africa before, during and beyond the period of its illegal military presence in Angola, the Council has persistently dragged its feet over bringing Savimbi to account for the appalling suffering and the cruel leadership he inflicted on those Angolans who lived within his fiefdom. Victoria Brittain's excellent book, *Death of Dignity*, tells this harrowing tale with great clarity.

Or look at the way in which President Mobutu Sese Seko of Zaire, one of the great plunderers of his people in post-independence Africa, was tolerated for years because his mineral-rich country was allied with the West throughout his dictatorship. (It is reputed that he ended his life – in Morocco, where he died of cancer shortly after being driven from office by the rebellion led by Laurent-Desire Kabila in 1997 – as one of the ten wealthiest people in the world).

The United Nations Security Council *must* treat the democratisation processes of Africa with greater determination than it has to date. It must be willing to understand *democracy* within the cultures and traditions of African groups and not seek to impose the broad Western model as the system to be adopted. In his excellent chapter, 'Uneven Ribs in

Zambia's March to Democracy', in P. Anyang 'Nyong' o's book, *Arms and Daggers in the Heart of Africa: Studies on Internal Conflicts*, Jotham C. Momba argues persuasively that, at least for a period, Kenneth Kaunda's one-party rule was an emancipating process away from the violence-riddled multi-party politics of the first years of independence, when parties were formed far more on tribal or regional rather than ideological lines; and that voters found it broadly acceptable, since there was a relative openness in the parliamentary election system.

I saw at first hand Tanzania's one-party system at work, especially in the late 1960s and early 1970s, when the *ujamaa* crusade was at its highest. To my mind, what TANU was seeking to achieve and the level of popular involvement in the political decision-making process it encouraged were very creative forces for open government, led by that remarkable president, Mwalimu Julius Nyerere. It is my belief that the relative openness of political discussion I continue to witness (at all levels of society) on visits to Tanzania and the fact that, despite their greater involvement in the government of Tanzania, the armed forces have never staged a *coup d'état* – really rather unusual in Africa since the 1960s – are among the fruits of that inclusive process.

It will not be easy for the United Kingdom, France, the United States of America and others on the Security Council, to debate seriously with African members what are the best democratic political structures for them to pursue at both national and local levels; but it *must* be done if a strong base for democratisation is to be created and its development assisted by the UN and others.

Threats to international peace and security

Second, the United Nations, increasingly working with and through the Organisation of African Unity (OAU) – recognised as it is as the foremost body for all-African security and co-operation issues under Chapter VIII of the United Nations Charter – has an *obligation*, as clearly spelled out in the UN Charter, to address situations that are a threat to international peace and security. In recent years, the Council's attitude towards conflicts in Africa has been very poor.

Somalia

I do not have time here to go in great detail into the success or otherwise of the United Nations Operation in Somalia (UNOSOM I and II). Suffice it to say that, from close monitoring of events there as they unfolded and from the UNICEF-based evaluation I made in March 1994 of the

UNOSOM experience, I came away relatively reassured that, given the extremely complex situation in which the Somalis found themselves after the final overthrow of the increasingly corrupt and tribal regime of Mohamed Siad Barre in January 1991 and the subsequent collapse of central government, the United Nations Mission could claim a number of important successes as well as frustration and failures.

In brief, the international media appeared all too often to confuse and equate the UNOSOM operation with that of the (UN Security Council-authorised) American Army Rangers and their attempts to capture a leading Somali warlord, Mohamed Farah Aideed, after a group – almost certainly of his militia – had murdered twenty-four Pakistani UN peace-keeping troops in Mogadishu on 5 June 1993. The decision to deploy the Rangers, who reported directly to their commander in the United States and who remained totally outside the UNOSOM command structure was, with hindsight, a disaster. This helped to destroy the attitude of many Somalis to UNOSOM and, after the tragic death of a number of Rangers and the unpleasant way in which their corpses were publicly reviled by an angry mob, led to the United States withdrawing from the country – and, in no small way, to the very negative attitudes of the US Congress (with which President Clinton seems to feel obliged to sympathise) towards UN peace operations elsewhere.

A turning away by the Security Council

The end result of the Somalia operations was a marked turning away by key members of the Council towards other major crises. This was in marked contrast to the new willingness of member states to involve themselves in strengthening UN missions in the euphoric atmosphere of the end of the Cold War in the late 1980s. At the time of the United Nations Transitional Authority in Cambodia (UNTAC) in the early 1990s; of the UNOSOM I and II missions in Somalia; of the UN-authorised military action against Iraq in the early weeks of 1991; of the intervention in Northern Iraq (Operation Safe Haven) in the late winter of 1991 and beyond in securing the protection of the Kurds of the area; of the intervention in Bosnia-Herzegovina, and of the intervention in Haiti, it seemed as if the member states of the United Nations were – at last – starting to use the UN more fully and effectively than had ever before been the case.

Sadly, the political will to continue this process did not last. Far from the Security Council seriously engaging in an ongoing process of acting *sui generis* in order to widen the interpretation of its mandate to inter-vene, it suddenly started to go into almost full reverse. Of course, the operations outlined in the previous paragraph were not undertaken without controversy; after all, they were, with the exception of the Iraqi invasion of Kuwait, *internal* disputes within the borders of individual member states of the United Nations.

Cambodia

The Security Council, as stated in Articles 33–51 (in Chapters VI and VII) of the United Nations Charter, has a mandate to take a variety of actions to end disputes that are 'likely to endanger the maintenance of international peace and security' (Article 33). In Cambodia, the United Nations offered to assist the process of renewed nation-building after many bitter years of both external and internal destruction, culminating in the fearsome Year Zero policies of the Khmer Rouge under the dreaded Pol Pot and his henchmen (1975–9); the Vietnamese invasion of December 1978; their forgetting, for some eleven years, to go back home again, and the Cold War stalemate in which Cambodia found itself trapped – with the civilian population once again being the main losers.

The UNTAC story is both creative and, in many respects, unique in the history of the United Nations. At the time (1990–3), it was the largest, most complex and most costly (around $2 billion) UN operation of all time.

Developing the doctrine of intervention

In Northern Iraq, Somalia and – at least, officially – in Bosnia-Herzegovina, the Security Council appeared to be advancing a doctrine that, if an overwhelming *humanitarian* crisis had developed, which the government(s) of the affected country(ies) could not – or would not – address seriously, then the international community could not just stand idly by and allow unimaginable, and often prolonged, human suffering to continue. In the case of Haiti, it appeared to be developing a similar doctrine in relation to *sustained human rights abuse*. No longer, it seemed, would the heinous abusers in the Killing Fields of Pol Pot's Kampuchea be allowed to 'get away with it'.

Rwanda

The genocidal killings in Rwanda in the summer of 1994 were, perhaps, the seminal turning point for the Security Council. There was already a United Nations Force in Rwanda – The United Nations Assistance Mission for Rwanda (UNAMIR) – following a comprehensive ceasefire between the government of Juvenal Habyarimana and the invading forces of the Rwandese Patriotic Front (RPF) the previous August.

However, further very serious outbreaks of violence and killings erupted in the wake of the murder of presidents Habyarimana and Cyprien Ntaryamira of Burundi on 6 April 1994, when their aircraft was shot down as they were approaching Kigali, the capital of Rwanda, on their return from an Organisation of African Unity (OAU) peace meeting in Dar-es-Salaam (Tanzania). The following day, the prime minister of Rwanda, Ms Uwilingiyimana, and ten Belgian UN peace-keepers within UNAMIR assigned to protect her were brutally murdered by Rwandan government soldiers during an attack on Ms Uwilingiyimana's home. Within days, the Belgian government had decided to withdraw its contingent – the largest national group within the Force from UNAMIR. Strenuous efforts by the UN Secretary-General, Boutros Boutros-Ghali, his UNAMIR Force Commander, Brigadier-General Romeo Dallaire (Canada), and others, such as the Secretary-General's Special Representative in Rwanda, Mr Jacques-Roger Booh Booh, to seek a substantial *increase* in the size of UNAMIR failed and they were left with a Security Council Resolution (No. 912, of 21 April 1994) which decided to *reduce* the size of UNAMIR to 270 personnel who would act as intermediaries in attempts to secure a ceasefire in what had once again become full-scale warfare.

The Secretary-General of the OAU, Salim Ahmed Salim, offered the fullest possible support of his organisation to the efforts of the United Nations to stop the bloodshed and terror. In a letter to Dr Boutros-Ghali dated 21 April 1994, he

> expressed grave concern after learning that some members of the Security Council might be contemplating a weakening of the UNAMIR presence or the possible withdrawal of the mission... Appealing to the United Nations to continue its efforts in Rwanda, the Secretary-General [of the OAU] said that a withdrawal of the United Nations mission at that point might be interpreted by African countries as a sign of indifference or lack of concern for the African tragedy. (*The United Nations and Rwanda 1993–96*, p. 42, para. 120)

On 1 May 1994, in a statement in Dar-es-Salaam, President Ali Hassan Mwinyi of Tanzania

> said that the decision to reduce UNAMIR to 270 troops had been 'one of the most unfortunate decisions' by the Council. It demonstrated that the tragedy in Rwanda was of no concern to the international community and stood in sharp contrast to the peace-keeping efforts

of the Organisation elsewhere. The President strongly supported [the UN secretary-general's] recent request that the Council review the status of UNAMIR. His country wished to draw the attention of the United Nations to the urgency of the situation in Rwanda and to highlight the obligation of the international community. (*The United Nations and Rwanda 1993–96*, p. 46, para. 125)

The subsequent decision of the Security Council to establish UNAMIR II, a force of 5500 with an expanded mandate, to impose an arms embargo on Rwanda and to establish a monitoring system for the embargo (Resolution 918 of 17 May 1994) was never implemented as envisaged and, on 19 June, the Secretary-General reported to the Council that it might well not be able to become fully operational for another three months. This stalemate led to the authorisation of a French–Senegalese initiative – *Operation Turquoise* – by the Council (by a majority vote – ten in favour and five abstentions) on 22 June (Resolution 929). This operation was highly controversial, not least because of France's long-standing relationship with the (Hutu-dominated) government of Rwanda for many years and the French supply of military and other support to it. Many people still believe that Operation Turquoise helped many *Interahamwe* killer groups flee successfully to Eastern Zaire, where they wrought havoc in the refugee camps...a situation which, in several ways, still persists today.

A failure of will

I have dwelt on the Rwanda crisis of 1994 at some length, since it displays a miserable failure both of any sense of *obligation* and of *political will* by the Security Council (with only one or two noble exceptions, including New Zealand). It would be a relief to be able to record that this was an isolated – if major and devastating – failure of will; but this is not the case...and Africa is the main victim of this state of affairs.

In Algeria, Angola, Burundi, The Democratic Republic of Congo (formerly Zaire), Lesotho, Liberia, Rwanda (with all its continuing violence and tension), Sierra Leone, Somalia (since UNOSOM's withdrawal) and South Sudan – forgetting crises in other parts of the world – the United Nations Security Council can in no way be described as being in the driving seat of efforts actively and decisively to seek a permanent cessation of hostilities in the short term and a proper post-conflict peacebuilding process as a major contribution to justice, reconciliation, community development and peace in the longer term. On a number of occasions in areas of conflict in Africa, windows of opportunity have opened which should have caused the Council to take immediate initiatives to build on them; but, time and again, delays and pusillanimity (a mixture of faint-heartedness and meanness of spirit) have prevailed. During a visit to United Nations headquarters in New York in October 1997 I had a long conversation with a member of the Secretariat in the Department of Peacekeeping Operations (DPKO). We studied together four such windows of opportunity that had opened that year – all in Africa: Burundi, Congo-Brazzaville, Congo-Kinshasa and Sierra Leone. On each occasion, the Security Council had asked the Department to prepare plans for seizing the situations that had developed. The Department duly complied; but for this reason or that – such as the United States' representative saying that any request to Congress for support would take a minimum of fifteen days for a reply – each of the windows closed while the Council dithered. A classic example of Nero fiddling while Rome burned. . . .

Restructuring the Security Council

This situation is simply unacceptable. Essentially, of course, the Council needs to be restructured in ways that will make it more fully and truly representative of the membership of the year 2000's United Nations rather than that of 1945. Africa certainly merits a permanent seat and – perhaps through the OAU – will have to decide how to fill it. The veto needs to be done away with – no mean challenge; but, perhaps as a start, the right to use it (presumably by any permanent member and not just the existing Five) might be limited to decisions taken under Chapter VII of the Charter. However, even while the turgid and non-consensual debate on such reform of the Council continues – and it *could* take years to complete – there *must* be a greater determination within the Council to support the resolution of crises *in all parts of the world* with much greater consistency and willingness than is the case at the time of writing.

Two 'soft' initiatives in 1998, but . . .

In 1998, there were two very modest '*soft*' Council initiatives in Africa – in the Central African Republic and Sierra Leone. Meanwhile, in the Democratic Republic of Congo (DRC), the Council withdrew its special team investigating charges of mass murder in the refugee camps of Eastern Zaire in 1996–7 during Laurent-Desire Kabila's rebellion against the Mobutu regime, because of the patent unwillingness of the Kabila Government to allow it to do its work. The issue of *impunity* immediately raises its ugly head at such moments, especially when there was a mass of evidence suggesting that Mr Kabila's troops, supported by regular units from the Rwandese national armed forces, were responsible for many of the atrocities. By the autumn of 1998 there were seven neighbouring governments that had sent troops to the DRC, five (Angola, Chad, Namibia, Sudan and Zimbabwe) on the side of the president and two (Rwanda and Uganda) with the Tutsi rebels in the east of the country – all with largely independent agendas.

In Angola, the Council finally started in 1998 to take seriously the threat to peace and stability in Angola and the surrounding region posed by Jonas Savimbi's monstrous behaviour – deemed by many observers to be another classic case of *too little too late*. This caused the government of Angola and UNITA to be locked in serious renewed fighting and the Council did nothing to intervene to stop the bloodshed and suffering.

In South Sudan, the Council has been very timid. Here was another clear-cut case of massive human suffering, caused by a combination of prolonged warfare and drought making for widespread food shortages.

Private security companies

A somewhat sinister and potentially disastrous result of the Security Council's current torpor is the growth of 'private' security companies, such as Executive Outcomes and Sandline, and their involvement in peace-keeping. In the 1960s, such mercenaries would have been less well organised – I recall the likes of 'Mad' Mike Hoare, 'Black' Jack Schramm and others in Congo-Kinshasa in the 1960s and the villainous mercenary groups operating a few years later in Angola – but the principle is the same: protection being purchased at a price and with no authorisation from the Security Council. One can, of course, argue that governments are entitled to make arrangements with such companies; but do rebel groups have the same rights? And what should be done about companies which, for motives of profit or whatever, decide to change sides? Such arrangements are clearly no solution at all.

Conflict prevention

In redefining its role for the twenty-first century, there are enormous challenges facing the Security Council – both in Africa and elsewhere. Conflict *resolution* is the top short-term priority, while the development of the United Nations' capacity to engage itself seriously in conflict *prevention* strategies must be the logical way forward. The UN needs to be encouraged and helped to enhance significantly its capacity to engage in conflict prevention. Modern warfare is too ghastly, destructive of (largely civilian) lives and the environment, and too costly to remain a serious option for the future; but, without international law being much more fully and consistently utilised than is currently the case, increasing anarchy will prevail – and we have already begun to witness it in crises such as that in the Democratic Republic of Congo and the decision of NATO to threaten to go it alone in Kosovo without any authorisation from the UN Security Council. These are *not* the way forward in a century that UNESCO has determined should be the age of education for the development of a culture of *peace* in place of the traditional culture of *war*. Even in Liberia and Sierra Leone, where the Council authorised the West African Economic Community (ECOWAS) and its military mission (ECOMOG) to lead international efforts to end the bloody war wrecking Liberia and to overturn the illegal *coup* in Sierra Leone, there was considerable unease that Nigeria, led at the time by a brutal dictatorship, was being allowed to gather weapons and so on for these operations, which could, in due course, be utilised for internal security needs (that is, repression) in defiance of the arms embargo in operation against the Nigerian regime.

Strengthening the capacity of the Organisation of African Unity

Alongside its own willingness to develop in the ways outlined above, the Council must now seriously enhance its pledges to assist the building of the capacity of the OAU to be able to play an ever-stronger role within Africa (in co-operation with the United Nations) in seeking to resolve and prevent deadly conflict. The twenty-first century must see an end to the rhetoric of such co-operation and a start to many more practical activities to achieve that end.

Sustainable development and environmental protection for poverty reduction

Third, the United Nations needs to increase acceptability by both donors and recipients (UN, governmental bilateral and non-governmental) for genuinely sustainable development and environmental protection programmes which prioritise poverty reduction as their over-riding objective. Closely allied to this approach must be serious initiatives to eliminate international debts, especially of the poorest countries. The Highly Indebted Poorest Countries (HIPC) initiative has been promulgated but at the time of writing is not yet being adequately implemented.

Additionally, in the future, there should be much more use in Africa of the World Bank's 'soft arm' – the International Development Association (IDA) – whose loans are, in reality, so soft that they are almost grants. Many African governments find the commercial terms of the World Bank itself very punitive.

Poverty is often deemed to be the world's greatest polluter, and I believe that statement to be basically correct. Without sustained – and sustainable – poverty reduction processes that target the *elimination* of the worst of poverty by agreed dates, the causes of conflict – social and economic injustice being high among them – and the resolution of existing deadly conflicts will never be properly addressed.

In the holistic approach which the United Nations in its various manifestations is now increasingly – and happily – taking, issues of corruption in government and civil society, elitism, nepotism and so on must also be addressed seriously. Efforts to encourage and assist the strengthening of good governance at all levels of society are vital, since, without it, none of the other measures discussed in this chapter will be attainable, as was stated at the beginning.

Sustainable development includes many complex and controversial issues, including the whole process of agrarian and land reform, ownership of such vital commodities as fresh water and adequate access to it, access to basic health care, universal primary education and vocational training, food self-reliance at both family and community levels, freedom of information and so on . . . the list is endless. Integrated into these processes must be environmental protection, again at all levels of society. Poverty can create disasters – how, for example, can you tell women that they should walk ever further distances to collect firewood in order not to strip nearby areas of vital trees and bushes, when they are already heavily overburdened in the never-ending battle to survive abject poverty?

In his report, 'The Causes of Conflict and the Promotion of Durable Peace and Sustainable Development in Africa', published in April 1998, UN Secretary-General Kofi Annan wrote:

> It is worth noting, for example, that because urban water supply is given preference over rural services, less than 20 percent of aid for water and sanitation services goes to rural areas or to low-cost mass-coverage programmes. Because higher education is given preference over primary schooling, less than 20 percent of aid percentages for education go to primary education. Because urban hospitals are given preference over primary health care, only about 30

percent of aid for health care goes for basic health services and facilities.

This is an appalling situation, which the UN agencies, funds and programmes need to address – not least with donors who often impose conditions that are more often than not working for their own interests (construction contracts for their national companies and so on) rather than in the interests of the very poor.

Gender issues are of primary significance in the process of securing genuine development. Women have traditionally been the repressed half of humanity in the great majority of societies and often remain thus. Without real and continuing efforts, gender issues will not be adequately resolved – and without this being done, genuine development will never result.

The much fuller integration of disabled people into society is another major challenge in Africa and, indeed, the whole world. Here again, special emphasis is still much needed on working *with*, rather than *for*, disabled people as they decide for themselves what they want to do in their lives.

The HIV/AIDS crisis is especially severe in sub-Saharan Africa. According to the UN Secretary-General's report on Africa, two-thirds of the people infected world-wide are in sub-Saharan Africa. The UN will have to expand its work on this crisis very considerably and urgently, co-operating with governments, NGOs and the whole of civil society, if the crisis is not going to become insurmountable. In the worst-infected countries, such as Botswana, some 20 per cent of the population is deemed to be infected. If not checked, the dramatic and catastrophic effect on the labour force of such countries can barely be imagined.

Although their end objectives need careful prior examination, nevertheless, as the Secretary-General's report states, most of Africa remains in great need of macro-level infrastructural support – for railways, port improvements, roads, telecommunications, computer systems and so on. For the UN, the drive to improve these facilities, working through the World Bank, the IDA and others, must form part of the ongoing agenda for the new century.

The United Nations must continue to seek and support the fullest use of African rather than expatriate expertise, whenever possible. Technical expertise was always supposed to be aimed at developing local capacity, but, as the Secretary-General's report says: 'It has been observed that today, after more than 40 years of technical assistance programmes, 90 per cent of the $12 billion a year spent on technical assistance is still spent on foreign expertise – despite the fact that national experts are now available in many fields.'

In this whole area, the United Nations will continue to have *the* key role to play in bringing governments, UN agencies, civil society groups and others together in order to debate and agree common strategies that are in harmony with each other. Without such a leadership role for the United Nations being accepted and supported, the exacerbation of the crises of poverty and environmental degradation is almost certain to continue – and time is desperately short to find and implement adequate solutions on such issues as global warming.

The redefining and clarifying of the UN role, alongside improved efficiency and co-ordination within the UN system, are a vital part of development capacity-building and implementation in the twenty-first century.

Human rights

Fourth, the UN must help by every possible means to develop a massive programme for human rights education, awareness and implementation. In sub-Saharan Africa there are still many gruesome abuses of human rights, and the assurances of many governments that people's rights are respected often leave much to be desired. The Nigeria of Sani Abacha was one obvious example as is the trauma initially created by the *coup d'état* in Sierra Leone in 1997 which overthrew the democratically elected government of President Kabbah.

Human rights – civil, political, economic, social and cultural – can never properly be compartmentalised. They are the umbrella under which all other activities should occur. If they are not enshrined comprehensively in them all, then those processes are defective. As the slogan for the fiftieth anniversary of the adoption by the UN General Assembly of the Universal Declaration of Human Rights (1998) proclaimed, 'All Human Rights for All!' That must be the challenge for the twenty-first century; and the United Nations High Commissioner for Human Rights has *the* key role to play in encouraging everyone in Africa to enhance human rights standards through awareness-raising and educational programmes that will result in much greater popular pressure being put on governments to *implement* those human rights conventions to which they have put their name. The UN's Decade for Human Rights Education is a vital channel for promoting this work.

Refugees and internally displaced people

For Africa, a key human rights challenge is the adequate protection of refugees and internally displaced people. The tragic history of Zaire/DRC from 1994 onwards is perhaps the starkest example of what can go wrong in refugee protection. The United Nations High Commissioner for refugees needs much more consistent support in carrying out a unique protection role throughout the continent.

A culture of peace

Finally, Africa needs much support in the development, with assistance from UNESCO and other partners, of a process of education for the development of a culture of peace as a major priority for the twenty-first century. This is, of course, a vital priority for the whole of human society, but Africa's bitter and continuing experience of widespread deadly conflicts and tensions demands that it be included fully in the process of fundamental attitudinal change.

Conclusion

In summary, the UN needs much more consistent political and practical support from its members in order to secure creative results in the struggle for human rights; political, economic, social and cultural justice; conflict resolution and prevention; enhanced democracy and a stronger civil society; the eradication of the worst of poverty; tackling the challenges of HIV/AIDS; environmental protection; helping to meet macro-level needs and securing the use of national rather than expatriate expertise; and the enhancement of the role of women as equal partners and of the disabled as fully integrated partners in all aspects of society.

It is an achievable target. As the new century starts, we can perhaps allow ourselves a moment of vision – of asking ourselves and each other what sort of a global society we want our successors to be living in at the end of it; and what are the steps that must be taken *now* in order to ensure that the road we all travel during our lifetimes is leading towards that goal. With sufficient political will and determination, whatever the setbacks along the way, we shall, as the freedom song of the 1960s assured us, overcome.

References

Anyang'Nyong'o, P. (ed.) (1993) *Arms and Daggers in the Heart of Africa* (Nairobi, Kenya: Academy Science Publishers).

Brittain, Victoria (1998) *Death of Dignity* (London: Pluto Press).

Dualeh, Hussein Ali (1994) *From Barre to Aideed* (Nairobi, Kenya: Stellagraphics).

Omar, Mohamed Osman (1992) *The Road to Zero: Somalia's Self-destruction* (London: Haan Associates).

Anonymous (1995) *Rwanda: Not So Innocent – When Women Become Killers* (London: African Rights).

Sahnoun, Mohamed (1994) *Somalia – the Missed Opportunities* (Washington, DC: United States Institute of Peace).

United Nations

UN Secretary General (1998) *The Causes of Conflict and the Promotion of Durable Peace and Sustainable Development in Africa: Report of the Secretary-General* (New York: United Nations).

UNDP, *Human Development Report*, series (New York: UNDP).

UNICEF, *The State of the World's Children*, series (New York: UNICEF).

The United Nations Blue Books Series

Volume VIII

The United Nations and Somalia 1992–96 (1996) (New York: United Nations).

Volume X

The United Nations and Rwanda 1993–96 (1996) (New York: United Nations).

12
International Health and Africa: Who is Leading Whom?

Susan Adong

Introduction

International health matters have been a rather neglected area of research in international relations. The onset of AIDS/HIV, a communicable disease (not a tropical malaise) has shown sub-Saharan Africa to be an area marginalised by the World Health Organisation's (WHO) rhetoric on 'universal health for all by the year 2000'. The trend currently is upwards in many other diseases such as tuberculosis, heart disease, cancer and other non-tropical diseases.[1] That it has lost its way and lead is not in dispute. Other factors, however, contributed to bringing the debate on international health reform on to the agenda of international relations:

1 The growth in multilateralism since the 1970s has called into question the role of the state in the crucial area of public health. The WHO, World Bank (WB), International Monetary Fund (IMF) and non-governmental organisations have formed an unlikely alliance in matters of international health in the Third World, wielding a huge amount of clout in the health policies of these countries, particularly in sub-Saharan Africa, Asia and Latin America.

2 International migration and increase in the mobility of people from one part of the world to another, has meant that health matters are no longer confined within the boundaries of one country. President Clinton of the USA used the term 'airport malaria' in describing these communicable diseases and the recognition of their international transmission nature as well as the need for collaboration in fighting their spread. Climatic changes have also had an impact on the

increase in these diseases, bringing new (non-temperate) diseases to temperate regions. However, the solutions to these problems must come from the African states themselves.

First, the argument is that, historically, public health has never been carried out by any actor(s) other than states. To try and invent something new for Africa as the WB and other multilateral agencies are prescribing is debatable – the Ugandan government has, for example, thrown out a WB proposal for privatisation of its entire health sector as something unthinkable in a developing country.

Second, the failure of the WHO to provide for the needs of the people in the Third World – especially in sub-Saharan Africa – has meant that African states must come up with their own solutions for health provision. The incidence of AIDS/HIV is decreasing in Uganda as a result of state action since the mid-1980s. The message is that state action and not WHO prescription is the most effective tool in the provision of health.

Third, culturally sensitive and appropriate means of health promotion in Africa, particularly in the area of AIDS/HIV, is one tool states in Africa can utilise. Songs, dances, poetry and theatre are some of the unique ways Uganda uses to get across the message of safe sex to its population. This has been a purely African initiative and not a WHO regulation.

Last, regional alliances provide a closer level of collaboration than the traditional regional demarcation set up by the WHO. The Great Lakes Regional AIDS Control Programme, which includes Uganda, Rwanda and Burundi, is one example of an African initiative that was set up on a cross-border co-operation basis. This initiative has shown that African regional co-operation based on the willingness of governments to find a common solution can and *does* work.

International health and its predecessors

In the era of globalism, universalism and internationalism, one thing that seems to define the disparity between the North and the South is the concept of international health. In prehistoric times, the ancient civilisations of Egypt, Assyria, Israel, Greece and Rome had public hygiene at their centre. Indeed, every race had some form of public hygiene as a social norm. The Western world had for years an agreement to control the diseases that had plagued them for centuries – the Sanitary Conferences were platforms where the Western world met from time to time and agreed on how to control any epidemic at hand. With Europe gaining colonies, the new lands (most of them in the tropics) had to be brought into the domain of 'world health'. Britain, France, Spain, Portugal, Belgium and Germany all had an interest in trying to control diseases from these parts. Medical research was carried out by these Western powers, who believed that 'medical researchers were fully aware that the future of imperialism lay with the micro-scope'.[2] Schools for the study of tropical diseases were established in Holland, Britain and France. Britain was, by the end of the nineteenth century, managing the health of its citizens and regularly published its scientific findings in medical journals such as the *Lancet* and *Empire Health*.

The unification of international health – from the League to the WHO

At the end of the Second World War, there were three international health agencies carrying out similar work: The Office International d'Hygiene; the United Nations' Relief and Rehabilitation Agency; and the League of Nations' Health Division. The former was created to protect Europe from the plague, yellow fever and cholera, which were an impediment to trade. By the time the League of Nations was formed, health had been established as an important part of civil society. After the end of the war, a clear framework under the new United Nations for a more unified agency was proposed, because of the need for a single world health organisation.

With the establishment of the United Nations, international health was universalised under its specialised agency, the World Health Organ-isation, the leading international agency, which was given the task of keeping the world's population healthy. Its mandate was 'to provide universal health for all by the year 2000'. The Constitution of the WHO states that 'the enjoyment of the highest attainable standard of health is one of the fundamental rights of every human being without distinction of race, religion, political belief, economic or social condi-tion'. The World Health Organisation defines health as 'a state of com-plete physical, mental and social well-being and not merely the absence of disease or infirmity'. Health and human rights is considered to be 'a holistic partnership'. Under this mandate, diseases that were considered to be epidemics were eradicated under the conceptual framework of co-operation among states under the leadership of the WHO. Smallpox was eradicated under this effort, becoming a global 'first', polio is currently on its way out. Other epidemics have since occupied this agency, with the most important one AIDS/HIV, which has occupied the WHO since the mid-1970s. Currently, there is a rising trend in most of the Third World, not only for this disease, but also for other non-communicable ones such as tuberculosis, and smoking-related ailments, including cancer. The WHO's priority is often, though not always, a concentration on communicable diseases. The overriding idea is that this is for the public good and serves the larger community. The historical basis of public health has always been rooted in this idea: international transmission makes co-operation and/or co-ordination among states important. It is for this reason that the eradication of smallpox was co-ordinated globally by the WHO. In the annual *World Health Report* for 1998, it admitted:

> However, progress has been far from universal. While health globally has steadily improved over the years, great numbers of people have seen little if any improvement at all. The prime concern of the international community must be the plight of those left furthest behind as the rest of the world steps confidently into the future. These are the many hundreds of millions of men, women and children still trapped in the grimmest poverty. They live mainly in the least developed countries, where the burdens of ill-health, disease and inequality are heaviest, the outlook is bleakest, and life is shortest.[3]

The WHO has traditionally concentrated on tropical diseases from sub-Saharan Africa. Diseases such as malaria, water-borne diseases and others, kept the WHO's policy clear-cut but, after fifty years, the WHO is having a mid-life crisis and is in need of major restructuring. Many observers have commented that it has in some way lost its direction along the way. The massive increase in the incidence of AIDS/HIV in the Third World and the relatively small increase in the developed world since the mid-1980s has shown the disparity between the rich and the poor parts of the globe – the disease is now known as 'a poor man's disease'. The developed world has only 10 per cent of the epidemic but spends 90 per cent of the global resources on fighting the disease; the Third World, on the other hand, has 90 per cent of the problem but spends only 10 per cent of global resources on fighting the disease. The WHO created the Global Programme on AIDS to co-ordinate national programmes around the world.

Multilateralism and international health

The growth in multilaterlism since the 1970s has brought into question the role of the state in the crucial area of public health. Robert O. Keohane defines multilateralism as 'the practice of co-ordinating national policies in groups of three or more states'.[4] Regimes such as the WHO, the WB, the IMF and non-governmental organisations (NGOs) have programmes that influence the health sector in Africa and the rest of the Third World. The WHO has many of the characteristics of a regime – it has procedures, regulations, rules and legitimacy accorded to it in the United Nations' Charter at the time of its conception.[5] States are, for example, required to notify the WHO of outbreaks of highly infectious diseases such as the ebolanius. Also, travellers from the tropics are required routinely to be inoculated when travelling to any other state. This is the procedure laid down by the WHO. In other words in matters of international public health, the citizens of a given state have to comply with WHO procedure and not states' procedures. State sovereignty comes second to regime regulation. This is the conceptual framework within which the WHO operates. The idea is that international transmission of diseases falls within the concept of public good.[6]

Recently, however, multilateralism has become a driving phenomenon in the field of international health as in international economic relations. The traditional role carried out by the WHO is being eroded by multilateral agencies. The WB, the IMF, the European Union (EU) and NGOs have come into the area of health. In the field of AIDS/HIV, the EC is, for example, providing aid under its Lomé Convention to Africa, Caribbean and Pacific countries to revamp the depleted national blood transfusion services to the beneficiaries. Among them are included Uganda, Malawi and Zambia. Global interdependence in the face of a common enemy has prompted self-interested actors (states) to act in combating a disease that is not tropical but is transmissable across borders. The developed world's response is self-interested rather than humanitarian. In regime theory as proposed by Stephen Krasner and John Ruggie, co-operation between states is often a by-product of self-interested motives. The evolution of co-operation among states often involved actor interests even in the absence of the high politics of conflict. Theorists in this field, such as Stephen Krasner, Oran Young and John Ruggie, have expounded this in their work. The field of international health is no different. Since the mid-1980s states have had to face the crisis of AIDS/HIV on a global scale: rarely a week goes by without some headline, often sensational, about the disease, whether it is the United States government barring Haitians, or a man on the loose in Sweden infecting women. For these reasons, the WHO's forum on the disease has legislation governing travel and civil rights.

The idealism behind this was that the agency would come up with a range of universal and harmonised policies to reduce the incidences of the disease around the world. The WHO has a legitimising code which enables states to act accordingly. Regime analysts call this the norms[7] and procedures that are used as their governing principles. This conceptual framework gives it the legitimisation it needs to carry out its work in the field of international health. It is this legitimising aspect of the United Nations system that makes states implement their actions. It is worth noting, though, that the WHO cannot enforce any of its legislation but only recommend. This is the reason why its critics argue that it is largely ineffective. The mandate that declares the universalism of health for all is found wanting. As empirical evidence has shown, developing countries rather than developed countries have borne the brunt of the crisis in AIDS/HIV.

International migration and the supersonic age we live in has brought the world together as a 'global village', so the control of transmissible diseases is a real necessity. Previously, epidemics in one part of the world might not have concerned another part, but now, the reverse is the case. All parts of the world can be in potential danger. Collaboration among states therefore makes sense, as infection can spread rapidly. The outbreak of the ebola virus in Kilkwit (a tiny village in the Democratic Republic of Congo), and the outbreak of 'chicken' flu in China all prompted swift action from the international health body, which illustrates the above point: tropical diseases rarely warrant a globally concerted effort, since the rich world perceive it as not being a problem for them. The developed world traditionally related to this matter as a charitable or humanitarian issue. But recently, the malaria parasite has been found in places not previously associated with the disease. Hence the WHO has launched a global strategy known as the Malaria Initiative. The world is becoming more interdependent in more ways than one.

Globalisation and the state of the state in sub-Saharan Africa

The concept of globalisation brings with it the idea of benevolence. However, in Africa and the rest of the Third World, it has reinforced inequalities and helps to maintain the status quo. The WHO *World Health Report 1998*, for example, states:

in general, the report offers an optimistic view of the future. It says that five decades of socio-economic development and major advances in health have benefited people in most countries, and are likely to continue in the 21st century, unless a major economic crisis arises.

Political economist, Susan Strange has argued that the state is in retreat. In Africa, multinational corporations rather than the state control vast sectors of public life. The crippling debt burden of most African states, has reduced the capability and capacity of the state to be truly independent. The new buzz words being bandied around are privatisation of health provision (something Britain has shied away from); the intellectual patenting of drugs; and private health insurance. These factors further marginalise the majority of Africans, who have a low disposable income. Moreover, the state in Africa often finds itself overwhelmed by these factors.[8]

State and health in Africa – indigenous initiatives and self help

Solutions to the problems brought on by globalisation must come from the African states themselves. Although the harmonisation of health legislation laid down by the international regimes suggest homogenous characteristics in these institutions, it is obviously not the case, given that developing countries have different socioeconomic structures. The *World Health Report 1998* admits:

> Some gaps in health between the rich and the poor are at least as wide as they were half a century ago, and are becoming wider still. While people in most countries are living longer, life expectancy is actually decreasing in some others. Between 1975 and 1995, 16 countries with a combined population of 300 million experienced such a decrease. Many of them were in Africa.

Current trends in AIDS/HIV reflect the disparity in state capability between the rich nations and poor ones. Disease surveillance systems are necessary to monitor the rate of infection but it has taken the developing part of the world most of the fifteen years or so since the mid-1980s to get this vital state machinery in order. Aid from donor nations and from non-governmental organisations had to be negotiated to rehabilitate depleted centres which had fallen into ruin thanks to debt-servicing. National blood services had to seek the same assistance, which takes time. Developed states only need to make very few adjustments, requiring a minimum of time. All the above interlinked issues and weak economies combine to reduce the effectiveness of any globally concerted effort envisioned by the WHO.

Examples from Uganda, Zambia, Ghana and Tanzania – self help at work

Prevention of HIV/AIDS infection has been possible in some states in sub-Saharan Africa. With governments taking the lead, Uganda, Zambia, Ghana and Tanzania have provided the political will needed to tackle this problem. Uganda, the first country to establish a national strategy to tackle the disease, has produced positive results. Beginning as early as 1986, the Uganda AIDS Control Programme embarked on an education and information campaign which has reached nearly all the population in the country. Most adults and even children have a good grasp of the issues surrounding prevention of infection: safe sex messages from billboards, radio broadcasting, theatre and traditional songs have helped reach the wider population, and, generally, this preventive method – the only workable tool in the absence either of a cure or a vaccine – has been incorporated into the fabric of everyday life.[9] Moreover, the Ugandan government is the only one in Africa – arguably one of the few in the world – where there is an independent AIDS Commission. This body, unlike others which tend only to involve the ministry of health, has ensured that eleven ministries are involved in AIDS/HIV in an integrated manner. The Ministry of Defence, for example, will not dismiss any HIV-positive soldier; and has a supportive policy.[10]

Through the initiative of a Ugandan woman, the largest organisation in the country, The AIDS Support Organisation (TASO), oversees counselling, testing, care and fostering of orphans using the traditional African culture of extended family rather than orphanages, an alien concept to most African societies. At the same time, TASO has been established in twelve other African countries including Zambia, Ghana and Tanzania. All these have been purely African initiatives and not ideas imported from abroad.[11] The Ugandan government has spared no efforts in its campaign against the disease. In a unique openness, the government brushed aside natural reservation and began to engage its population on issues regarding sex. It has also managed to deal with objections from religious groups, especially the Catholic Church, which is the largest provider of healthcare in the country, as in other parts of

Africa. In this manner, condom distribution has been widely encouraged; free testing is available; and many people have used these facilities, which has helped to reduce infection and to let individuals know whether or not they are infected.[12] A government-owned newspaper, *The New Vision* distributes a newsletter, aptly titled *Straight Talk* aimed at teenagers. This discusses sex in explicit ways and describes ways of reducing infection. On the main roads, huge billboards recommend fidelity and abstinence from casual sex, and warn about the effects of alcohol on peoples' judgement about sexual encounters. In public buildings, posters to the same effect are used. Prominent Ugandans who test positive for the virus give personal testimony. Two most notable ones are the late Philly Lutaaya, an international Ugandan pop singer, and an army major called Ruranga Rubarima. The latter, after testing positive has involved himself in counselling other soldiers, then helped to set up a network linking all infected individuals. He has a regular radio spot, 'Captain Doctor', which offers frank safe sex advice and has reached millions of Ugandans.[13]

With the leadership of President Museveni, who personally recorded radio and television messages – possibly the only head of state to do so – the general mood in the country is one of positive optimism. By December 1996 over 300 000 Ugandans had voluntarily presented themselves for testing. This is truly a remarkable achievement in a relatively short time – ten years, considering the problems of the society and its previous shyness in discussing sex matters. The government has managed to change cultural and social systems and reversed the trend. Some fifteen years later the rate of infection is now taking a nose dive.[14] Other African countries have made similar actions possible. In Zambia, the National AIDS Prevention and Control Programme promotes health messages. Cabinet ministers, Members of Parliament and other political leaders have taken part in workshops and seminars on AIDS. Over 700 anti-AIDS clubs, with over 27 000 members, have been started in primary and secondary schools, in companies and church congregations. The former president, Kenneth Kaunda, gave a personal testimony when his son died of the disease. This went a long way in dispelling the stigma attached to the disease.[15]

In the West African country of Ghana, the Ghana AIDS Control Programme has formed an integrated policy whereby health workers from non-governmental institutions such as the Catholic Mission Hospital get their salaries paid by the Ministry of Health. This provides a vital service which could otherwise be unavailable. Again, this illustrates the way that individual African countries deal with this issue in a way that suits their own situation and which clearly varies from country to country.[16] The newer issues of private health care have negative effects on the public sector. The middle-income countries were targeted to branch out into privatisation. In the case of Uganda, it was state action on health promotion in the media that turned the AIDS/HIV crisis around. As a typical debtor state, it has been implementing the structural adjustment programme of the IMF and the WB since 1980 and spends $4 per person per annum on health. Most of its export revenue is spent on debt-servicing. It had to find an original way of managing health promotion without any new money. The National AIDS Commission was launched in 1988, early in the crisis, and Uganda was one of the first countries in the world to develop a national strategy to deal with the disease during the 1980s. The use of the media in the form of radio, posters, songs, poetry and theatre in the Ugandan context proved more effective than the other traditional methods used elsewhere. In parts of Africa where the state has not taken action, the incidence of the disease is on the increase. A case in point is that of South Africa, where the government did not take any action until the end of the 1990s. African states need their own initiative and not recommendations from outside. A well-known international public health and human rights professor articulates the problem:

> However, in the current climate of separatism, work to address societal factors; governmental, socio-cultural, and economic, has been fragmented and generally ineffective. There is no common, coherent conceptual framework to describe and analyse the nature of the essential societal factors; nor is there consensus about the necessary direction of societal change required to reduce vulnerability to HIV/AIDS. As a result, the current approach is essentially tactical, not strategic; it is a collection of isolated efforts, not a public health movement; and it remains isolated from other, and broader health issues.[17]

Conclusion

It is other, broader, health issues that are coupled with economic ones to force African states to take drastic actions; health is given low priority because of the factors of globalisation. Other internal factors, such as internecine conflicts and unstable state systems, make it difficult to have a coherent health policy, or indeed any policy at all. The most notorious, but well-documented decaying state is that of the former Zaire, now the Democratic Republic of Congo. For nearly three decades since the 1960s, most of the state sectors have been depleted and that state – the size of Western Europe' – , has almost a non-existent centralised health sector. To turn it around will require the stamina of the new government. Uganda and her neighbours have shown that African initiatives can work.

States bordering each other need to form alliances based on mutual vulnerability brought on by their close proximity. This will create closer levels of collaboration than the traditional regional demarcation set up by the WHO. The Great Lakes Regional AIDS Control Programme, which includes Uganda, Rwanda and Burundi, is an example of a purely African initiative based on cross-border co-operation. Also, the East African Community, comprising Kenya, Tanzania and Uganda, is being revived and is collaborating in issues that are of mutual benefit to the three states. Southern African, Western African and Central African Alliances specifically based on health could complete the picture and provide a new pan-Africanism.

Notes and References

1 The World Health Organisation has since its conception catalogued incidences of diseases according to their being tropical or non-tropical ones. For example, cancer, heart disease and other non-communicable diseases were, until recently, common in developed non-tropical parts of the globe.

2 Quoted from Lyons Maryinez (1992) *The Colonial Disease, A History of Sleeping Sickness in Northern Zaire* (Cambridge: Cambridge University Press), p. 21.

3 *The World Health Report 1998.* This is the annual World Health catalogue of the state of the world's population's health; since 1948 there has been an annual report with such divisions as age, demography and so on.

4 Robert O. Keohane (1990) 'Multilateralism: An Agenda for Research', *International Journal*, vol. 45, no. 731, Autumn.

5 Robert Keohane and Joseph Nye define regimes as 'networks of rules, norms and procedures that regulate behaviour' Robert O. Keohane and Joseph Nye (1989) *Power and Interdependence* (New York: HarperCollins), p. 19.

6 World Bank (1997) *Confronting AIDS, Public Priorities in a Global Epidemic* (Oxford and New York: Oxford University Press).

7 Norms can be defined as 'standards of behaviour defined in terms of rights and obligations': See F. Kratochwil and J. Ruggie (eds), (1994) *International Organisations: A Reader* (New York: HarperCollins), p. 7.

8 The World Bank's recommendation for African states to privatise is brought to light in a chapter by Sam Agatre and Joanna Macrae (1995) 'Whose Policy Is It Anyway? International and National Influences on Health Policy Development in Uganda', *Health Policy and Planning*, vol. 10, no. 2, pp. 122–32 (Oxford: Oxford University Press).

9　'Uganda Determined Not To Be Aids Victim', *Guardian*, London, 30 November 1994.
10　Ibid.
11　Hampton, Janie (1990) *Living Positively With Aids*, Strategies for Hope Series No. 2, The Aids Support Organisation (TASO), Uganda (London: Actionaid and AMREF), p. 5.
12　'Straight Talk for Survival', *Financial Times*, London, 31 December 1996.
13　Ibid.
14　Ibid.
15　Glen Williams (1990) *From Fear to Hope, Aids Care and Prevention* at *Chikankata Hospital, Zambia*, Strategies for Hope Series No. 1 (London: Actionaid and AMREF), p. 5.
16　Hampton, Janie (1991) *Meeting AIDS With Compassion, AIDS Care and Prevention in Agomanya, Ghana*, Strategies for Hope Series No. 5 (London: Actionaid and AMREF), p. 8.
17　Jonathan Mann, Professor of Health and Human Rights, Harvard School of Public Health, 11 July 1996.

Bibliography

Ghana AIDS Control Programme, Ministry of Health, Ghana.
Hampton, Janie (1990) *Living Positively with AIDS*, The Aids Support Organisation, (TASO), Uganda (London: ACTIONAID).
Krasner, Stephen (ed.) (1995) *International Regimes* (Ithaca, NY; London: Cornell University Press).
Kratocwhil, F. and Edward D. Mansfield (eds) (1994) *International Organisations, A Reader* (New York: HarperCollins).
Ministry of Health, Tanzania, National AIDS Control Programme.
World Health Report 1998 (Geneva: WHO).
Uganda AIDS Control Programme Series, Entebbe, Uganda: The Aids Control Programme, Ministry of Health.

13
UNESCO: A New Role in Africa?

Sagarika Dutt

Introduction

When UNESCO[1] was established in 1945 only one African state – Egypt – participated in its creation, and by 1958, UNESCO still had only eight member states from this region: Egypt, Ethiopia, Ghana, Liberia, Libya, Morocco, Sudan and Tunisia. However, following decolonisation, the African states joined UNESCO in large numbers, mainly in 1960/1, and at the time of writing number fifty in total. This chapter traces the history of UNESCO's involvement in Africa's development in response to African member states' needs and expectations, and UN initiatives. It argues that UNESCO's approach to peace and development is particularly appropriate for Africa as it stresses the development of endogenous capacities and the cultural dimension of development[2] rather than neo-liberal models of development often imposed on African countries by international financial institutions, which have not brought peace and prosperity to Africa. UNESCO believes that peace and development are 'indissolubly linked' and are 'two sides of the same coin'.[3] Peace, in the longer term, is not dependent on successful peacekeeping, as Malcolm Harper pointed out in Chapter 11 of this volume, but on 'constructing the defences of peace in the minds of men' as the preamble to UNESCO's constitution asserts.[4] Since the late 1980s UNESCO has considered Africa to be a priority and this trend is likely to continue well into the twenty-first century. UNESCO's medium-term strategy (1996–2001) has four priority groups: Women, Youth, Less Developed Countries, and Africa. The medium-term strategy and the programme and budget for 1996–7 and 1998–9 were based on the recommendations made and standards and targets set by the Africans themselves in 1995 at the Audience Africa Conference, and the UN system-wide initiative on

Africa that was launched in 1996. The emphasis is, however, on education, since that is UNESCO's main field of activity, and on the 'acquisition, sharing and transfer of knowledge'[5] because UNESCO believes that 'a peace based exclusively upon the political and economic arrangements of governments would not be a peace which could secure the unanimous, lasting and sincere support of the peoples of the world, and that the peace must therefore be founded, if it is not to fail, upon the intellectual and moral solidarity of mankind.'[6]

UNESCO's initial action in Africa

It would be slightly inaccurate to say that UNESCO's role in Africa began only after the African countries joined UNESCO, as it had played a role in bringing about decolonization in Africa. Numerous strongly-worded resolutions were passed by the UNESCO General Conference between 1960 and 1972. At its eleventh session in 1960, the General Conference passed a resolution entitled 'The role of UNESCO in contributing to the attainment of independence by colonial countries and peoples', which declared that 'colonialism in all its forms and all its manifestations must be speedily abolished, and that accession to freedom and independence must not be delayed on the false pretext that a particular territory has not reached a sufficiently high standard in economic, social, educational and cultural matters'. It also declared that 'UNESCO has a vital part to play in promoting the freedom and independence of colonial countries and peoples through its programmes in the fields of education, science and culture', and that 'one of UNESCO's *most urgent tasks* is to help the newly independent countries, and those which are preparing for independence to overcome any harmful after effects of colonialism, such as economic, social and cultural underdevelopment, illiteracy and the serious shortage of trained personnel'.[7]

UNESCO asserted that the formal educational system in Africa was in transition from the colonial to the post-colonial period. Warning against cultural hegemony, UNESCO criticised both metropolitan powers and local African elites who had been brainwashed by European education into devaluing their peoples' own culture. UNESCO argued that the schools in Africa were an extension of the metropolitan structure, as were the economy, polity and social structure. As long as the national bourgeoisie in its colonial role dominated the domestic pyramidal structure, we can expect that the education system would prevent liberation on two levels: liberation from the definition of culture and development by the high-income imperial nations; and liberation from the domestic pyramidal structure.'[8] Michael Barratt Brown points out that it is the profound conviction of African thinkers and writers that there is an African road to development that cannot be the European road. In the words of the Senegalese economist, E. S. Ndione, 'One must not impose the norms of a system on persons who function according to the norms of another system.' Technology has to be cleared through cultural customs, as Karl Polanyi would insist, and African culture is not European culture and cannot simply be transplanted.[9]

UNESCO's action in Africa was originally twofold. On the one hand, it was involved with emergency aid, the best example of which was its participation in the United Nations emergency operation in Zaire. It involved sending hundreds of teachers to that country, reopening existing primary and secondary schools and creating higher-education institutions. On the other hand, UNESCO developed its medium-term policy, initially for education, whose inception was marked by the adoption of the first Plan for African Educational Development by the Addis Ababa Conference in 1961.[10] This was the first of a series of regional conferences at ministerial level that were to define the scope of both the member states' actions and UNESCO's involvement.

The Addis Ababa Plan emphasised that a break had to be made with the past and the system of colonial education. It recommended that 'the authorities in charge of education revise the content of their education as regards the programmes, school text books and methods, taking into account the African environment, the development of the child, his cultural heritage and the requirements for technical progress and economic development, especially of industrialisation'.[11] The long-term (1961–80) objectives of the plan were as follows: (a) primary education will be universal, free and compulsory; (b) secondary education will be given to 30 per cent of the children who have completed primary education; (c) higher education will be given to about 20 per cent of the youth who have completed their secondary education; and (d) the improvement of the quality of African schools and universities shall be a constant aim. The Conference recommended that the percentage of the national revenue reserved for funding education should be raised from 3 per cent to 4 per cent between 1961 and 1965, and to 6 per cent between 1965 and 1980.[12] Between 1960 and 1972 the number of students attending school at primary, secondary and higher levels in forty-four African countries rose from 17.8 million to 37.6 million. The number of girls and young women in education also more than doubled. Moreover, syllabuses and textbooks were Africanised: that is, redesigned to meet the realities and needs of Africa rather than those of Europe.[13]

Between 1961 and 1989, UNESCO convened four other conferences on education; one on the conservation and use of natural resources; two on science and technology for development (CASTAFRICA I and II); and two devoted to culture and communication, respectively (AFRICACULT and AFRICOM). The recommendations of these regional conferences constituted one of the bases for the preparation of UNESCO's programme. Their implementation was financed either under UNESCO's own budget for programme activities or by funds made available to the organisation by other institutions such as the World Bank, UNDP, regional development banks and certain governments.[14]

Building on the Addis Ababa Plan, the Harare Conference (1982) which brought together for the first time ministers of education and high-level officials responsible for economic planning in African states, underscored the link between development policy and educational strategy. Its central theme was 'Education and Endogenous Development in Africa: Evolution, Problems and Prospects'. However, it noted that while considerable progress had been made in the eradication of illiteracy, the absolute number of illiterates was still increasing and the objective of schooling for all children had not been attained. Moreover, few African countries had succeeded in founding a truly decolonised new school, based on the rediscovered cultural identity and taking into account the cultural values of African societies. The Conference adopted a declaration and a series of eighteen recommendations, dealing mainly with the elimination of illiteracy in Africa before the end of the twentieth century; improvement in the teaching of science and technology and strengthening the role of higher education in the training of high officials; the development of research; and the promotion of national cultures.[15] In spite of the slow progress made, it reaffirmed the pivotal role assigned to 'the democratisation and renovation of education in order to enable all African children and adults of both sexes to exercise fully their right to education, a prerequisite for the fulfilment of individual potential and for the progress of society'.

In the area of *science and technology*, the tasks that UNESCO set itself as priorities in Africa were the systematic expansion of the research capabilities of the African member states, and the application of science and technology to the solution of a number of development problems. UNESCO's action in the *social and human sciences* involved strengthening the relevant infrastructure and institutions in Africa; encouraging the flow of information through the dissemination of research findings; training personnel; promoting co-operation between researchers and institutions at the regional level; assisting in the struggle against apartheid and for human rights; furthering the participation of women and young people in development; and advising on population matters. In the field of *culture*, UNESCO has contributed to the gradual change in thinking on the cultural dimension of development which has taken place in Africa, as well as to the formulation of cultural agreements between African states.[16]

Priority Africa: UNESCO's response to the United Nations Programme of Action for African Economic Recovery and Development (UNPAAERD)

By the late 1980s, UNESCO decided to intensify its efforts in favour of Africa. So, how and why did this come about? Widespread concern throughout the United Nations system and among member states over the critical economic situation in Africa in the 1980s led to the convening in 1986 of a UN General Assembly special session on Africa. The General Assembly adopted the United Nations Programme of Action for African Economic Recovery and Development, 1986–1990 (UNPAAERD) which sought to mobilise political and financial support for economic reforms.[17] This led to the UNESCO General Conference adopting the 'Priority Africa' Programme (1990–5) during its twenty-fifth session, as the contribution of UNESCO to the implementation of UNPAAERD.[18] At the beginning of the general policy debate with which the proceedings of the General Conference customarily open, Mr Frederico Mayor recalled that immediately after his election to the post of director-general he had stated his intention to 'commit myself personally to ensuring that Africa is a priority for UNESCO'.[19]

At its twenty-third plenary meeting on 2 November 1989, the General Conference adopted a resolution stating that 'despite the many efforts made by African countries and the international community, the latest reviews of Africa's economic and social situation by the multilateral development institutions point to a persistent slowing down in the global growth of African economies and to a constant deterioration in the living conditions of the populations of that continent'.[20]

It is worth noting here that the economic crisis in the African continent and the structural adjustment programmes imposed on them by international financial institutions (which led to a reduction in public expenditure) reduced the resources available for financing development. This is mainly due to the fact that public investment in development had traditionally been higher than private investment. Education thus had to compete with other sectors for fewer and fewer resources. As a result, the expansion of education at all levels stopped in the 1980s. A UNESCO report states that experiences in various African countries – for example, in Cameroon and Nigeria – show that the disengagement of the state from education was responsible for the abandonment of their studies by children from poor surroundings, girls being generally the first victims of the high cost of education.[21]

The General Conference thanked the director-general 'for his initiative in personally looking into the economic and social situation of the African continent and proposing in the document "Priority: Africa" the implementation, within UNESCO's fields of competence, of a programme of action, whose objectives and strategies are highly relevant to the African countries' current concerns', and encouraged him to pursue his efforts by giving each member state concerned the support it needed to draw up a plan of priority activities to be undertaken under this programme and to implement these activities.[22] In addition, the director-general was requested to identify resources that could help to launch this Programme.

The draft resolution was submitted to the delegates by Mr Aliyu, chairman of the Africa Group and the permanent delegate of Nigeria to UNESCO. He paid tribute to the director-general, whose action had brought UNESCO into the mainstream of the concerted efforts of the UN and its agencies to implement the UNPAAERD. He added: 'Priority Africa further underscores the immense burden which African States must bear, but which they accept, in the primary responsibilities to develop their own region and their societies; but it also points to the need for and the possibilities of international co-operation on the subject – in this case through UNESCO under its regular budget as well as through extra-budgetary resources, making use of the Organisation's capacity...to co-ordinate assistance from its Member States.'[23] The resolution adopted by the General Conference emphasised the urgency of developing African member states' national capacities to manage national human and financial resources. Thus, 'Priority Africa' was to be implemented by the Africans themselves. UNESCO was to act as an adviser, an animator, and a catalyst of intellectual, human and financial resources drawn from a wide variety of sources: international, intergovernmental and non-governmental organisations, financing bodies, governments and institutions, all of which would be invited to co-operate with African governments at the latter's request. Also, African states were themselves expected to make a special effort to compare and collate their experience and their approaches, and to intensify their co-operation, either in the context of the numerous regional and subregional organisations concerned with the continent's development, or on an *ad hoc* basis.[24]

However, UNESCO was to make resources available for the implementation of the 'Priority Africa' programme. On 16 May 1990, the director-general of UNESCO informed the 134th session of the UNESCO Executive Board that, in accordance with the relevant provisions of 25 C/Resolution 27, he had allocated US$300 000 to this programme from savings, and reserved US$1 500 000 for it under the Participation Programme. Added to the US$860 000 already assigned to it in the Approved Programme and Budget, it brought the total to US$2 660 000. This sum would be used mainly to assist member states in the preparation of joint projects designed to mobilise the extra-budgetary funds necessary for their implementation. He added that the 'Priority Africa' programme 'deserved to be further reinforced. Projects aimed at developing technical co-operation among African Member States as regards distance education, computer science in schools, the rehabilitation of African universities, the training of engineers, combating desertification, and self-sufficiency in food are being prepared and should be launched by June 1990'.[25]

The programme was also meant to provide a 'bonus' for activities already being undertaken in the various major programme areas by encouraging regional and subregional co-operation, mobilising extra-budgetary resources, and supporting interdisciplinary and intersectoral activities *in fields considered a priority by African member states themselves*.[26]

In 1990, the Conference of the Ministers of the Africa Economic Community (AEC) adopted a resolution at its sixteenth meeting, asking all African member states to co-operate towards the implementation of the 'Priority Africa' programme. In 1991, the Treaty of Abuja was adopted by the chiefs of state and government of the Organisation of African Unity (OAU), which established the AEC. In 1991, the UN General Assembly reviewed the UNPAAERD and concluded that the critical economic situation in Africa was continuing and called for a New Agenda for the Development of Africa in the 1990s (UN-NADAF). In 1994, the UN adopted an Action Plan for the UN system for the economic recovery and development of Africa, reflecting the new imperatives because of a revision of the Agenda. UNESCO was designated as leader for the chapter of the plan concerned with 'development of human resources and capacities'. In order to co-ordinate the action programmes for Africa and favour the implementation of the UN-NADAF and the Action Plan, the United Nations decided to create the

'United Nations Inter-Agency Task Force on African Economic Recovery and Development'. UNESCO participated actively in this.[27]

A review of the progress made in Africa by the mid-1990s

The year 1995 in Africa was characterised by the continuation of the democratic process and the pursuit of economic stabilisation. However, this process was subjected to serious shocks: the devaluation of currencies in the region; and political and civil upheavals. Some countries such as Angola, Mozambique and Ethiopia, emerged from civil conflicts and started the 'arduous business of nation-building', but civil strife continued in others, such as Rwanda and Burundi. The political and social remedies applied in most of the countries of the region 'were yet to show signs of attacking the malaise associated with poverty by the time the year [1995] ended'.[28]

In UNESCO's fields of competence, the year marked the half-way point between the Jomtien Conference on Education for All (1990) and the target year of 2000 AD. As a number of countries in the region engaged in Jomtien mid-term reviews, they were also faced with the problem of strikes by teachers and students. A number of countries even witnessed the *année blanche*. In the field of science, the year was marked by improved rainfall in the Sahel, but drought again ravaged the countries of Southern Africa. Science, research and technological infrastructure remained in a poor state. Even though there was increased awareness about the environment everywhere, projects developed to meet the demands of Rio's Agenda 21 could not attract funding. The field of culture witnessed creativity within the civil society, in spite of gruelling economic hardships. Even though the major development partners did not seem to show sufficient concern for cultural issues, a number of major continental cultural events were organised (for example, the Ouagadougou film festival; the Accra African and Black writers' congress and so on). The continuing dynamism of the civil society was the main achievement in the social science sector. Although talents in the sector were badly affected by brain-drain, pan-African NGOs such as the Council for the Development of Economic and Social Research in Africa (CODESRIA) and the Fédération des Associations de Parents d'élèves et Étudiants (FAPES) continued to maintain a high profile. In the information and communication sector, Africa's communication problems persisted, in spite of improvements in telecommunications in a number of countries. The 'explosion' of the private media continued unabated, though quality suffered in many instances. There was a greater awareness of the need to promote freedom of expression, but it is also on record that this freedom was bitterly suppressed in a number of countries. African countries participated in the three World Summits: in Cairo (population and development); Copenhagen (social development), and Beijing (women), and worked hard to make their voices heard, subscribed fully to the charters and plans of action, while hoping that the post-summit period would see an end to their current difficulties.[29]

UNESCO's achievements in Africa

UNESCO's achievements in Africa in the 1990s may be summarised as follows:

Education sector

1 Assistance to member states in the organisation of mid-term reviews of the post-Jomtien achievements;
2 Promotion of studies on the education of girls and women; and
3 Regional activities in the areas of Science 2000+ (its African version POPSTAFRIC) and the International Project on Technical and Vocational Education, and higher education.

Science sector

1 Training in desertification control (Southern African countries); and
2 Strengthening of Man and the Biosphere committees;

Culture sector

1 Book development: (a) assistance to higher institutions for the production of authoritative texts; and (b) regional training programmes in publishing management; and
2 Continuation of the translation into Hausa and Kiswahili of UNESCO's *General History of Africa*.

Social and human sciences

1 Co-ordinating Africa's contribution to the Copenhagen Summit on social development; and
2 Assistance to the regional and national effort for the strengthening of democracy, youth, development and human rights.

According to a report by the UNESCO Office at Dakar, the rate of execution in all areas was quite high (90–100%). This was made possible by the devotion of staff members, the active co-operation of the intellectual community, and institutions and NGOs/IGOs in the region. The Dakar Office also enjoyed the kind support of UNESCO National Commissions and all the UNESCO Offices in the region. Extra-budgetary projects remained a major source of strength to the Office during 1995.[30]

Listening to Africa: the audience

The most important initiative UNESCO took in the 1990s with regard to Africa was the convening of an international conference entitled Audience Africa, held at the UNESCO headquarters in Paris from 6–10 February 1995. It aroused great interest throughout the African continent and marked a turning-point in the organisation's work for Africa. The conference was attended by Africans from a wide range of social and occupational backgrounds: independent figures from civil society; political leaders and policy-makers; and representatives of international, regional, non-governmental, intellectual and scientific organisations. They examined the whole question of development and development priorities in their continent on the eve of the World Summit for Social Development (Copenhagen, March 1995), enabling them to determine for themselves the priority fields for UNESCO's action in Africa over the coming years.[31]

Reporting on the Audience Africa meeting, George Ola-Davies of West Africa wrote: 'Audience Africa is a radical departure from the special six-year-old Africa's Priority programme instituted by UNESCO's Director-General, Mayor. Until now, explains Basile Kossou [head of UNESCO's African bureau for external relations], this priority Africa – which is itself an addition to UNESCO's general programme – has been elaborated by officials within the organisation's secretariat. Audience Africa will attempt to show where the Africa priority programme has gone wrong.'[32] Essentially, the conference diagnosed Africa's problems, assessed the situation in the fields of education, science, communications and culture and made recommendations for the future.

The participants stressed that Africa was facing a serious situation as the new millennium begins to usher in new models. The globalization of markets and the growing reinforcement of regional blocs would intensify commercial, financial and cultural competition, and scientific and technological rivalry on an unprecedented scale. They envisaged that the industrial nations would 'further their development in a spirit of individualism and egoism' and that international assistance would be granted on draconian terms, inspired by a thinly disguised desire to create situations of hegemony or dependency. Africa will therefore have to rely increasingly on its own strength. Its 'true future lies in its children's ability to design, forge and enhance a process of renewal of liberation and progress, without which it will never participate as a credible, responsible and respected partner in international relations'.[33]

Participants pointed out that the African continent was still seriously handicapped by four centuries of slave trading and 'the ever-present weight of colonial and neo-colonial domination'. However, it cannot be denied that since 1960 Africa has made progress in education, science, culture and communications, 'which can be fully appreciated when set against the performance of the colonial era, over a much longer period of time.'

However, they also admitted that the continent has failed in a number of areas. It has the highest general mortality and infant mortality rates, the lowest life expectancy, the lowest rates of economic growth, the lowest income per capita, and the highest population growth. The African continent also has extremely low school enrolment rates and particularly high illiteracy rates: 'We are considerably under-equipped and development of the communication media is still in its infancy. Education, training, culture, information and health budgets are constantly being whittled down, while defence, security and arms budgets are constantly being expanded.' Moreover, African administrations are often blighted by ethnic preference, a partisan approach, cronyism, nepotism, corruption, absenteeism, laxness, and low rates of return and efficiency. Misappropriation of public funds, wastage and chaos are not sufficiently discouraged. They felt that Africans were themselves responsible for these lapses and that they must all make a firm and resolute commitment to reverse this trend by 'breaking with the past and formulating a completely new endogenous development policy.' However, they must first share a number of convictions.

The ten convictions

1 The African continent is not poor. It has great natural wealth.
2 Independence is not an end in itself but a means of improving a situation.
3 Africa will never be built by foreigners. The end purpose of assistance is to make it possible for assistance to be phased out.
4 Only Africa can decide its own destiny. Africans must take the initiative in solving their own problems.

5   As long as Africans have no confidence in themselves, in their culture, abilities or values, they will never make full use of the resources
of creativity and inventiveness that lie dormant within them.

6   Three decades of difficulties, mistakes, hesitant experimentation
will not have been in vain if we have the courage to carry out a
critical assessment of the situation, and make an effort to draw, with
humility, all the appropriate lessons from it with a view to a new
start.

7   Structural adjustment plans should rapidly give way to genuine
development programmes based on growth, full employment and
justice, devised and carried out by the citizens of the countries
themselves for the benefit, in particular, of the most disadvantaged
sections of society.

8   The centralisation of power or seizure of power by a minority operating through a single party or a state-party is harmful. Africa needs
democracy. However, democracy is not a model to be copied but
rather an objective to be attained.

9   Africans need an inflexible political will to reverse a serious and
ongoing trend of political instability and war.

10 In a world dominated by economic blocs 'engaged in cut-throat
competition', micro-states have no chance of becoming significant
and credible forces unless they unite.

With its population of 640 million people at the time of writing, who
will number more than 1.2 thousand million consumers in around
twenty years' time, we can be sure that Africa, with the wealth in
its soil, its subsoil, its seas, its forests and its tourist and cultural
potential, will never be marginalised if its people have the necessary
negotiating skills to turn such undoubted benefits to commercial
advantage.[34]

The recommendations of the Conference

The Conference made a number of recommendations to, on the one
hand, African governments, and on the other to UNESCO and other UN
specialised agencies. It also made several recommendations to African
organisations such as the OAU, AEC and the African Development Bank
(ADB), and to the intellectual and political elites, civil society and
territorial communities. The recommendations and priorities, which
were quite comprehensive and wide-ranging, fell under the following
headings:

1 Training and sharing of knowledge: which schools and which universities for tomorrow's Africa?
2 Science, technology and sustainable development: Africa and the world.
3 Regionalization and development.
4 Communication and development in the rural environment: the cultural dimension of development in Africa.
5 Democratisation in everyday life: the culture of peace.

Training and sharing of knowledge

Audience Africa considered the impact of structural adjustment plans on education systems and observed that after a period of expansion of some twenty years, education and training had been marked in recent years by the emergence of wide disparities between rich and poor, urban and rural areas, and girls and boys. That was being compounded by the inability of education systems to move with the times and adapt to the requirements of an ever-changing world.

It recommended to African governments that the systems inherited from the colonial era must be rebuilt, which will mean redefining goals, content, structures, methods, approaches and values as part of a mould-breaking strategy. The basic aims must be that education should be of a high standard and that it should be relevant to the sociocultural context. Education of girls should be treated as one of the chief priorities of the reform.

The reform of education systems will be an opportunity for African countries, with regard to the financing of education, to redefine new partnership strategies providing for burden-sharing and cost-sharing between states, regions, provinces, municipalities, rural communities and families on bases that have been jointly negotiated and are mutually acceptable.

The meeting endorsed the conclusions of the Jomtien conference on Education for All (1990) and recommended that basic education should be given priority, and that 20 per cent of the budget should be directed towards it. It was also suggested that a law on compulsory schooling should be introduced wherever this has not already been done. People should be made aware of the importance of developing African languages for use in schools, the media, journals and so on. It was recommended that UNESCO and member states should establish research centres and language academies to develop these languages, as education, relevance, understanding, self-reliance, and so on will result directly from using an individual's language with parents, teachers and so on.

Audience Africa recommended that UNESCO should help African states to prepare a programme for the regionalization of higher education and the creation of regional centres of excellence. These should provide a response to concerns regarding African authenticity, and should aim to attain the specific objectives to be assigned to them with regard to contributing to the solution of the problems people come across in everyday development. UNESCO Chairs should be created for the teaching of human rights in order to foster a culture of peace and democracy.[35]

It was also recommended that private enterprise, elites and financial backers also had a role to play in education. With reference to the United Nations, it was proposed that the guidelines laid down by the revised Programme of Action in the United Nations New Agenda for the Development of Africa in the 1990s, adopted by the General Assembly of the United Nations in Resolution 49/L.44/Rev.2 of 22 December 1994, should be taken into account in implementing the recommendations of Audience Africa.[36]

Science, technology and sustainable development: Africa and the world

The Committee that dealt with science, technology and sustainable development for Africa and the world based their recommendations on the argument that, in spite of their diversity, African countries had common problems and it was therefore necessary to devise common strategies.

Audience Africa recommended to African governments that they should formulate a coherent science policy and a concrete plan of action at both national and regional levels. African governments should promote science and technology teaching from primary school onwards, and centres of excellence throughout the African continent. They should also develop, improve and diversify infrastructures with a view to achieving autonomy and self-reliance in science and technology. They should also allocate a minimum of 0.4 per cent to 0.5 per cent of their country's GDP to research for development. They should endeavour to facilitate access by African researchers and academics to data banks through computer networks, finding appropriate partners for them.

The Conference recommended to UNESCO that it should promote twinning operations between research institutes and laboratories, with a view to setting up viable scientific partnerships between the scientific communities of the North and the South, and among those of the South in areas of concern to them. Possibly its most significant recommendation to UNESCO was that it should contribute to the definition of a new paradigm for endogenous development, geared to the priority needs of populations, practicable, and drawing on endogenous resources.

UNESCO was also encouraged to contribute to the improvement or establishment of centres of excellence and fellowship programmes for this purpose, and provide strong support to women scientists from African countries – for example, through the African unit of the Third World Organisation for Women in Science (TWOWS).

UNESCO was also urged to give priority to science and technology in Africa during the following two years and throughout the period covered by UNESCO's medium-term strategy. In this connection, special interest should be taken in the applications of solar energy and other sources of renewable energy for sustainable development and environmental protection through the establishment of an African solar programme. Audience Africa asked the UNDP to ensure that 3 per cent of all African national allocations was earmarked for research and development. Finally, UNESCO was urged to continue efforts to secure extra-budgetary resources for the fund set up by the director-general for the development of science and technology in Africa.

Regionalization and development

The Committee that considered the theme of regionalization and development asserted that regional co-operation was a decisive factor in the achievement of peace and stability in Africa, and an essential condition for its development:

> Audience Africa took full note of the fact that regionalization implied the creation of a climate of confidence, tolerance and mutual respect within each African State and also between all of those States. It also supposed respect for commitments entered into within the framework of a State based on the rule of law and upheld by the force of the law. On that basis, regionalization would be a matter for the people concerned. It would enable all Africans to learn how to live together and to know each other, to respect and talk to each other, to mix and work together, to exchange goods and services and to communicate, irrespective of their language, religion, ethnic origin or the colour of their skin.

As regards the strategy that should be adopted to carry out this policy, Audience Africa stressed the importance of community projects based on geographic or other forms of proximity, to support all joint institutions which had proved their effectiveness, and to work to improve the performance of those that were essential to the future of the African continent, even if they were experiencing temporary difficulties.

Audience Africa took the view that African integration should be conceived in pragmatic terms, with a gradual transfer of responsibilities and sovereignty to common institutions, and with the strengthening of inter-African co-operation and seeking to establish ties with communities of African origin in other continents, without forgetting horizontal South–South co-operation. In this connection, Audience Africa welcomed the adoption by the General Conference of a resolution providing for the convening of an intergovernmental meeting of experts on South–South co-operation in 1995.

The Conference recommended to African governments that they should provide effective support for the continent's institutions such as the OAU, the UN Economic Commission for Africa (ECA) and the ADB, by paying their contributions, carrying out their resolutions and making use of their services in their fields of competence in order to endow them with the necessary authority. They were encouraged to develop joint projects relating to training, infrastructure, communication and so on, in order to reduce costs and maximise efficiency, as well as to formulate and execute jointly, at regional and subregional level, strategies for the protection of the environment and for the joint exploitation of natural resources, specifically in the fields of energy, water, forestry and so on.

Popular participation was encouraged in order to make a success of integration, and emphasis was put on promoting tolerance through education and in training citizens in the context of the enhancement of the culture of peace. This would lead to greater awareness of the obligations, duties and rights of every individual and a greater understanding between Africans, which would be a guarantee of calm and constructive cohabitation.

Private enterprise too had an important role to play in the success of the integration process. In addition to governments and civil society, private businesses must be in contact with each other, establish working practices based on trust, moral probity, respect for commitments, a liking for efficiency, and a commitment to jointly established regulations and standards. They must also pool information, experience, capital, managers and infrastructure in order to undertake joint ventures and explore options for co-operation in all fields.

UNESCO was invited to work with the OAU, AEC and ADB to implement the Lagos Plan of Action,[37] and to encourage the practical application and effective implementation of the Treaty of Abuja establishing the African Economic Community. Other agencies of the UN system were urged to join UNESCO in supporting in a variety of ways and in their respective fields of competence the sub-regional and regional programmes initiated by African states and the joint institutions running them.[38]

Audience Africa made it quite clear that Africa's development was not dependent upon a few actors but rather a variety of actors at local, regional and international levels whose co-operation and active participation was needed if Africa was to achieve its goals.

Communication and development in the rural environment; the cultural dimension of development in Africa

Audience Africa noted the inadequate development of communication in Africa and its limited involvement in the development efforts of African countries. It ascribed this to the low level of priority accorded to communication by African governments and to the insufficient resources allocated to its development.

The Conference emphasised the vital role of communication in all aspects of development and rural activity, and recommended that UNESCO and other international organisations should work with African governments to establish a policy making communication a major priority aim of development.

As regards the cultural dimension of development in Africa, the Conference reaffirmed the need for Africa and Africans to display independence and initiative of thought and action in the areas of study, invention, the production of ideas, concepts, values, symbols and references.

Democratisation in everyday life: the culture of peace

Audience Africa noted that democratisation was on the agenda everywhere on the African continent. In some countries, democratic change had occurred without violence. In others, the democratic process was taking place 'in an extremely fragile context, mainly because of the absence of any democratic culture, the intensity of tribal and ethnic antagonisms, the weakness of new parliaments and the persistence of fundamentalism and outbursts of violence'.

The Conference requested that UNESCO should bear in mind that African history and culture should be used as the main inspiration for democracy in Africa, and should denounce strongly dictators in Africa, and invite a group of African experts to prepare an African covenant on democracy, governance and respect for fundamental human rights.

The participants declared themselves to be opposed to the use of religion and ethnicity for political and terrorist ends, and called for the development of religious and moral values and ethics as fundamental elements and catalysts in the culture of peace. It welcomed the efforts made by the Angolan government to hasten peace and national reconciliation on the basis of the Lusaka Protocol, as well as the efforts made towards national reconciliation in Sudan, Liberia, Sierra Leone, Burundi, Somalia and Eritrea, and urged the parties to co-operate with regional and international bodies trying to find peaceful solutions to the conflicts in those countries.

It is worth noting here that national culture of peace programmes were launched in several African countries in the 1990s – for example, in Mozambique and Burundi. The national programme in Burundi was launched in December 1994, with the opening of a House of a Culture of Peace in Bujumbura, staffed by a multi-ethnic team. The house provides both a symbolic expression of the national desire for peace and a material structure with the means and institutional power to put it into practice. It has already become a centre for many individuals and groups working for peace. Despite the violence that has afflicted the city, work has continued on peace seminars for journalists, government administrators, educators and representatives from NGOs and the UN.[39]

The message from Africa

The ideas expressed by Audience Africa were reiterated by the Organisation of African Unity in the Cairo Agenda for Action adopted in June 1995.[40] Both Audience Africa and the Cairo Agenda reaffirmed that Africa's development is, first and foremost, the responsibility of the governments and people of Africa themselves, but that international partners could enhance the development prospects of Africa through an understanding and appreciation of Africa's development efforts.

The United Nations system-wide special initiative for Africa

On 15 March 1996 the UN Secretary-General, Boutros Boutros-Ghali along with the executive heads of all UN agencies and organisations represented in the Administrative Committee on Co-ordination (ACC), launched a ten-year, \$25-billion UN system-wide special initiative on

Africa. Designed to accelerate African development, the Special Initiative aimed over the following decade to expand basic education and health care greatly, to promote peace and better governance, and to improve water and food security. It was the UN system's most significant mobilisation of support ever for the development activities of the African continent. A live link-up to Addis Ababa enabled Meles Zenawi, prime minister of Ethiopia and Chairman of the Organisation of African Unity (OAU), and OAU Secretary-General, Salim Ahmed Salim, to provide an official response on behalf of Africa. Mr Zenawi said the Initiative was 'fully in line with Africa's priorities and interests', and was being launched at a time when there was a need for steps to ensure its development.[41] By Resolution 51/32 of December 1996, the General Assembly emphasised the complementarity of the United Nations System-wide Special Initiative on Africa and UN-NADAF.

The UN clearly emphasises that the Special Initiative is not a call for action by UN Agencies; rather, it is a call to support the priorities determined by Africa and to galvanise international support for Africa's efforts and for the successful implementation of Africa's programmes. It consists of fourteen distinct programmes which are to be implemented by joint and concerted actions of UN agencies.[42] Within this framework, UNESCO is the co-ordinating agency for three programmes: *basic education for all African children; communications for peace-building; and harnessing information technology for development*.[43]

The recommendations adopted at Audience Africa, together with the programme of the United Nations System-wide Special Initiative on Africa launched in March 1996, were taken into account in drawing up the Medium-Term Strategy (1996–2001) and thus formed the framework for UNESCO's action in Africa and the main guidelines for 1996–7 and 1998–9. This fact was also stressed by Ashgar Husein, Director of the Priority Africa division of UNESCO.[44] There are five main tendencies: priority is given to programmes to encourage *regional integration and co-operation* and the setting-up of regional and sub-regional networks; *basic education for all African children; science and technology and sustainable development*; all activities relating to the *culture of peace*; and the *role of African women* in the continent's development.[45]

Africa in UNESCO's programme and budget (1996–7)

Programmes for Africa in the period 1996–7 were in the following areas: elimination of illiteracy among women and young girls in rural areas; technical and professional education; access to higher scientific and technological education and scientific careers; scientific publications for young people; technological development and university–research–industry relationships; the environment and the development of natural resources; the management of social transformations, taking into account the cultural dimension in development projects; training in the areas of creation and handicrafts; development of community media; training in the field of communication; development of data processing/computer science; support to democratisation processes; and intercultural dialogue.[46]

The 1996–7 budget allocation for activities relating to African member states under the regular programme amounted to some $15 million. UNESCO claims that this is a substantial sum in view of the fact that it was intended primarily to serve as seed money for the purpose of providing impetus, selecting and preparing projects, launching pilot projects, organising training, and mobilising other resources to broaden, generalise or continue activities later. In addition, the allocation of $6.7 million under the Participation Programme enabled 340 projects to be implemented in African member states.[47]

From the start of the two-year period to the end of September 1997, $40.2 million from extra-budgetary sources were used to fund sixty-four regional projects and ninety-four country projects in Africa. To these sums may be added staff and running costs for the Organisation's African offices, making a total budget of some $100 million devoted to Africa. Lastly, UNESCO points out that it should not be forgotten that UNESCO, as adviser, facilitator and 'moral conscience' of the United Nations system, also acts in intangible ways that are difficult to evaluate in budgetary terms, although they have financial implications (missions, negotiations, appeals by the director-general, press releases, and so on).[48]

In 1996, UNESCO initiated twenty-nine special projects for four priority target groups (women, youth, least developed countries, and Africa) for a total of US$5 613 200 from its regular budget. Most of these projects included activities involving African countries, but seventeen of them were designed exclusively for Africa and six specifically for young people: enhancement of learning and training opportunities; music cross-roads; science reading for young Africans; video libraries for young people in Africa; enhancing the contribution of youth to development; and intercultural dialogue in everyday life. Two other special projects also have a dual priority, targeting African women and girls: scientific, technical and vocational education of girls in Africa; and women and water resource supply and use. UNESCO claims that the rate of execution is greater than 80 per cent for virtually all these projects, which will last between two and six years.[49]

The period 1998–9, which is the second stage of the implementation of the medium-term strategy (1996–2001), also gives priority to Africa in its programmes and continues the initiatives started in the previous two years. The programme and budget include several special projects for African countries.[50] These include: promoting girls' and women's education in Africa; scientific, technical and vocational education of girls in Africa; women, higher education and development; biotechnologies for development in Africa; women and water resources supply and use in sub-Saharan Africa; a museum outreach programme in Africa; African Itinerant College for culture and development; improving communication training in Africa; women speaking to women; and women and a culture of peace in Africa.[51]

Conclusion

UNESCO's policy towards Africa in the 1990s and into the new millennium is that, first, Africa must develop its endogenous capacities. This was also the 'conviction' of the Audience Africa conference, which declared that Africa will never be built by foreigners. Only Africans can decide their own destiny. However, as long as Africans have no confidence in themselves, or in their culture, abilities or values, they will never make full use of the resources of creativity and inventiveness that lie dormant within them. Second, both UNESCO and its African member states agree that Africans must determine their own priorities and set their own targets. This was the main objective behind the Audience Africa Conference. However, African member states have accepted UNESCO's fundamental thesis regarding the relationship between peace and development, and subscribe to the liberal principles enshrined in its Constitution while at the same time emphasising their own cultural identity and practices. Third, both UNESCO and its African member states agree that Africa needs the support of the international community to achieve its goals. UNESCO, therefore does not seek to replace African organisations and authorities but to serve as an adviser and a catalyst of intellectual, human and financial resources drawn from a wide variety of sources. At the seventh conference of ministers of education of African Member States (MINEDAF VII) held in Durban from the 20th to the 24th of April, 1998, the following declaration was adopted which embodies these policies: 'We, the Ministers of Education of African Member States, conscious of our commitments...are resolved to work together towards regional integration within the framework of OAU and the African Economic Community, and call upon UNESCO and our regional and international partners to give priority support to our capacity-building and reform efforts, so that together we can shape Education as the lead instrument for the fashioning of the African Renaissance.'[52]

Notes and References

1　UNESCO (United Nations Educational, Scientific and Cultural Organisation) was set up to 'contribute to peace and security by promoting collaboration among the nations through education, science and culture in order to further universal respect for justice, for the rule of law and for the human rights and fundamental freedoms that are affirmed for the peoples of the world, without distinction of race, sex, language or religion, by the Charter of the United Nations' (Article I, Constitution of UNESCO).

2　The director-general of UNESCO stresses that UNESCO has always stressed the importance of the cultural dimension of development and sought 'to look beyond the purely economic aspects of development and assign to human beings their rightful place in this process so that they become not merely an object or instrument but also the ultimate goal of development' (UNESCO (1989) *UNESCO and Africa* (Paris: UNESCO), p. 4).

3　UNESCO (1996) *Medium Term Strategy – 1996–2001*, Document 28/C4 (Paris: UNESCO), p. 9, para. 36.

4　UNESCO's cross-disciplinary project, 'Towards a Culture of Peace' brings together the activities UNESCO intends to carry out in order to promote adherence to values that are at the heart of the 'spirit of peace': respect for human rights and democratic principles; the rejection of violence and all forms of discrimination, including discrimination between men and women; attachment to the principles of freedom, justice, solidarity, tolerance and understanding, both between peoples and between groups or individuals; and to foster the acquisition of the knowledge, skills and attitudes which reflect and embody these values (see UNESCO (1997) *Approved Programme and Budget for 1998–1999*, Document 29/C5 (Paris: UNESCO), p. 121).

5　To facilitate the acquisition, sharing and transfer of knowledge of the means of eliminating the obstacles to development is one of the priorities of the medium-term strategy. Other priorities include: encouraging the development of human resources; assisting in the creation or reinforcement of endogenous capacities; ensuring access by all to science and technology while halting the brain drain; reinforcing communication capacities and facilitating the free flow of information; and fostering social cohesion and democratic participation (UNESCO, *Medium-Term Strategy, 1996–2001*).

6　See preamble to the Constitution of UNESCO: *Basic Texts* (1998) (Paris: UNESCO); p. 7.

7　S. Dutt (1995) *The Politicization of the United Nations Specialized Agencies: A Case Study of UNESCO* (Lampeter; Lewiston: Mellen University Press), pp. 82–3.

8   See Michael Barratt Brown (1995) *Africa's Choices* (Harmondsworth: Penguin), pp. 3–4.

9   Ibid., p. 4.

10 This was the first regional conference of ministers of education and economic planning in Africa (MINEDAF I). The themes of the following MINEDAFs were as follows: MINEDAF II (1964): Funding of National Education Plans; MINEDAF III (1968): Science and Technology Education; MINEDAF IV (1976): Educational Reforms and Innovations; MINEDAF V (1982): Eradication of Illiteracy; MINEDAF VI (1991): Basic Education for All in Africa.

11 UNESCO (1997) *Report on the State of Education in Africa – 1997* (Dakar: UNESCO Regional Office for Education in Africa (BREDA)), November, p. 97.

12 Ibid.

13 Basil Davidson (1994) *Modern Africa*, 3rd edn (London and New York: Longman), p. 186.

14 UNESCO (1989) *UNESCO and Africa* (Paris: UNESCO), p. 6.

15 UNESCO, *Report on the State of Education in Africa – 1997*, pp. 99–100.

16 See UNESCO, *UNESCO and Africa*, pp. 13–24.

17 United Nations (1995) *Basic Facts about the United Nations* (New York: United Nations), p. 138.

18 Eva Sankale, 'UNESCO and Africa, "L'action de l'UNESCO en Afrique: un bref rappel",' available at: http://www.unesco.org/africa/, accessed 1 May 1998. It should, however, be noted that UNESCO went through a crisis in the mid-1980s, when the USA and the UK withdrew from the organisation, taking more than 25 per cent of the budget with them. UNESCO's financial constraints and ensuing staff reductions in the Secretariat prevented the organisation from launching a new programme specifically designed on the basis of the UNPAAERD programme. Nevertheless, UNESCO endeavoured to group together and strengthen those of its activities that fell within the scope of the Programme in order to respond as far as possible to the appeal made to the specialised agencies of the United Nations system (UNESCO, *UNESCO and Africa*, p. 25).

19 UNESCO (1990) *Priority: Africa, News Bulletin*, no. 1, July, p. 5.

20 UNESCO (1989) *Records of the General Conference*, 25th session, Resolutions, Document 25/C, p. 188; Resolution 27, 'Co-operation with Africa'.

21 UNESCO, *Report on the State of Education in Africa – 1997*, ch. II, 'Education and Economic Crisis', pp. 32–60.

22 UNESCO (1989) *Records of the General Conference*, 25th session, Resolutions, Document 25/C, p. 188, Resolution 27, 'Co-operation with Africa'.

23 UNESCO (1990) *Priority: Africa, News Bulletin*, no. 1, July, p. 6.

24 Ibid., pp. 6–7.

25 Ibid., p. 7.

26 UNESCO (1997), *Review of UNESCO's Activities in Africa (1996–1997)*, Priority Africa Department (Paris: UNESCO), October, p. 1.

27 Eva Sankale, 'UNESCO and Africa...'.

28 UNESCO (1995) *Rapport Annuel* (Dakar: UNESCO Regional Office), p. 7.

29 Ibid., pp. 7–10.

30 Ibid.

31 UNESCO, *Review of UNESCO's Activities in Africa*, pp. 1–2.

32 George Ola-Davies (1995) 'Calling All Africans', *West Africa*, London, 23 January.

33 UNESCO (1995) *Audience Africa, Social Development: Africa's Priorities*, Final report, Document BRX-95/CONF.006/7 (Paris: UNESCO), p. 2.

34 UNESCO (1995) *Voices, Values and Development: Re-inventing Africa (South of the Sahara)* (Paris: UNESCO), p. 8.

35 The UNITWIN/UNESCO chairs programme was launched in 1991 with the aim of promoting the transfer of knowledge and the institutional development of higher education, and mitigating the negative impact of the brain drain, especially in the least developed countries, through the establishment of inter-university networks. These networks are mainly inter-regional, but co-operation among institutions in different developing countries (South–South co-operation) is particularly encouraged. More than forty UNESCO chairs have been set up in Africa so far. These include Education for Human Rights and Democracy (Addis Ababa University); Democracy and Human Rights (University of Namibia); Oliver Tambo Chair of Human Rights (University of Fort Hare, South Africa); Culture of Peace, Preventive Diplomacy (University of Durban, South Africa); Human Rights and Democracy (National University of Benin); and Peace Education and Peaceful Conflict Resolution (University of Burundi). See UNESCO, *Review of UNESCO's Activities in Africa*, p. 9 and annexe III.

36 This Programme of Action lays emphasis on research, higher education, information exchange, inter-university co-operation, the promotion of quality and innovation, and the steps to be taken in the context of preventive education against AIDS. In this regard, UNESCO should play a vigorous role as lead agency for the implementation of the priority programme 'Human Resource Development and Capacity-Building', by the United Nations system.

37 The Lagos Plan of Action for the Economic Development of Africa, 1980–2000 was based on an African perspective. It committed members of the OAU to nothing less than the establishment by the year 2000 of an 'African Economic Community, so as to ensure the economic, social and cultural integration of our continent'. It was to be the basis for discussions between African governments and outside bodies, donors, investors and international institutions on Africa's development (see Brown, *Africa's Choices*, p. 130).

38 Audience Africa also had recommendations for the international financial community, which was urged to give absolute priority to the funding of regional integration projects in Africa. For a single decade, 0.7 per cent of the gross national product (GNP) of the industrialised countries should be allocated to official aid for the development of Africa, in line with United Nations resolutions. Addressing the IMF in particular, Audience Africa requests it to grant African states a substantial allowance in the form of special drawing rights (extended facilities) in order to deal with the problems raised by the implementation of a new development policy based on the construction of regional integration, which opens up the prospect of greater co-operation and promises growth in the future.

39 UNESCO (1997) *UNESCO and a Culture of Peace* (Paris: UNESCO), p. 50.

40 Relaunching Africa's Economic and Social Development: The Cairo Agenda for Action. In 1995, at an extraordinary session of the Organisation of African

Unity (OAU) Council of Ministers, an African Agenda for Action was adopted. This was subsequently endorsed by the June 1995 Summit of the African Heads of State and Government in Addis Ababa. The Cairo Agenda reaffirmed that Africa's development is, first and foremost, the responsibility of the governments and people of Africa themselves. It also affirmed that priority must now be given to the implementation of the strategies and programmes for the development of African countries which have been adopted at national, regional and continental levels. The Agenda identified a set of priority issues that governments are committed to address, and for which international support is required. They include:

- governance, peace, stability and development;
- food security;
- human resources development and capacity building;
- resource mobilisation;
- regional economic co-operation and integration; and
- the structural transformation of African economies.

International partners could enhance the development prospects of Africa through:

- an understanding and appreciation of Africa's development efforts;
- mitigating the adverse consequences of the Uruguay Round (trade agreements);
- taking measures to reduce the continent's debt burden; and
- stimulating both economic and social development in Africa.

These themes were echoed at the July 1995 meeting of the ECOSOC High-level Segment on Africa. There is an emerging consensus that while Africa needs external support, it is the Africans themselves, men and women, who must take charge of their destiny and who should have the fundamental responsibility for bringing about development on their continent (see UNA-UK, Agenda for Development Study and Discussion Pack, *The United Nations System-Wide Special Initiative for Africa*, February 1997, pp. 3–4; United Nations, *Document on the United Nations System-Wide Special Initiative on Africa*).

41 'The United Nations System-Wide Special Initiative on Africa: Ten-year, $25-billion Drive for Development', *UN Chronicle*, vol. XXXIII, no. 2, 1996.

42 These fourteen programmes are as follows: peace-building, conflict resolution and national reconciliation; external support for Africa's economic transition; internal resources mobilisation, domestic savings and investment; harnessing information technology for development; basic education for all African children; health sector reform; employment and sustainable livelihoods; expanding the capacities for transparent, responsible and effective governance; strengthening civil society for development; food security and drought management; assuring sustainable use of and equitable access to fresh water; household water security; freshwater assessments; and water for food production.

43 UNESCO is also a supporting agency for eight other programmes conducted within the remit of the Initiative, particularly as regards solar energy, and

participates in ten other components. It is involved in activities carried out in this context, such as the special programme 'L'Alliance pour l'industrialisation de l'Afrique', launched by UNIDO in October 1996 and adopted by the Summit of Heads of State and Government of the OAU in Harare in June 1997.

44 Interview with Mr Ashgar Husein at UNESCO, Paris on 29 July 1998.
45 *Review of UNESCO's Activities in Africa*, p. 2. Pursuant to the Audience Africa recommendations, the director-general of UNESCO set up an International Committee to follow up Audience Africa, which, at its first meeting on 10–11 September 1996, stressed that it was essential for Africa to take and sustain the initiative for its own development. The Committee, which acts as an observatory for the situation in Africa in UNESCO's fields of competence and advises the director-general on further action, has identified a number of key fields for social development in Africa: promotion of a culture of peace; strengthening of co-operation and acceleration of the process of regional and subregional integration; improved resource management; education, especially of girls and women; training, science and technology; promotion of a maintenance culture; use of new information and communication technologies; universal health policy; and action to combat poverty in general.
46 Eva Sankale, 'UNESCO and Africa', part IV, 'L'Afrique dans le programme de l'UNESCO'.
47 *Review of UNESCO's Activities in Africa*, p. 2.
48 Ibid.
49 Ibid.
50 See UNESCO (1997), *Approved Programme and Budget for 1998–1999*, Document 29C/5 (Paris: UNESCO).
51 Ibid.
52 UNESCO, *The Durban Statement of Commitment*, Seventh Conference of Ministers of Education of African Member States (MINEDAF VII), Durban, April 1998, p. 9.

14
Africa: What does the Future Hold?*

Jack Spence

Introduction

This chapter considers the legacy of the Cold War, the problems facing African statehood, and the modest solutions that are being prescribed by institutions – for example, the World Bank. Attention is also given to the weaknesses of the African political economy and the problems of poverty. Finally, the chapter discusses the 'failed state' issue and the need for African solutions to the problems of peace and security.

The global context

Since the end of the Cold War, Africa has suffered mixed fortunes. Western preoccupation with the implications of the collapse of Communist rule in the former Soviet Union and its satellite empire, together with the unresolved issue of 'widening and deepening' the European Union (EU), have contributed to the marginalisation of Africa on the foreign policy agendas of the major powers. Africa too has lost its orthodox strategic significance as an arena of competition between the super-powers.

Yet the demonstration effect of 'people's power' in Eastern Europe and the emergence of an incipient civil society underpinned by opposition groups (students, trade unions, and the Churches) forced free, externally monitored elections on to discredited regimes anticipating the creation of a new political order. Pressure from below was reinforced by external insistence (first voiced by the World Bank (WB) and the International Monetary Fund (IMF) in the 1980s) that the price of continued aid, technical assistance, investment and debt rescheduling was a sustained commitment to the principles of good governance, the liberalisation of decrepit command economies and the application of structural adjustment programmes designed to promote lasting growth and wealth creation. Thus, in 1990, Douglas Hurd, Britain's foreign secretary, in defining 'political conditionality' emphasised that 'in future, aid policy would favour democracies: countries tending towards pluralism, public accountability, respect for the rule of law, human rights and market principles, should be encouraged'.

For many African states, following the achievement of a 'second independence', the task of transformation in terms of these criteria has proved to be formidable: in effect, their peoples, expecting great things from newly-elected governments, have been asked to defer the satisfaction of basic needs in the short run for the sake of ultimate benefit in the long run. After all, restructuring an economy and making multi-party democracy autochthonous and legitimate, are enterprises which take time to reach their full potential and deliver the benefits of stable government and sound economic practice. The problem is compounded by competition for the resources and the assistance of the rich North from a host of new claimants in Russia and Eastern Europe, and the continued attraction of the Asian Tiger economies and China for overseas investment.

Thus the African state is poised at a critical juncture in the continent's history: will it (can it?) recover from decades of economic mismanagement, corruption, the vices of one-party statehood and military dictatorship? Alternatively, will the new mood of African 'self-reliance' articulated by a new, dynamic generation of leaders herald a revival of the continent's fortunes? The signs are modestly encouraging: it is no longer fashionable to blame Africa's ills on colonialism or to rely on aid handouts to rescue hard-pressed economies. Instead, the emphasis is on self-help designed to transform African states into 'emerging markets, capable by dint of their own efforts of profiting from the freer flow of trade in the global economy'.[1] Thus the economies of sub-Saharan Africa grew by 4.4 per cent in 1996, with Uganda's reaching a record 8 per cent.

So far, so good. But abundant harvests and firm commodity prices are only part of the answer. Such benefits – important as they are – cannot be capitalised upon without an effective political and legal order to create conditions for maximising wealth, and for ensuring its sensible and sustained distribution to the citizens. But at least there is now a widespread acknowledgement that, without such an order offering the citizen physical security and a legal structure providing rules (and by definition consistency and certainty of social outcome in their application) for regulating economic transactions both at home and abroad, statehood in Africa and elsewhere in the Third World will remain an empty shell incapable of protecting people or property. There is also a recognition that much remains to be done if this parlous outcome is to be avoided.

In this context, the 1997 World Bank's *World Development Report* makes salutary reading and is worth quoting at length:

> Africa faces a crisis of statehood which cannot be resolved without international help... The majority of African countries now have a lower capability (including state capability) than they did at independence... A minimalist state would do no harm, but neither could it do much good... Markets and governments are complementary. [NB the experience of the 'Asian Tigers' in this context]. The state is essential for putting in place the appropriate institutional foundations for markets... An institutional vacuum of significant proportions has emerged in many parts of Africa, leading to increased crime, and an absence of security, affecting investment and growth.[2]

First, some general propositions are offered, namely:

- That a degree of cautious optimism about the continent's future is justified in view of the progress made so far in establishing democratically elected governments in some thirty-five out of forty-eight countries since 1990.
- That although efforts had been made – with varying degrees of success – to liberalise African economies, the exercise is by no means complete, as demonstrated by the tardy progress of South Africa – one of the two most advanced economies on the continent.
- That an end to Africa's civil wars is crucial, not simply to get the task of reconstruction under way, but also to check the effects of near disastrous spill-over into neighbouring states caused, for example, by the plight of refugees and the absorption of scarce resources in ameliorating their wretched condition.
- That what is required by way of external assistance is the creation of an enabling environment to help fragile democracies strengthen their political and economic capabilities.
- That grandiose schemes of salvation are inappropriate.
- That, to quote Mr Wolfensohn, the president of the World Bank, even in the worst situation, very small steps towards a more effective state can have a large impact on economic and social welfare. The

challenge for states is neither to shrink into significance, nor to dominate markets, but to start taking these small steps.[3]

- That partnership with African governments, preferably organised on a multilateral basis, is the appropriate mode for rendering assistance, rather than neo-colonial paternalism.

- Finally, that the fragility of African institutions is compounded by the impact of global economic forces: footloose multinational companies able to pick and choose congenial economic environments, together with impersonal judgements of the world's financial markets. Such pressures affect all states – rich and poor, weak and strong – in varying degrees and impose severe limits on the exercise of absolute sovereignty as traditionally defined. In these circumstances, states have to 'box clever', but this is increasingly problematic for states with inadequate capability to hold their own in a global market-place imposing free market disciplines.

Reform of the polity

It is fair to say that the African political experience was fractured at the time of independence, with the imposition of Western models of democracy rooted in European history and experience. In effect, Africa's political development was denied an evolutionary process of change in which traditional 'habits' – in an Oakeshottian sense – of political behaviour might have melded successfully with colonial experience to produce a peculiarly African mode of democratic politics. The elites who took power in the 1950s and 1960s were thus faced with the twin tasks of simultaneous state and nation-building and – not surprisingly – in view of Europe's very different historical experience over an extended period of time, their efforts proved fruitless. The result, in many cases, was degeneration, into one party and/or a military dictatorship.

It is a mistake to believe that state failure is a recurring, permanent condition. It is all too easy to generalise from the experiences of the former Zaire, Somalia and Liberia, and ignore the encouraging attempts to revive democratic rule during the 1990s. The South African experience in this context is also a refreshing reminder of what can be done by way of state transformation via the mechanism of negotiation and compromise, although, unlike other African states, the post-apartheid regime has inherited a set of institutions and traditions with autochthonous roots: parliamentary government; strong statehood; and a vibrant civil society, all of which have survived the battering of apartheid.

What was crucial in this context is to avoid any suggestion to African peoples that there is only one, Western-inspired, model of democracy worth striving for. Indeed, African leaders and their peoples must be encouraged to find their own individual democratic path, drawing on local traditions where appropriate. The key ingredient in any such system must be the capacity to evolve, as time and circumstances dictate – a Burkean view of politics – but one that is especially relevant in societies such as Uganda, where the absence of political parties does not preclude their ultimate emergence. To condemn President Yoweri Museveni for not adopting a Western model as the basis for political reform fails to recognise that economic change allows the citizen to raise his or her head above the subsistence parapet with a corresponding expectation of wider and more effective political participation.

In this context, the 'Asian Tiger' model is sometimes cited approvingly with regard to its relevance as a neat and exact parallel, but scepticism is expressed about this view, given the very different cultural and historical experiences of East Asia. Nonetheless, there is a link between economic transformation and its political counterpart. However, the view – voiced by some African intellectuals – that African states should return self-consciously to their pre-colonial past in search of appropriate structures, is not shared. True, many of these were destroyed by colonial rule, but in an era of globalisation, the African state has no choice but to modernise and devise institutions capable of adaptation to external pressures. But, above all, it is the belief that democracy must be viewed as a process with a variety of local modes to assist those beginning the long march to political rejuvenation. South Africa, Botswana, Benin and Mali are all states with viable institutions, different in the style of day-to-day governance, but all, nonetheless, recognisably democratic.

What is essential, is that an African version of democracy should incorporate values that are – by and large – 'deemed to be self-evident': participation; accountability; transparency; the rule of law; the protection of minorities; and free and effective media. Writing these values into a constitution is one thing, but, as James Maddison remarked, constitutions are 'parchment barriers'. If they are to flourish and take root, the values they enshrine must be institutionalised in the wider body politic to articulate and assert them against the claims of the state to be the sole judge of what is right and proper in particular circumstances. Hence the importance of fostering civil society, namely that network of private and public associations – trade unions; women's groups; the media; the Churches and the universities; the professions;

and non-governmental organisations (NGOs) of all kinds – which provide the social glue to hold society together and provide a healthy diversity of view and aspiration. By themselves the grand institutions of government and public administration can only do so much; for institutional structures to take root and respond to individual needs, the political process must be vigorous and diverse. Happily – as I remarked earlier – the new governments that came to power in the 1990s were swept into office by a resurgent civil society. But their continued success depends on restraint and tolerance of opposition. The spectacle of Kenya's police beating up students in July 1997, because of demands for constitutional reform, is an alarming portent of what happens when state authorities overreach themselves. Yet another example – although less distressing – is the tendency of Western donors to switch support from local NGOs in South Africa to the ministries responsible for the delivering of social goods.

Western governments therefore have a role to play in helping Africa build the institutional capacity essential if these values are to be given full expression and lasting protection. Many examples can be cited: one is the provision of training for bureaucrats (and, indeed, would-be politicians) to enable them to cope more effectively with the increasing technical nature of modern government. The World Trade Organisation (WTO), for example, runs courses for those who will have to negotiate their country's participation in an increasingly global free market; the Commonwealth of Nations via a host of private and public associations, links lawyers, doctors, engineers and so on in durable and mutually beneficial networks. (Indeed, in this context, the Commonwealth has been well described as an incipient global civil society.) The British Ministry of Defence has assisted in the training of African armies in the theory and practice of peace-making and peace-keeping. NGOs of all kinds provide advice and assistance on new projects in the realm of agricultural reform, and the better utilisation of water and other basic resources. This 'small step' approach is not to be despised, even if its achievements go unreported in the world's media.

One interesting feature of the debate on democratisation is the assertion that Africa must move away from 'cultural denial' and recognise the reality of ethnicity as a factor in its political experience. Thus the notion of the highly centralised unitary state is being questioned; indeed, the idea of federal and confederal structures is acknowledged to have value in societies divided by ethnic particularity.

True, the record of federation in Africa is poor; East Africa and Nigeria in the 1960s are cases in point. But what is striking is the renewed interest in federal arrangements, especially for states such as the Democratic Republic of the Congo (formerly Zaire), where it is clear that the writ of central government under former president Mobutu was barely acknowledged outside the metropolis. Here, the South African model has some relevance: nine provinces under the ultimate control of a central government, but with the capacity to evolve as ambitious leaders press for more power and resources from the centre. Thus – following a Burkean prescription – the long-term outcome might be a 'federalism by stealth' as *de facto* changes in circumstances and personnel compel *de jure* changes in constitutional principle. This, after all, is how constitutions elsewhere, for example the USA, have been modified over time, confirming the earlier view that democracy is, indeed, a process and not a static condition.

Another preoccupation of external observers is the possibility of regional groupings to provide a safety net for weak states. It is often argued that a putative new world order might well be one in which regional associations in varying degrees of integration will constitute major actors in their own right, with a corresponding decline in the power and legitimacy of the solitary sovereign state. This is, at best, a speculative proposition and, in any case, the theory and practice of regional integration as applied in the context of the European Union must – to a degree at least – be regarded as *sui generis*. Parallels with European experience can be misleading; the histories and cultures of the original six and those that subsequently joined the Community were profoundly different from those of African states. One critical difference between Europe in the 1940s and 1950s and contemporary Africa was the absence of any single power capable of dominating the rest; by contrast, in Africa – with the possible exception of East Africa – hegemonic powers (for example, South Africa and Nigeria) have to combine 'sensitivity and restraint' (Nelson Mandela's phrase) with subtle and skilful leadership of a disparate group of states characterised by uneven development.

The trade-offs for both the weak and the strong in West and Southern Africa will not be easy to engineer. Functional integration as in the European Community (EC), employing a step-by-step approach, depends on the successful application of the principle of structure following substance. As transnational transactions multiply across borders, the need arises for supranational institutions to establish a level playing field for all the actors involved – be they traders or investors – to regulate their interaction. This is turn assumes trade and resources complementarity and a harmonisation of legal, judicial and regulatory systems – conditions that do not yet exist to any significant degree, as the

Southern African example demonstrates. Thus regional integration of a sophisticated kind must remain a long-term aspiration.

What is possible in the short run is intergovernmental co-operation on specific issues such as transnational crime, enforced migration, environmental degradation, and transportation linkages. The hope must be that, over the long run, particular regions will be locked together in a network of such agreements, making the transition to integrated supranational structures seem an inevitable and desirable progression. Here again, the West can help by training the technocrats of the future – the African Monnets and Spaaks – without whose creativity and charisma regional integration will remain a distant dream.

Finally, in a discussion of the prospects for successful democratisation, the role of women as agents of productive change is crucial. Traditional African culture relegated women to subordinate roles; yet their current and potential contribution to the enhancement of decent values is vital as the role of women in the Liberian peace process and the elections in Sierra Leone demonstrate.

Economic development: incentives and constraints

Inevitably, discussion of this theme overlaps with the scrutiny of the political realm. Some alarming statistics emerge: Africa, for example, has 10 per cent of the world's population, but attracts only 2 per cent of its investment. Furthermore, assuming growth rates of Africa and the industrialised world remain the same, Africa would take some 700 years to achieve 50 per cent of the GNP of the latter.

Clearly, there is a very strong case for giving increased investment a higher priority if the trends noted above are to be reversed. But this, in turn – echoing discussion of the political constraints – requires capacity building at a variety of levels. Western countries could, for example, increase their efforts to help in crime prevention – a major deterrent to investment in Africa – as South Africa and Nigeria (the two strongest economies in Africa, with 50 per cent of the continent's GNP) have found to their cost. Similarly, more could be done to help construct local mechanisms to support small business development. There is no shortage of potential entrepreneurial skill as the growth of the informal economy throughout Africa demonstrates. The key to success is the establishment of basic training programmes to foster skills in accountancy, marketing, literacy, artisanship and credit management. NGOs clearly have a role to play here, but continued aid is important in this context, providing for capacity building at relatively low cost to donors, especially at the local level.

There is less agreement on the role of the IMF: some have argued in its favour on the grounds that structural adjustment programmes (SAPs) have had the desired effect in forcing African governments to put their economic houses in order. Others argue that, while being important, the impact of the IMF is limited – given that the real weakness in African economies is the failure to attract investment, and this will not be remedied unless and until radical improvements occur in the social and physical infrastructure. The importance of accelerating privatisation is stressed, on the grounds that productive resources will be released for social and economic development.

On the contribution that increased trade can make to Africa's economic progress, few dispute that the restrictions imposed by the industralised world on the continent's exports – especially with regard to agricultural products and textiles – impose severe impediments to growth. This issue highlights the need to improve the external enabling environment by reducing protectionism and providing greater access to Western markets. Here, responsibility lies squarely with the rich states of the North.

The question of debt relief is also of crucial importance. Official debt is estimated to represent between 40 per cent and 50 per cent of general revenue in sub-Saharan Africa. Debt alleviation via the mechanism of the heavily indebted poor countries' (HIPC) programme is one solution, as is the use of debt swaps. There is, a strong consensus in favour of the Group of Seven (G-7) countries co-ordinating their efforts to find the right mix of proposals for assisting particular countries, especially those with some record of success. This would involve examining the major sources of capital flows (aid, trade, investment and debt relief). The efforts of the US government to establish a joint strategy involving a variety of key governmental actors in preparation for the G-7 summit in Denver was in 1997 a hopeful portent for the future.

Finally, there is the expectation that sub-Saharan Africa is a potential emerging market. The West has a clear and vital interest in fostering the continent's growth, not simply because of the value placed on its fossil fuels and strategic minerals, but because failure to assist would perpetuate a morally and politically unacceptable division between the rich North and its neighbours to the South. Some commentators point to the example of Latin America where, after decades of corrupt military government and the failure of a variety of economic panaceas, civilian successors have 'bitten the bullet' of liberalisation and become attractive candidates for investment. Therefore, creating a more favourable climate for investment and all that this implies in terms of capacity-building, training and debt relief, is the key to Africa's future success.

The poverty problem

Poverty contributes to environmental degradation and disease. Again, some alarming statistics set the scene for debate: 1.3 billion people live on less than US$1 a day. Here too education is seen as being vital, on the grounds that, without skilled training and basic literacy and numeracy, individuals have little, if any, prospect of lifting themselves above the poverty line. Again, the importance of education for women is stressed. Without a gender balance, women will continue to have unequal access to productive assets – which is a waste of valuable human resources.

With regard to environmental degradation, three primary causes can be identified:

- poverty compels individuals to use renewable resources in an unsustainable way;
- lack of education means that people – especially in rural areas – lack environmentally appropriate management techniques; and
- the failure of planners – again an education deficiency – to take into account the environmental impact of large infrastructural projects.

Many African states are caught in a profound dilemma: short-term exploitation of natural assets for foreign exchange often conflicts with long-term environmental needs. There is no immediate solution to hand to deal with this problem, but there is the growing awareness by some multinationals of the need to follow sensitive environmental practice. In this context it is worth mentioning in passing that there is increasing pressure on multinationals to issue ethical codes of practice and provide for independent monitoring of the degree to which they are observed in the developing world.

Education too is acknowledged as having a critical role to play in eliminating disease. AIDS – to which Africa has been particularly prone – tuberculosis, meningitis and malaria have all taken a heavy toll. Access to decent medical care is often difficult, and governments with slight budgets have few resources to spare for improving their peoples' health. Yet sensible provision for training healthcare workers would reap enormous benefits out of all proportion to the costs involved. Similarly, improving the salaries earned by doctors and nurses is vital if the tide of professional emigration to the developed world is to slow down.

Peace and security

In the past, the 'image' of Africa projected to the outside world – largely through sporadic and at times sensationalist media reporting – has been reminiscent of Joseph Conrad's despairing 'heart of darkness' vision: civil war; famine; government coups; and social and economic stagnation. Yet the fact remains that the establishment of a modicum of peace and physical security remains a *sine qua non* for the sensible and profitable exploitation of Africa's human and material resources – whether by indigenous efforts or in combination with external entrepreneurial skills.

What is required is a climate of confidence in the capacity of governments – newly elected after the ravages of civil strife – to begin, complete and sustain the task of economic and social rejuvenation. Thus who can doubt the damage done to a variety of states: Sudan, Angola, the Democratic Republic of the Congo, Rwanda, Somalia, Sierra Leone and Liberia, scattered across the continent and worn down by the enervating and destructive impact of violent conflict. What is striking about all these examples is the persistence of conflict over many years and yet there is some consolation – however bleak it may be – that all wars (and Africa is no exception) do eventually end – often when the protagonists recognise that the cost of continuing conflict outweigh the benefits of negotiation and compromise.

In this context, so called 'contact groups', whether diplomatic or NGO-led, can and do take advantage of the window of opportunity provided by the spectacle of mutual exhaustion. The presence of such groups is a strikingly innovative feature of the post-Cold-War scene: they exist to 'knock heads together', to be available and experienced enough from long familiarity with the conflict to kick-start negotiations. Peace-keeping to police a precarious truce then becomes an option, as in Angola, Namibia, and Mozambique. We should also note the capacity and the considerable efforts made by key African states such as Nigeria and its allies in the Economic Commission for Africa Cease-Fire Monitoring Group (ECOMOG) to *enforce* a peace in both Liberia and Sierra Leone.

Some commentators have proposed more radical solutions: in the early 1990s, Douglas Hurd, British foreign secretary, speaking at the General Assembly of the UN, mused about the possibility of restoring

UN-sponsored 'benign imperialism' to collapsed states. Similarly, Ali Mazrui suggested 'external re-colonisation under the banner of humanitarianism'. He went on to argue:

> Countries like Somalia and Liberia where central control has collapsed may invite an inevitable intervention... although colonialism may be re-surfacing it is likely to look rather different this time round. A future trustee system will be more genuinely international and less Western than it was under the old guise. Administering powers for the trusteeship territories could come from Africa and Asia, as well as from the rest of the membership of the UN.[4]

Indeed, the issue of the 'failed state' and what to do about it cuts across the general view that resources should be devoted to capacity-building in those states that have begun to show a commitment to democracy and the liberalisation of their economies. In other words, reward success rather than failure – a harsh doctrine but an inevitable one, given the competition for scarce external resources. Interestingly, there is evidence of theoretical discussion about alternatives to the state as the vehicle for political organisation. In this context the reader is referred in particular to a penetrating analysis by Jeffrey Herbst in a recent edition of *International Security*.[5]

Yet what is abundantly clear, however, is that Western governments (and this applies equally to Russia and China) are adamant in their reluctance to intervene in so-called 'failed states' enduring civil war. In this context, the US experience in Somalia in the early 1990s was crucial in reinforcing a traditional inhibition about peace-enforcement operations in distant parts of the globe. The public abroad have no appetite for enterprises of this kind; the best that war-torn African states can hope for is humanitarian assistance under a UN rubric.

There is also a conviction, shared by both civil authorities and their military advisers in the West, that intervention in civil wars cannot be justified in terms of the classic criteria for success in such ventures: the need to set and maintain a limited objective and the political will to achieve it; available resources; and the prospect of rapid disengagement – that is a clear exit strategy. Perhaps the most important, if rarely articulated, objection to military involvement charged with peace enforcement (as distinct from peace-keeping), is the reluctance to follow up such intervention with a long-term programme of state reconstruction involving the deployment of substantial political and bureaucratic resources.

Clearly, the 'failed state' syndrome is a disturbing one, not least for investors and traders abroad. Their willingness to be helpful, and to engage in trade and investment, will depend ultimately on their perception of the capacity of a new government to provide physical security and a reasonably reliable political and legal order. And most important of all must be the availability of economic resources, whether mineral, agricultural or state enterprises ripe for privatisation – for successful and mutually profitable exploitation. Measured in these terms, Angola, therefore, may seem a better bet than Sudan; and, similarly, Mozambique more attractive than Liberia or the Democratic Republic of the Congo. But, in the last analysis, what will influence potential investors is the extent to which states demonstrate a commitment to capacity building, to establishing a viable set of democratic structures and a commitment to the liberalisation of their economies. In other words, this applies to all African states, not only those that have recently emerged from the trauma of civil war. Success in these areas of development will be rewarded, and failure punished, by external indifference to their social and economic needs. This may seem a harsh doctrine, but it is an inevitable one, given the fierce competition for external resources – whether investment, trade, aid, technical assistance, or debt relief.

Yet just as the new breed of African leaders, the so called 'renaissance' generation have indicated a genuine willingness to come to terms with the pressure of a global market-place, so one detects a similar spirit of self-reliance with respect to the security needs of the continent. There is a general recognition that the continent's problems in this regard will have to be solved by African means and African commitment. Thus real efforts are being made via the Organisation of African Unity and its regional offspring to devise a peace-keeping and peace-enforcement doctrine appropriate to local African conditions. This is likely to take a regional form, drawing on the experience of the Nigerian-led ECOMOG, which – as was argued earlier – has been remarkably successful. As for the West, there is a willingness to help with logistic support, training and appropriate weapon systems. The USA, France and Britain have all been active in this area. The new South Africa too might have an extended role to play beyond its immediate hinterland. Yet external expectations that it would help to save the continent from itself were confounded by the cautious approach of the Mandela Government and the constraints of domestic needs and priorities.[6] Of more doubtful utility is the use of private armies by African governments resisting rebellion – for example, Executive Outcomes. This is certainly an example of free enterprise and is symptomatic both of the weakness of governments trapped in a vicious cycle of civil war, and the reluctance of their counterparts abroad to intervene directly. Yet while such organisations may have short-term utility in particular circumstances (witness the recent operations of Sandline in Sierra Leone), the difficulty is that they are ill-equipped once military success has been achieved to engage in helping with the work of social and economic reconstruction. This surely must remain the responsibility of the international community, or individual states in particular regions. (The role of the British army in rebuilding Bosnia's shattered infrastructure is a case in point).

Conclusion

This paper has attempted to highlight the major themes in the debate about Africa's future. Capacity building at both national and local level is crucial, as is education and training in virtually every area of public and private activity. Aid should be targeted specifically, in the hope that over the long run an enabling environment can be created in which African leaders and their peoples are able to maximise their potential.

What is required is greater co-ordination of Western responses to the African condition, and this applies equally to NGOs. Close partnerships rather than distant patronage between the West and Africa is essential. Grandiose blueprints serve no constructive purpose. In the last analysis, perhaps what is required is a greater public awareness in the West of the success that has attended African development during the 1990s. Here, the media and those who control them have a major responsibility to help educate Western electorates, to forgo the 'heart of darkness' image and by so doing stimulate their governments into sustained concern, practical help and a re-ordering of the global agenda.

Notes and References

*   This chapter is an edited version of a plenary address to a conference held at the University of Pretoria, South Africa in August 1997. It also contains material from a report written by the author about the proceedings of the Addis Ababa Forum on *Attracting Global Capital to Africa*.
1   'Emerging Africa', *Economist*, 14 June 1997.
2   'Africa Faces a Crisis of Governance', *Financial Times*, 26 June 1997.
3   Ibid.
4   A. Mazrui (1993) 'The Bondage of Boundaries', *Economist*, 11–17 September. An article along similar lines by Matthew Parris appeared in *The Times*, 15 August 1997.
5   J. Herbst (1997) 'Responding to State Failure in Africa', *International Security*, vol. 21, no. 3.
6   Note, however, the possibility of South African involvement in the OAU peace-keeping efforts in the Democratic Republic of the Congo.

Index